DEVELOPING BUSINESS APPLICATIONS IN THE '90s

4GL-based Software Development
Using Thoroughbred IDOL-IV ™

Jeffrey L. Zickler

Project Manager:	John M. Irwin
Editorial:	Kathleen Sinnott, Steven Stewart, Lisa McCarty
Cover Design:	Larry Smith & Diane Thoma
Production Supervisor:	John M. Irwin
Production:	Melissa Schmidt, Laura Wolf

This book was typeset using Xerox Desktop Publishing Series: Ventura Publisher Edition. Camera-ready copy was produced on a NEC Silentwriter LC-890 printer. Illustrations were created using ZSoft Publisher's Paintbrush and the Canon IX-12 Image Scanner.

Thoroughbred, Concept Omega, IDOL-IV, SCRIPT-IV, REPORT-IV, DICTIONARY-IV, and Thoroughbred BASIC are trademarks of Concept Omega Corporation.

Informix is a registered trademark of Informix Software, Inc. Basic Four, MAI, and Application Software Corporation are registered trademarks of Management Assistance, Inc. UNIX is a trademark of AT&T Information Systems. ORACLE is a trademark of Oracle Corporation. Unify ACCELL is a trademark of Unify Corporation.

Copyright © 1988 by Jeffrey L. Zickler

Published by:

AdvanceWare, Inc.
1411A Warner Avenue
Tustin, CA 92680
Telephone: 714-259-1761

All rights reserved. No part of this work covered by the copyright hereon may be reproduced, transmitted, or used in any form or by any means — graphic, electronic, or mechanical, including photocopying, recording, taping, or information retrieval systems — without permission of the publisher.

ISBN 0-9620847-0-0

The author and publisher make no warranty of any kind, expressed or implied, with regard to the programs and documentation contained in this book. The author and publisher shall not be liable in any event for incidental or consequential damages in connection with, or arising out of, the furnishing, performance, or use of the programs contained in this book.

For more information on **Thoroughbred IDOL-IV** contact:

Thoroughbred
Concept Omega Corporation
19 Schoolhouse Road
P.O. Box 6712
Somerset, NJ 08875-6712

Telephone:
201-560-1377
800-524-0430

Telex: 910-3808-394
Fax: 201-722-7958

CREDITS:

Figure 1.1, page 6 adapted from James Martin, FOURTH GENERATION LANGUAGES, Volume I, Principles, © 1985, Figure 1.2, page 17, by permission of Prentice Hall, Inc., Englewood Cliffs, NJ.
Figure 4.1, page 42 based on C.J. Date, AN INTRODUCTION TO DATABASE SYSTEMS, Volume I, Fourth Edition, ©1986, Figure 11.1, page 233, reprinted by permission of Addison-Wesley Publishing Company, Inc., Reading, MA.
Screen representations from the Thoroughbred 4GL Environment are printed with permission from Concept Omega Corporation.

Table of Contents

PREFACE ix

How This Book is Organized x
Objectives of This Book xi
Audience xii
How To Get the Most From This Book xii
About the Author xii
Acknowledgements xiii

1 INTRODUCTION 1

A Historical Perspective 1
Earlier Generations of Computer Languages 3
Fourth Generation Languages (4GLs) 4
Two Additional Technology Advancement Issues 7
New Software Development Tools 8
Notes and References 9

2 A PHILOSOPHY OF HIGH TECHNOLOGY BUSINESS APPLICATIONS DEVELOPMENT 11

Major Philosophical Issues 12
How Much Can Really be Done with a 4GL? 13
How Will a 4GL Affect The Life Cycle of a Software Project? 14
Development of a New Generation of Application Software Packages 20

Fourth Generation Languages and the Value of Software Activities 21
Conclusions 22
Notes and References 23

3 OVERVIEW OF THOROUGHBRED IDOL-IV 25

Application Development Terminology 25
Some Terms Defined 26
DICTIONARY-IV: IDOL-IV Design Dictionaries 28
IDOL-IV Database Maintenance 30
Screens, Views, and Links 31
IDOL-IV Menus 32
Special Screen Features 33
REPORT-IV 34
SCRIPT-IV 35
Conclusions 37
Notes and References 37

4 THE BUSINESS APPLICATIONS DESIGN PROCESS 39

Introduction to Data Normalization 40
Relational Data Modeling 40
Data Normalization Rules 43
IDOL-IV and Data Normalization 50
A Quick Overview of Structured Design Issues 51
A Sample Applicant Tracking System (ATS) 52
ATS: The Database Design 53
ATS: A Functional Overview 55

Conclusions	57
Notes and References	57

5 IMPLEMENTING THE DATABASE DESIGN 59

Global Dictionary	59
Formats	64
Help Text	66
Text Fields	66
Message Lists	67
Links	68
Secondary Keys	69
Conclusions	70
Notes and References	70

6 DATABASE MAINTENANCE IMPLEMENTATION AND USE 73

ATS: Database Maintenance Specifications	74
Creating a Default Screen	75
Designing a Custom Screen	76
Screen Formula Capabilities	78
Using IDOL-IV DBM With a Custom Screen	79
Types of SCRIPT-IV Scripts	82
A Simple SCRIPT-IV Data Entry Script: Its Operation	84
A Simple SCRIPT-IV Data Entry Script: Main Procedure	86
A Simple SCRIPT-IV Data Entry Script: Get Record Procedure	90
A Simple SCRIPT-IV Data Entry Script: Add Record Procedure	93
A Simple SCRIPT-IV Data Entry Script: Display Record Procedure	95

A Simple SCRIPT-IV Data Entry Script: Delete Record Procedure 98
More Complex SCRIPT-IV Data Entry Scripts: Organization 98
More Complex SCRIPT-IV Data Entry Scripts: Operation 99
Conclusions 107
Notes and References 108

7 DESIGNING AND USING A VIEW OF A FILE 113

Creating and Saving the View Definition 113
View Display and Record Selection Functions 117
Mass (Groups of Records) Functions 118
Parameterization of View Functions 118
Conclusions 119
Notes and References 119

8 DESIGNING AND IMPLEMENTING REPORTS 121

ATS: Report Specifications 122
Creating a Simple Report Definition 123
Creating a More Complex Report Definition 126
Other Reporting Capabilities 130
Conclusions 131
Notes and References 132

9 DESIGNING AND IMPLEMENTING MENUS 135

ATS: Menu Specification 136

Designing and Implementing a Menu Screen 136
Creating the Menu Definition 138
Some Special Menu Features 139
Conclusions 140

10 DESIGNING AND IMPLEMENTING UPDATE PROGRAMS 141

ATS: Update Specifications 141
Collecting the Target Requisition 143
Searching for Matching Applicants 146
Conclusions 150
Notes and References 150

APPENDICES

1. ATS Global Dictionary 1-1
2. ATS Format Definitions 2-1
3. ATS Message Dictionary 3-1
4. ATS Link Definitions 4-1
5. ATS Screen Definitions 5-1
6. ATS Data Entry Scripts 6-1
7. ATS Sample Code File Data 7-1
8. ATS Report Specifications 8-1
9. ATS Report Definitions & Sample Output 9-1
10. ATS Menu Definitions 10-1

INDEX

List of Illustrations

1 Introduction
Figure 1.1 Development Effort for Creating Programs 6

2 A Philosphy of High Technology Business Applications Development
Figure 2.1 Traditional Software Project Life Cycle 15
Figure 2.2 New Software Project Life Cycle Using Prototyping 18
Figure 2.3 Objectives of Vertical Market Software Packages 21

3 Overview of Thoroughbred IDOL-IV
Figure 3.1 Relationship Between the Global Dictionary and Fields in a Format 30

4 The Business Applications Design Process
Figure 4.1 The Relational Data Structure 42
Figure 4.2 Sample Personnel Requisition Form 44
Figure 4.3 Unnormalized Personnel Requisition File 45
Figure 4.4 Sample Sales Order Entity Showing a Repeating Group 46
Figure 4.5 First Normal Form of Sales Order Files 47
Figure 4.6 Second Normal Form of Sales Order Files 48
Figure 4.7 Personnel Requisition Files in Third Normal Form 49
Figure 4.8 Sample Employment Application Form 54
Figure 4.9 Applicant Files in Third Normal Form 55
Figure 4.10 Functional Breakdown of Applicant Tracking System 56

5 Implementing the Database Design
Figure 5.1 Global Dictionary Definition Screen 60
Figure 5.2 Format Definition Screen 65
Figure 5.3 The Function of a Link 68

Figure 5.4 Link Definition Screen 69

6 Database Maintenance Implementation and Use

Figure 6.1 Default Screen Layout Example 75
Figure 6.2 Custom Screen Layout Example 76
Figure 6.3 Recruiter Code Screen Showing Mode Selection 79
Figure 6.4 Recruiter Code Screen After Mode Selection 80
Figure 6.5 Recruiter Code File Displayed as a View 81
Figure 6.6 Salary Grade Record Selection 85
Figure 6.7 Salary Grade Record Editing 86
Figure 6.8 Main Body of ATSGMM0 Script 88
Figure 6.9 GET-RECORD, SET-FILE-KEY and Error Procedures 91
Figure 6.10 ADD-RECORD Procedure 94
Figure 6.11 DISPLAY-RECORD and Other Edit Mode Procedures 96
Figure 6.12 DELETE-RECORD Procedure 98
Figure 6.13 Applicant Masterfile Maintenance Browse/Add Screen 100
Figure 6.14 Applicant Masterfile Maintenance Main Lookup Window 102
Figure 6.15 Applicant Masterfile Maintenance Retrieved Record 102
Figure 6.16 Applicant Masterfile Maintenance with Experience Code Lookup Window 103
Figure 6.17 Applicant Masterfile Maintenance with Requisition Number Lookup Window 103
Figure 6.18 Applicant Masterfile Maintenance Select Message 105
Figure 6.19 Applicant Masterfile Maintenance Screen 2 105

7 Designing and Using a View of a File

Figure 7.1 First Step in View Definition 114
Figure 7.2 Completed View Definition 116

8 Designing and Implementing Reports

Figure 8.1 Report Specification for Report #3 122
Figure 8.2 Report Specification for Report #6 123

Figure 8.3 Report Definition Screen 124
Figure 8.4 Report Definition of Open Requisitions Summary Report..............125
Figure 8.5 Sample Output from Open Requisitions Summary Report 127
Figure 8.6 Report Definition of Recruitment Costs Report 128
Figure 8.7 Sample Output from Recruitment Costs Report...............................131

9 Designing and Implementing Menus

Figure 9.1 Main Applicant Tracking System Menu Screen 137
Figure 9.2 Applicant Tracking System Reports Menu Screen 137

10 Designing and Implementing Update Programs

Figure 10.1 Specification of Search for Applicants by Requisition 142
Figure 10.2 Data Declaration for the Update Scripts 144
Figure 10.3 Main Procedure from ATSRCH0..144
Figure 10.4 Requisition Number Entry Screen 145
Figure 10.5 Target Requisition Confirmation Screen 145
Figure 10.6 EDIT-RECORD and SET-TERM-KEY Procedures
from ATSRCH0..147
Figure 10.7 Continuation Update Script Part 1 148
Figure 10.8 Continuation Update Script Part 2..149

PREFACE

Business Applications Software for small to medium-sized businesses is a topic of significant importance to those of us who make our living designing, developing, and installing multi-user business applications. This is by far the largest segment of the business software marketplace, and the approaches being used today are much the same as those that were used when we developed applications for the very first "minicomputers". The economics of this business have changed dramatically in the past fifteen years (generally in the form of increased expenses and reduced sales prices) while attendant technology (or other) improvements have failed to keep pace.

Developing Business Applications in the 90s deals with exactly these issues. It examines what has happened to the applications software development business, and discusses what needs to be available in the way of new technology (as well as what business practices need to change) to position a software developer to meet the end user requirements of the next decade.

Developing Business Applications in the 90s uses as the basis for its analysis and discussion, applications development oriented around the Business BASIC language and recent improvements in this market place. This language is almost completely ignored when the issue is the evolution of existing software (and its users) through the use of advances in software technology. COBOL is usually the language that receives the most attention, but it is important to remember that a very large percentage of the successful business applications for small- to medium-sized companies has been written using Business BASIC.

Much has been said in the trade press, and many product announcements have been made, that ostensibly refer to solutions to current applications software development problems. However, significant results have not been seen by those of us who have stood on the "bleeding edge". A solid answer for the applications developer who has a large investment in Business BASIC applications has not existed until very recently.

PREFACE

A relatively new set of applications software development tools has become available from the Thoroughbred division of Concept Omega Corporation. This tool set, called Thoroughbred IDOL-IV, is utilized extensively throughout this book in examples of how applications development should be accomplished today and in the future. Only with a clear understanding of how this can be done, will developers of business applications be able to maintain and expand their businesses over the next ten years.

Developing Business Applications in the 90s should be of interest to anyone, regardless of programming background, who plans to develop and maintain multi-user applications software over the next decade. It deals with a number of essential business factors that are largely independent of the specific tools in use. It also uses as its technology example a tool set that is one of the best currently available anywhere.

Computer software is becoming a "mature" industry with all of the related characteristics of other industries at this life cycle stage. It is important that business people serious about staying in this industry be able to make informed decisions about how their specific enterprise utilizes the technology available to all participants. Only in this way can individual businesses, as well as the industry as a whole, grow and succeed.

How This Book is Organized

Before any new technology can be examined in detail, the philosophy behind its use must be understood. The first two chapters of this book discuss the issues surrounding the development of applications software in the light of recent technology advancements. A quick historical look is taken to set the stage for where technology has come from and is going. A number of new ideas are evaluated as to how they might be of use in improving the overall design and development processes. A specific tool set is described that offers the best opportunity for embracing this new technology.

The objectives that all software developers should have for the successful operation of their business are itemized, and suggestions are made as to how these objectives can be met. Economic, as well as technological, factors are examined. A number of business organizational and procedural issues are reviewed with the goal of making a significant impact on the productivity and effectiveness of the software operation.

Chapter 3 of this book contains an overview description of each of the Thoroughbred IDOL-IV components highlighting their major features. Each component of the tool set is examined in relation to how it supports the objectives outlined in the previous chapters. Key terminology is defined as it relates to IDOL-IV and to the Fourth Generation application development process itself. Examples are included to show the basic capabilities of each component.

PREFACE

The first step in the development process, and a step supported to a larger extent by these new types of tools compared to previous approaches, is designing the target application system. Chapter 4 describes the process of designing an example application solution and how IDOL-IV aids this process. It is divided into sections that contain a brief treatment of each of the various aspects of this design and development project. An actual application is employed in this and subsequent chapters to emphasize just how easily this new technology can be put to use.

Chapter 5 discusses designing the sample application's database. One of the most important features of a tool set such as IDOL-IV is the availability of a centralized repository for design and implementation information. This is usually kept in a set of dictionaries or an "encyclopedia." The various aspects of the IDOL-IV dictionaries are discussed in this chapter as they relate to supporting the definition of existing, as well as new, application files and processes. Features of IDOL-IV that significantly enhance this important design function are examined.

Chapters 6 through 10 describe the processes used to design and implement the various types of programs that comprise a suite of applications software (e.g., data entry, report, menu, and update programs). These design and development processes are considered from the point of view of new applications development as well as of adding newly designed and developed programs to an existing application system. Throughout these chapters, the unique features of IDOL-IV are highlighted in detail.

At the end of the book are a number of appendices which include documentation on the sample application system. These appendices may be used to examine in detail what is being done in a particular chapter, if the development software is not available. In addition, a detailed index is included to help you find topics that are of specific interest.

Objectives of This Book

After you have finished this book you should be able to:

- Better understand the process of embracing the new application development technologies as they continue to become available

- Develop all the various portions of a business applications system using Thoroughbred IDOL-IV

- Make a more informed decision when choosing technology improvements for your own use

- Better understand how to approach the applications development business in the future so as to take economic advantage of the results of these new technologies

Audience

This book is written with the assumption that you have at least a fundamental understanding of computer programming. In other words, you have used some kind of programming language to write at least a few programs. It is helpful if you understand the basic concepts of data modeling and database design, but it is certainly not required. A detailed understanding of Business BASIC is also not a requirement, but may be of some use to you should you wish to get deeper into some of the details later in the book. The book has been written so that you can either review its concepts and ideas without digging into specifics or go further into all the details.

How To Get the Most From This Book

It will become obvious to you very quickly that the best way to utilize the information in this book is to have access to Thoroughbred IDOL-IV and the sample application system while you are going through each chapter. However, the book has been written to stand alone without the software, and you can certainly gain a good understanding of the capabilities of these types of tools by reading the book by itself. Of course, the business and economic discussions are, to a large degree, independent of the software as well.

About the Author

Jeffrey L. Zickler was first introduced to computers while an undergraduate Aerospace Engineering student at The University of Texas at Austin in the late 1960s. He became interested in the business uses of computers while taking his masters degree in Business Administration, and began teaching a graduate seminar relating to this topic. For several years following graduate school Mr. Zickler sold, installed, and supported accounting systems written in Business BASIC on Basic Four® computers.

He then joined a company that developed and distributed Business BASIC applications software packages worldwide. This company was acquired by MAI® Basic Four, and became MAI Application Software Corporation®. Mr. Zickler served as director and vice president of Marketing and Operations of MAI ASC, and was promoted to president of the company in early 1983.

PREFACE

Mr. Zickler has spent the past five years dealing with the economic and business issues of applications software development as they relate to advances in software technology. In 1983, while president of MAI Application Software Corporation, Mr. Zickler led the company to an international announcement of a set of Data Management and Applications Development Tools that are in widespread use within the MAI Basic Four community today.

In 1984 Mr. Zickler joined Peregrine Systems, Inc., as vice president of Applications Engineering, and was instrumental in the final design and development of a Fourth Generation Language and Relational DBMS. He then directed the creation of a suite of applications systems developed with these tools. These applications are now being sold to Fortune 500 companies to automate many of the functions within a company's Data Centers.

Most recently Mr. Zickler has gained a broad base of experience, while acting as an independent consultant, with several of the Fourth Generation Languages and Relational DBMSs available under the UNIX™ Operating System (e.g., ORACLE™, Unify/ACCELL™, and Informix®). Mr. Zickler has written a number of articles, and currently teaches a course at UCI (University of California, Irvine) Extension, on Fourth Generation Languages. This course is one of the seven required courses in the Certificate in Advanced Software Technologies, one of two certificates in the Information Technologies Program offered by UCI Extension.

Mr. Zickler is currently president and chief executive officer of AdvanceWare, Inc., a software development, distribution, and consulting company in Southern California that specializes in advanced technology consulting and business software products developed with Fourth Generation Languages.

Acknowledgements

I am greatly indebted to all the people at Concept Omega for their help and patience during the creation of this book. I would especially like to thank Roger Sparks for introducing me to the company and its new development system, and John-L Johnson for his ready and unselfish sharing of ideas and his amazing stamina. It has been a joy to work with such top-notch professionals, and I have, as always, learned a lot from associating with such people as these two.

Many others had a hand in getting me and this book through the weeks and months from start to finish. As an alpha test site for IDOL-IV, I had the opportunity to see the product and its documentation take shape. I would like to thank Veronica Cannon for listening to all my problems and for keeping me up-to-date with the "latest version". I

PREFACE

would also like to thank Bill Clarke and all the others in Product Development who responded so rapidly when I did find a problem. And, I am deeply indebted to Nancy Dempsey for taking care of all the myriad details over the months that, without her help, would have been forgotten or missed.

I would also like to thank Janice Forsythe and John Irwin for all their help and encouragement from the very beginning, for editing the endless drafts, and for all their ideas for improvements. John and his staff did a wonderful job in final editing and layout, and actually put the whole thing together. And, of course, the book would never have gotten to final draft form without Janice's constant support. She saw the book through every step of development with me, and being the kind of person she is, never faltered in her belief that I could do it.

JLZ

1

INTRODUCTION

Advances in the technology with which business applications software is created have been appearing on the market over the past few years at an amazing rate. Unfortunately, some have not really been "advances", but rather "warmed over" versions of previously available technology. And, on occasion what appeared at first glance to be a real advance, turned out not to be "real" at all.

One frustrating aspect of many of the "real" technological advances is the inherent assumption that no applications software already exists that should be taken into consideration. In other words, many products recently available require that entire applications systems be redeveloped from scratch, and assume that any integration with currently installed software will seldom be done, if at all.

For an applications developer, embracing a new technology must always be an economically justifiable decision. Only quite recently have advances in applications software development technology become available that clearly meet this criterion. This book discusses in detail one of the few products that fits in this category.

A Historical Perspective

For the past fifteen years or more a large percentage of all business applications software available for true multi-user, medium-scale computers[1] was written in a language called Business BASIC. This language was pioneered by several individuals and organizations in the early 1970s, and became a powerful business applications development language. By far the largest number of applications originally written in the language were created for one particular proprietary hardware system — the Basic Four computer.

1 INTRODUCTION

In the late 1970s, a move in the industry began toward standardization in operating systems and a wider choice among hardware manufacturers. As a result, many developers of Business BASIC applications began searching for a way to salvage their investment while following these industry trends. Much time and money had gone into the creation of their applications, and reimplementation in another proprietary environment was highly undesirable. Soon, a Business BASIC interpreter became available on all the "standard" operating systems. Also, a new operating system appeared that took the best possible advantage of the functionality of the Business BASIC language. That operating system is available today on at least as many different hardware systems as are all the various versions of UNIX.

At roughly the same time as this "standardization" trend was developing, another advancement began to make some major headway. This was the idea of utilizing a Database Management System (DBMS) to store the definition of, and control the access to, application data, replacing more primitive file systems. Again, a DBMS soon appeared that worked with any application developed in the Business BASIC language, regardless of whether or not it was originally intended to be used with a DBMS.

In the early 1980s, a third technological advancement began getting a lot of press. This one centered around the somewhat fuzzy ideas of "the automatic generation of applications software" combined with "end user applications software development." Only quite recently have these concepts begun to be clarified and understood by the computer industry, and significant development capabilities are finally becoming available.

End user software development has generally evolved into the functions of inquiry and retrieval of application data, and has avoided the more complex issue of developing "complete" applications systems. This evolution has been accomplished through the recent availability of query systems or languages, and report creation tools (e.g., report writers, report generators, etc.) that a user may employ.

The idea of "the automatic generation of applications software" has generally evolved into something called Fourth Generation Languages — computer programming languages that are much more powerful than those previously available. It is in this area of technological advancement that many of the serious disappointments have occurred. It is also in this area that much of the "real" advancement has been required.

Earlier Generations of Computer Languages

Fourth Generation Languages (4GLs) get their name from the fact that (according to most people) there have been three previous "generations" of computer programming languages. First Generation Languages were completely machine-specific binary languages, usually called "machine languages". All programming was accomplished by stringing the appropriate 0's and 1's together to make the hardware accomplish a particular function. With added mnemonic codes (signifying a specific hardware operation) and the ability to declare storage locations (registers) within memory, machine languages became a little less cryptic, but still were utilized successfully by a very small number of computer programmers.

Second Generation Languages (usually called "assembler languages") were also hardware-specific, but had a significant improvement over 1GLs. This improvement was called "symbolic addressing,"[2] and was the ability to name data that was being stored in memory. These names were called "variables", and are still used in all computer programming languages — even 4GLs. The number of potential computer programmers increased by at least an order of magnitude with the advances in 2GLs, but this was still a relatively small number.

Third Generation Languages started to become available in the 1960s, and contained the first real breakthroughs in computer programming technology. One such breakthrough inherent with most (but not all) 3GLs was machine independence. COBOL was one of the first widely used machine independent computer programming languages. On the other hand, Business BASIC (another 3GL) did not acquire machine independence until after a large number of applications had already been written in it.

Another improvement that had a sizable impact on programmer productivity was the advent of "high level" language commands.[3] Rather than making the programmer take care of each specific "bit" in storage, 3GLs provided commands that did much of the necessary housekeeping automatically, freeing the programmer to concentrate on the larger aspects of the program, such as screen layout, input validation logic, etc. Very large commercial applications were easier to create with 3GLs (compared to 1GLs and 2GLs), even though large numbers of lines of programming code were still needed for most business application functions.

A third improvement that came with most 3GLs was increased verbosity, and therefore increased human readability, of the language statements. This was not universally true, but again COBOL and Business BASIC contain good examples of this characteristic. All in all, these improvements allowed a much larger audience (again, something close to an order of magnitude increase) access to the art of computer programming, and commercial applications software development really began in earnest.

Despite these improvements, 3GLs contain at least two serious disadvantages when compared to earlier computer programming languages. One is the lack of the programmer's ability to cause the target computer to do all of the specific functions that a 1GL or a 2GL could do. In other words, with machine independence and high-level commands came a compromise — a programmer just could not do all the things with a 3GL that he or she could do with a 1GL or 2GL. The justifications for this compromise were valid (improved usability of the language, and removal of functions not really needed for commercial applications software development), but they still created obstacles to widespread acceptance. This disadvantage was considered so severe that many 3GLs provide access to "lower level" functions through the mechanism of a subroutine call to a 1GL or 2GL.

Another 3GL compromise, caused by having the computer do more of the work, was that a program written in a 3GL did not usually execute as fast as an equivalent program written in a 1GL or 2GL. As a result, software tools called compilers and linkers are used to convert 3GL source code into the equivalent 1GL code before execution, in an attempt to recover throughput to earlier language levels.

These two compromises caused a number of programmers to doubt the real usefulness of 3GLs for many years. In fact, it was many years after its initial introduction that COBOL gained widespread acceptance in the data processing industry, even though it offered orders of magnitude improvement in development time over earlier techniques.

Fourth Generation Languages (4GLs)

With all their improvements, 3GLs still have serious limitations when it comes to creating commercial applications software systems. 3GLs require large numbers of lines of code to accomplish most business functions. For the most part 3GLs were designed to be used by technically trained professionals. It is extremely difficult and time consuming to debug, and virtually impossible to modify, most complex applications systems written with a 3GL

The creation of an application function requires a significant translation from the specification of the user's requirement to the 3GL code. In fact, the developer of a 3GL-based application is required to make thousands of detailed decisions every day about "what the user really wants". This "distance" between the specification of user requirements and the end result 3GL code in the application allows an incredible amount of variation to be introduced, and is the major cause of errors (other than logic errors) in the developed system.

Fourth Generation Languages were created in response to these problems to meet the following objectives:

- To speed up the applications development process

- To reduce the cost and difficulty of application maintenance

- To minimize debugging problems

- To create bug-free, "accurate" code from high-level specifications of user requirements

- To expand the audience of users who can put computers to work by at least another order of magnitude[4]

One of the primary ways that 4GLs attempt to meet these objectives is through the use of relatively few, even higher level, commands. More programmer housekeeping is taken care of by the computer, and, thus, more ground can be covered by a 4GL programmer than an equivalent 3GL programmer.[5] Relatively little choice is available in deciding how to accomplish a particular function, so a 4GL programmer is free to concentrate on the design of the application rather than on how to construct a program segment.

A very important use of these capabilities is the construction of an application model or prototype, which can be used to verify user requirements **before** system development commences. The concept is no different from model construction in any other engineering discipline, but is rarely possible with a language less powerful that a 4GL. An important result of prototyping is the narrowing of the distance between user specifications and the encoding of these requirements into a program. This allows a 4GL programmer to make many fewer decisions regarding user needs without input from the user.

One early issue in the development of 4GLs was procedurality vs. non-procedurality. It was first thought that a 4GL had to be almost completely non-procedural to be considered a "new generation" language. However, developers using these early 4GLs

1 INTRODUCTION

quickly proved that complete business applications cannot be created without procedurality. Thus, the proper mix of non-procedural and procedural commands make up today's full-function 4GLs. Figure 1.1 illustrates the productivity tradeoffs between procedurality and non-procedurality in 4GLs as compared to a typical 3GL, such as Business BASIC.[6]

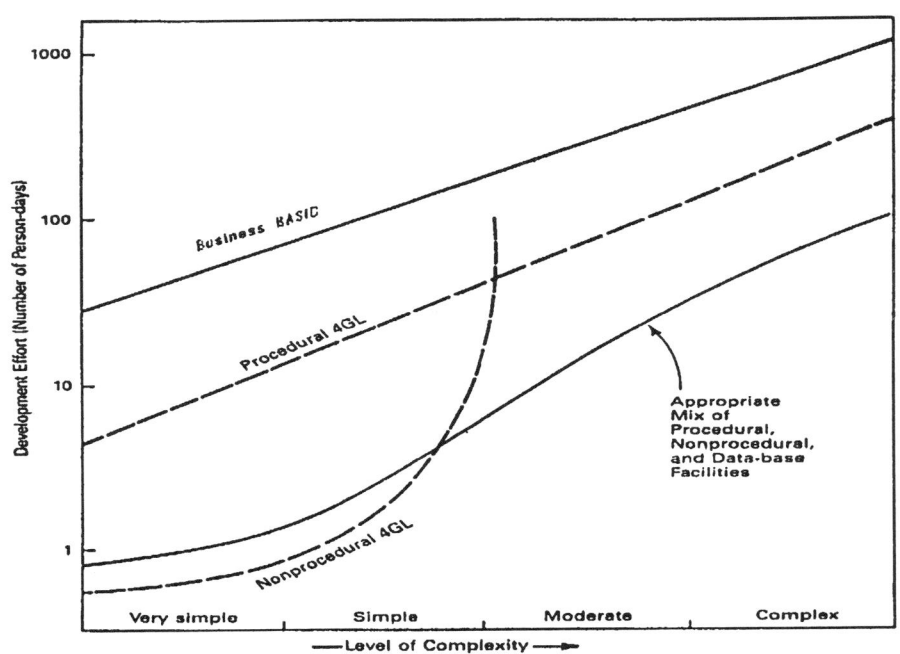

Fig. 1.1 Development Effort for Creating Programs

A number of additional principles are important in the design of a 4GL, among them: access to a data dictionary or encyclopedia within which to store application development data, avoidance of obscure or misleading syntax, the human factoring of the developer and user interfaces, and orthogonality (non-overlap) of the language constructs. (These design principles are covered in detail in other texts.[7])

As a result, most "good" 4GLs utilize a combination of procedural and non-procedural commands, and have access to some type of data dictionary within which to store the definition of both application data and common logic or business rules. These 4GLs comprise a wide variety of approaches to command structure, syntax, and developer interface, and range in power from end user query languages to full-function business applications development languages.

Two Additional Technology Advancement Issues

Two additional technological advances should be mentioned here to complete this discussion, although neither will be addressed in any detail elsewhere in this book. These issues involve Fifth Generation Languages/Systems, and the automation of the requirements analysis and initial design of applications systems.

Fifth Generation Languages/Systems can generally be categorized in the following ways.[8]

- expert systems

- knowledge-based systems

- inference engines

- the interpretation and processing of human languages

In a fifth generation system, knowledge is encoded in such a way that the computer can appear to make decisions based on current parameters and user input. There are some applications of such systems today, but in general most business applications are not readily adaptable to today's fifth generation technology. (One of the current uses that is gaining acceptance is the interpretation and processing of human language commands for query, reporting, and execution of pre-programmed functions.)

In addition to fifth generation systems, a new category of software product, especially targeted for personal computers or workstations, has appeared in the past couple of years. A new buzzword has also developed around this category of software — CASE, for Computer-Aided Software Engineering — that appears to encompass the whole gamut of automated support for applications analysis, design, development, and maintenance. Unfortunately, as yet no one offers a Software Engineering tool kit that seamlessly integrates all of the required functions from analysis through maintenance.

1 INTRODUCTION

In the meantime, individual items of software are becoming available that assist in the initial analysis and design activities in a fashion similar to the way 4GLs assist in the detailed design, implementation, and maintenance stages of an applications development project. These "front end" tools are generally divided into two types: those that support the ideas of "software engineering" and those that support the ideas of "information engineering". Software Engineering refers to a procedure-driven approach to applications development, utilizing such methodologies as data flow diagrams and structure charts. Information Engineering, on the other hand, refers to a data-driven approach that "maps out" an organization-wide information strategy as the basis for applications development.[9]

Again, these software products have not been integrated into complete development tool kits to date, but are standalone tools that do a specific analysis or design function. As such, they do offer significant value in the correct environment, but they are not **by themselves** in any way the ultimate answer to automated support of the entire software development process. Eventually, all three of these concepts (4GLs, 5GLs, and CASE) will merge together into a fully integrated, automated Software Engineering Support System that will change the shape of computer programming completely. However, that day is still a few years away, at least.

New Software Development Tools

Until very recently a software developer who had a significant investment in applications created with **any Third Generation Language** had no choice but to move to an entirely new (and significantly different) 4GL, and begin all over again. Furthermore, no matter which 4GL he or she chose, much of the redevelopment would again be done with a 3GL, such as COBOL or C, as the 4GL could not do enough of the procedural work. No "real" alternative was available to take advantage of existing applications designs while employing development tools that would support the migration to new technologies. Fortunately, this is no longer the case.

A new set of application software development tools is now available from the Thoroughbred Division of Concept Omega Corporation that satisfies this requirement. The tool set is called Thoroughbred IDOL-IV — **Interactive Definition Oriented Language, Fourth Generation**. Its components are: DICTIONARY-IV, the IDOL-IV Design Dictionaries; IDOL-IV Database Maintenance, a powerful DBMS and Data Entry application; REPORT-IV, a developer and sophisticated end user report writer; and SCRIPT-IV, a set of powerful Fourth Generation Language constructs seamlessly integrated with Thoroughbred Business BASIC as well as the other IDOL-IV components. Together, these tools comprise a very substantial Applications Development System, or full-function 4GL, that should be of interest to any 3GL development enterprise.

The main objective of this book is to analyze the new 4GL technology, and to examine, using Thoroughbred IDOL-IV, how it can be put to use immediately to start a business applications developer on the road to Fourth Generation Applications Development. Using this type of technology is the only realistic way for a software development business to survive the next decade.

Notes and References

[1] These were once called minicomputers, but now encompass everything larger than single-user PCs up to, but not including, "mainframes" (usually from IBM).

[2] J. Martin, <u>Fourth Generation Languages, Volume I, Principles</u>, Englewood Cliffs, NJ: Prentice Hall, Inc., 1985.

[3] In fact, 3GLs were originally called "higher level languages". <u>Ibid</u>.

[4] <u>Ibid</u>.

[5] 4GLs have also been called "high-productivity languages". <u>Ibid</u>.

[6] Taken from a similar figure in Martin, <u>Ibid</u>, page 17.

[7] <u>Ibid</u> being among the best.

[8] <u>Ibid</u>.

[9] John Desmond, "Case Transfixes Users", <u>Software News</u>, April 1987.

2

A PHILOSOPHY OF HIGH TECHNOLOGY BUSINESS APPLICATIONS DEVELOPMENT

No matter how the estimates are made, there can be little argument that there is a significant need for additional business applications software, hence improved applications development technology. All major corporations admit to explicit programming backlogs for new applications of three to five years, and this does not account for the **implicit** backlogs (those requests that are simply not made because the explicit backlog is so large).

Numerous studies have been published in the past few years that show the cost of producing a "**working** line of 3GL code" to be approximately $10. An average 3GL programmer can produce only 10 to 15 such (again, the operative word here is **working**) lines of code PER DAY. And, a single 3GL program contains hundreds to thousands of lines of code. Furthermore, during the life of a typical 3GL program, the cost of a line of code increases to approximately 10 to 20 times the cost of creating it (mainly through maintenance and enhancements).

These programming statistics have not really changed for the past 10 to 15 years, while the improvements in the production of computer hardware have been rather astounding. It is generally accepted that the cost of the hardware required to execute one MIPS (million instructions per second) has been reduced by approximately 50 percent during **EACH** of the past five years. Also, many of the processes required to manufacture computer hardware have been automated to an amazing degree, while the majority of business applications software is still handcrafted by individuals or teams of increasingly more expensive programmers.

2 A PHILOSOPHY OF HIGH TECHNOLOGY BUSINESS APPLICATIONS DEVELOPMENT

Finally, with the proliferation of "personal computers" and the general improvement in computer literacy, the requirement for well designed, flexible, adaptable business applications software is increasing at an accelerating rate. The lack of this type of software is becoming the computer industry's largest problem.

For those who recognize and can take advantage of it, this lack offers a massive business opportunity — by utilizing the new advances in software development technology. However, several major issues must be examined in the process of considering any of the new applications development technologies for use in a software development enterprise.

Major Philosophical Issues

The first and foremost issues at hand are probably the most obvious ones, but, unfortunately, are many times thought to be the **only** issues to be considered. They **are** of primary importance, but other matters must also be taken into account that can result in a better business decision overall. These two primary issues are: (1) what computer environments (hardware and operating systems) are targeted for the 4GL and its resultant software?, and (2) can a 4GL or ADS (Applications Development System)[1] **really** do everything that is needed to create complete commercial business applications?

The first issue can be resolved fairly easily. Portability of applications software is not a new issue, and most developers of 4GLs take it into consideration to some degree. The first task then is to determine which 4GLs are available on the various hardware and operating systems of interest to you. This results in a much shorter list than considering every available tool set on the market today.

Unfortunately, there is not so simple an answer to the second question, as it depends largely on the application problem that is to be solved, and the tool (or tools) chosen to do the job. This issue is discussed in detail below.

The other issues relating to this decision are as much business and economic issues as technological ones. They include such questions as: how will a 4GL affect the way that software projects are dealt with? What will be the nature of the software solutions delivered to customers in the next five to ten years? How will "packaged software" be affected? And, how will the use of a 4GL affect the economic structure of the typical applications developer business?

Each of these issues is examined in this chapter, as we formulate a new business philosophy for dealing with business applications development in the next decade.

How Much Can Really be Done with a 4GL?

Can Fourth Generation Languages available **today** be used to develop **complete** commercial business application systems? Typically the answer is "Yes, if...". The "if" part of the answer has to do with how much you are willing to compromise on how the developed software functions, how it appears to the user, how much control you feel is required over the layout of screens and reports, etc. It is also related to what mechanism you are willing to use to write those intricate procedural functions that all business applications include. Finally, it is related to how sensitive you (and your customers) are to throughput (i.e., response time).

Each 4GL commercially available today has some potentially negative impact on these factors. Many 4GLs have serious performance penalties for any application other than simple data entry or reporting. It is not unusual at all to experience response time increases of 25 to 100 percent in simple data entry or reporting functions, and as much as 400 to 2000 percent in transaction processing functions, such as order processing or payroll pay cycle updating.

Many developers of 4GLs have made assumptions about the type and nature of the applications that will be developed with their tools. Developing an application that differs, even a little, from these assumptions may be very difficult, if not impossible. While it is true that there are only four or five major types of application programs in all business systems, the style and structure of these types of programs differ significantly from system to system and developer to developer. This makes it possible for companies to differentiate their products from others and encourages developers to add new functions to traditional business systems. Using someone else's ideas of the style and structure of your applications may not be in your best interests.

Many 4GLs "allow" the developer of a complete business application to "escape" to a 3GL (typically COBOL or C) for any intricate programming. Simple procedural functions can usually be created with the 4GL, but any significant procedural logic is beyond the capability of the language. As we discussed earlier, a full-function 4GL must have an inherent procedural capability, but requiring the developer to revert to an external 3GL is a very poor way of providing this functionality. Certainly many 3GLs provide good procedural capability, but the integration of procedural and non-procedural functions is vitally important. The 4GL tool set must be consistent and logical for maximum productivity gains to be achieved.

4GLs vary widely in their non-procedural components as well, with many 4GLs providing such a narrow range of non-procedural functions that an applications developer must resort to using procedural capabilities (such as an external 3GL) all too often. This, again, negatively impacts any productivity gains that might be achieved.

Very few 4GLs make any allowances for existing applications from a format/layout, user interface, or data storage point of view. New, **stand alone** applications can easily be created and delivered to end users who have existing software, but improved functionality or additional functions integrated with that existing software are virtually impossible.

The only rational alternative to this whole issue, then, is to pick a 4GL or ADS that provides as much of the new technology as possible with minimum detrimental impact on current activities. In other words, you should choose a 4GL with the following general characteristics: (1) that provides the throughput and response times that you and your customers expect and require, (2) that allows you to develop application programs in a multitude of styles and structures, (3) that provides a simple, but powerful, procedural language as an **inherent** part of the 4GL, not as an after thought, and (4) that allows you to develop applications that easily integrate with existing software in format/layout, user interface, and data storage.

How Will a 4GL Affect The Life Cycle of a Software Project?

Figure 2.1 contains the outline of a traditional software project life cycle that might be used by an applications development enterprise employing a 3GL.

A very traditional allocation of total project resources (manpower and time) through the first three phases of this life cycle might be 15 percent in Phase I, 60 percent in Phase II, and 25 percent in Phase III. Those of us who have spent any significant amount of time accomplishing these types of projects have long recognized the requirement to increase time spent in Phases I and III, and to decrease the time spent in Phase II. We have also recognized the need to reduce the artificial barrier between analysis and development, and to get better, more informed user feedback to the proposed system design.

Many software developers in the multi-user marketplace are not engaged in the development of single-customer systems. Rather, they are attempting to create systems that can be sold and installed in a number of customer companies. Irrespective of these issues, the software project life cycle must still be managed.

Step	Activities
	Phase I - Analysis and Design (15%)
1	Study the problem; interview user(s); make written notes as to user requirements
2	Accomplish data analysis and produce system design documentation (data flow diagrams, structure charts, screen and report layouts, etc.)
3	Review analysis and design documentation with user; upon approval, design is "fixed"
	Phase II - Development and Testing (60%)
4	Create new programs; modify existing programs; accomplish unit/program testing
5	Integrate all programs into new system
6	Accomplish system test and quality assurance
	Phase III - Delivery, Installation, and Training (25%)
7	Demonstrate new system to user; user reviews system to ensure it adheres to design
8	Make final adjustments to system components based on demonstration feedback
9	Finalize system documentation and create user documentation, if any
10	Deliver and install system; train users and system administrator
	Phase IV - Maintenance and Support
11	Provide ongoing maintenance and support for system problems

Fig. 2.1 Traditional Software Project Life Cycle

2 A PHILOSOPHY OF HIGH TECHNOLOGY BUSINESS APPLICATIONS DEVELOPMENT

One traditional solution to resource allocation (using 3GLs) was to design highly flexible, "parameter-driven" applications packages that could be "tailored" to a particular user's needs without as much programming as would be required with "hard-coded" applications systems. This solution was only possible, of course, to the extent that a "standard" applications package could be defined, designed, and implemented for a particular class of users. Thus, it was much of the driving force behind the concentration of applications developers into selected vertical market areas.

Although this approach did succeed in many cases, it has some serious drawbacks when used as the sole solution to this problem. First of all, to design a "good" vertical market software package requires that the designer fully understand all aspects of the target market, or the resultant system will not be applicable to all potential users in the market segment. This is a very rare person indeed.

And, even a well thought out and implemented package can be too restrictive in many instances. When many modifications must be made to apply it to a user's requirements, the functioning of many of the parameters can be destroyed. Sometimes it can get to the point where it would be better to start over and develop a custom system rather than modify a package.

Finally, testing a software package with a large number of parameters is virtually impossible. Successfully testing a "hard-coded" applications system is difficult enough. As a result, much of the testing of a parameterized package really occurs during each user installation. This can cloud the economic issues associated with the development and distribution of the package, as well as upset the users who perceive they are acquiring a "well tested" system.

What, then, can be done to improve this situation by using a 4GL? First, a 4GL provides the ability to create new programs very quickly. Therefore, new applications development can occur with less resources. If a "package" has been developed using a 4GL, changes to existing programs can take advantage of the same improvement in productivity.

Most 4GLs provide the ability to store system design information in their data dictionary or encyclopedia. This allows design documentation to be kept more up-to-date than when it is kept manually. Data analysis and system design tools can be utilized in conjunction with a 4GL to aid this activity even further. With many 4GLs no additional technical documentation is required other than that created in the process of developing the system.

Because 4GL "programs" are created with higher-level commands than are used in 3GLs, the likelihood that logic and significant programming errors will occur is reduced. Also, these higher-level commands are automatically "closer" in meaning and power to the specification of the user's requirements. Thus, less **translation** is required by the programmer between the system design and the actual programs. The system will more closely resemble the design and be easier to test as a result.

In addition to reducing the amount of resources required to accomplish the Phase II activities shown in Figure 2.1, a 4GL also provides a realistic alternative to the "fixed design" problem of the traditional 3GL life cycle. This alternative is called "prototyping", and encompasses an iterative design-development-design process (see Figure 2.2). The analyst/designer works with users to determine initial system requirements. The analyst/designer then creates a model or prototype of the system using the 4GL. This can take as little as an hour or as much as a few days.

When the prototype is ready for review, the analyst/designer and the user work together to understand how the system will function by analyzing the functioning and design of the model. The user really begins to understand what the system is capable of, and enhances his or her ideas for system needs as a result of seeing the model function. The analyst/designer better understands the user's problems and how the system might solve them. In essence, the user and the analyst/designer have a common tool to use to understand each other's language — the model or prototype. Further development and testing can be done by the analyst/designer or by a programmer.

At first it appears that this new life cycle will take longer than the one shown in Figure 2.1. However, what is not apparent from Figure 2.2 is that Phase II in general, and specifically Steps 5 and 6, will take fewer resources after thorough prototyping has been accomplished. The analyst/designer will have a much clearer idea of what the system is to do, and a much increased probability of success in meeting the user's requirements. It is even conceivable that Step 5 will essentially be complete at the end of the prototyping activities.

Step	Activities

Phase I - Analysis and Design (50%)

1. Study the problem; interview user(s); make written notes as to user requirements
2. Accomplish data analysis and produce system design documentation (data flow diagrams, structure charts, screen and report layouts, etc.); create initial prototype
3. Review prototype with user and get user feedback
4. Enhance/modify prototype and repeat Steps 3 and 4 until entire system has been prototyped and approved

Phase II - Development and Testing (20%)

5. Complete development of all system functions; accomplish unit/program testing
6. Integrate all programs into new system
7. Accomplish system test and quality assurance

Phase III - Delivery, Installation, and Training (30%)

8. Demonstrate new system to user; user reviews system to ensure it adheres to design
9. Make final adjustments to system components based on demonstration feedback
10. Finalize system documentation and create user documentation, if any
11. Deliver and install system; train users and system administrator

Phase IV - Maintenance and Support

12. Provide ongoing maintenance and support for system problems
13. Contract for modifications and enhancements, if any

Fig. 2.2 New Software Project Life Cycle Using Prototyping

Also, a new type of technical position begins to emerge — the "analyst/designer" mentioned above is more a business expert than a detailed programming expert. He or she must be able to understand user requirements and restate them in terms of the 4GL. At the same time, he or she accomplishes much of the task of the traditional "programmer".

As a result of this new approach to software development projects, the distribution of resources over the first three Phases might be as follows: 50 percent (or more) in Phase I, 20 percent in Phase II, and 30 percent in Phase III. These changes in the allocation of project resources have a marked impact on the validity of completed systems and user satisfaction. They also provide more time for creating better user documentation, accomplishing more detailed user training, and in general creating a more satisfied customer.

A programming task that might have been estimated to take 15 to 20 hours with a 3GL may only take 1.5 to 4 hours with a 4GL, with some or all of the work being accomplished during prototyping. The programmer will be able to accomplish the same task in a fraction of the time with a 4GL compared to a 3GL and will have much less to "code".

The other major impact of prototyping on the software project life cycle is on Phase IV. Prototyping encourages a system's design to evolve slowly as both user and developer better understand each other's requirements and capabilities. A system developed with a 3GL is usually quite difficult to change after installation and production use has begun. The use of a 4GL and prototyping techniques, however, starts the evolution of the system early in the project life cycle, and provides a mechanism for it to continue well after installation. Basically, this means that the user can begin to receive benefits from the system much quicker, as early versions of the system are made available, and can continue to receive increased benefits from the system as it evolves over time into a better and better solution to his or her problem.

Of course, there are also economic ramifications related to using this approach. These, as well as other business considerations, are discussed in the last section of this chapter.

Development of a New Generation of Application Software Packages

At this point it should become obvious that the prototyping technique described above combined with the advantages of a well-designed vertical market applications software package would make an extremely powerful business approach for software developers and installers. The amount of prototyping can be reduced by the existence of a software package targeted to the needs of a specific class of users, and the prototyping and development that is required can be done very quickly with a 4GL. All this leads us to the next logical question: what changes should be made in the design and development of such a 4GL-based software package (in relation to currently available 3GL-based packages)?

First and most important, the number of parameters required in a 4GL-based software package can be substantially reduced. Specifically, all parameters that have to do with changing the "cosmetics" of the system are no longer needed. A good 4GL will provide three capabilities that make these types of parameters obsolete: the ability to create and modify screen and report formats easily, the ability to separate these formats from the applications programs that use them, and a DBMS underneath the programs that handles the storage and formatting of data elements. This last capability also eliminates the need for parameters directed toward determining what data to store and how it is to be formatted.

The design activities used to create a 4GL-based vertical market package will concentrate on two primary issues — the data and information required to be stored and manipulated by the system, and the critical functions required to accept the data into the system and return the information in the proper form. Layout of screens and reports will still be important for initial acceptance, but will not be as critical, as they can be changed for each user with very little effort. Also, fewer application programs will need to be created, as users will expect to create many of their own reports. In some industries, users may even determine additional data items to store. In general, these factors will make it easier to develop a vertical market software package, but, of course, will not replace a good understanding of the industry and its potential users.

The list of objectives for a vertical market applications software package (see Figure 2.3) are not really any different when a 4GL is used than when a 3GL is used. The main difference is that many of the objectives can now be realistically achieved. A good 4GL provides the power and flexibility not only to create the package efficiently but also to maintain and enhance it over time so that it continues to meet the needs of its potential users.

- Portability across a wide range of computers maximizes the potential value of the package.
- Broad-based horizontal functionality allows an entry-level system to be installed and added onto as needs expand.
- Standardization of critical components among all users makes it possible to keep up with industry trends and maintain a consistent customer base.
- Ability to tailor cosmetics for each user allows the user to receive "high value" from the system while still utilizing a "package."
- Layered vertical functionality allows additional functions to be added to a user system as specific industry requirements and user growth dictate.
- Efficient supportability and maintainability makes it possible for the user to acquire economically feasible enhancements and modifications to the system over time.

Fig. 2.3 Objectives of Vertical Market Software Packages

Fourth Generation Languages and the Value of Software Activities

The last major issue that we will deal with in this chapter has to do with what impact a 4GL will have on the "value" of various software activities. Much of the income generated by both software developing and software installing companies comes from hourly billings. The amount of this income can be jeopardized when a 4GL is utilized, and especially a 4GL in conjunction with a 4GL-based software package, if proper planning does not take place. On the other hand, when planned for correctly, the utilization of a 4GL can have a healthy effect on a company's profitability.

It should be clear by now that one significant result of using a 4GL is productivity gain. A programmer will be able to accomplish the same task in 10 to 25 percent of the time with a 4GL compared to a 3GL. For example, a customer wants a change to his or her software that will take 10 hours with a 3GL. This work might traditionally be priced at $750 ($75 per hour). The same change may only take 1 to 2 hours with a 4GL (and 4GL-based package or system). Is the price to the customer still $750? Or is it now only $75 to $150?

2 A PHILOSOPHY OF HIGH TECHNOLOGY BUSINESS APPLICATIONS DEVELOPMENT

There is no simple answer to this question, but the "price" of the project mentioned above should be based on the "value" of the project to the customer, not necessarily on **either** hourly "estimates." Certainly the number of hours required to do the actual programming has some bearing on this value, but it never takes into consideration all the expense to the software developer or installer. All essential factors should be considered, such as documentation, testing, ongoing support, etc.; the 4GL should simply increase the probability of profit for the project. Using a 4GL should also offer you many more opportunities to do such work for your customers at a much higher probability of success overall.

The same "cost vs. value" issue arises as a result of the changes that a 4GL can have on the project life cycle discussed above. As a result, hourly billed steps in a software project should probably be replace with fixed priced steps. This approach will reduce the overall impact on the "top line" of the company while strengthening profitability of each project.

Another economic consideration when using a 4GL is that it generally takes people less time to learn to use a 4GL for development than a 3GL. It also requires a less accomplished programmer, in general, to create programs with a 4GL than with a 3GL. It is therefore possible for less experienced programmers to create quite good systems, and for programmer turnover to be less costly to the company. Because of the self-documenting aspects of 4GLs, their programs are usually easier for someone other than the original programmer to figure out and to modify, again reducing the cost of those activities.

Basically, a 4GL should be viewed, from an economic point of view, as the means to produce a higher quality product using less resources. When integrated correctly into the economic structure of a software enterprise, it can have a very positive effect on the "bottom line". Increased profitability is, of course, a significant advantage to both the company and its customers.

Conclusions

In the next decade business applications developers must utilize improved technology to be both operationally and economically effective. An Applications Development System must be chosen that satisfies the business requirements of the enterprise and contributes to its economic stability. This ADS must have the following characteristics:

(1) It must be able to accomplish all of the programming tasks that are required, in the style and structure chosen by the company's designers, offering the requisite response times for critical functions.

(2) It must support a prototyping-based software project life cycle.

(3) It must provide all of the capabilities necessary with which to develop a new generation of vertical software packages that can take advantage of this improved technology.

One of the very few Applications Development Systems that has all of the characteristics listed above is Thoroughbred IDOL-IV from Concept Omega Corporation. In addition, it has the relatively unique feature of allowing a developer who already has some applications developed in Business BASIC to evolve them into 4GL-based applications over time. A complete rewrite is **not required** to get started with this new technology. For someone with no Business BASIC investment, IDOL-IV offers a better alternative to 4GL-based applications development than most other 4GLs available today. In the following chapters we will examine exactly how these tools work and what types of applications development can be accomplished with them.

The utilization of a 4GL can have substantial impact on a company that develops or installs software and/or software packages. The major economic issue to remember is that the improved technology in the 4GL underlying a customer system has added significant value to that system by virtue of its inherent capabilities. In general, work done with a 4GL, and systems produced with a 4GL, have a higher intrinsic value than similar endeavors that use a 3GL.

Notes and References

[1] The term Applications Development System (ADS) will be used throughout the rest of this book as a synonym for 4GL. The author feels that it sometimes better expresses the true nature of many of the available products.

3

OVERVIEW OF THOROUGHBRED IDOL-IV

Before we get into the details of the application examples that comprise the remainder of this book, it will be helpful to examine in summary the various components of the tool set we will be using in later chapters. As well, we will discuss some terminology in this chapter that will be important to your understanding of the various design and development activities that follow.

As previously stated, the components of Thoroughbred IDOL-IV are: 1) DICTION-ARY-IV, the IDOL-IV Design Dictionaries, 2) IDOL-IV Database Maintenance, a sophisticated Data Base Management System; 3) REPORT-IV, used for creating reports and listings; and 4) SCRIPT-IV, used for creating any programs that are required in an application system that the other three components do not cover. These four components are described in summary fashion in this chapter, with examples that show the basic capabilities of each. The next chapter outlines a specific application problem and solution that will be used to examine in detail each component's features.

Application Development Terminology

In any applications software development environment there are a number of terms used to describe the various developmental activities and the objects on which these activities occur. In the next section we will review these terms as they are used in the Thoroughbred IDOL-IV development environment.

Any application program comprises a group of objects. These objects are generally thought of as: the application source code, the executable code, the screen or report definitions (if any), the file or table definitions (if any), menus that allow access to the program, and any descriptive information about these various objects (usually stored as

3 OVERVIEW OF THOROUGHBRED IDOL-IV

text, help, messages, dictionaries, etc.) that may be required to document their functioning. An application program created within the Thoroughbred IDOL-IV development environment is no different. It is, therefore, important to learn what each of these objects is called, so that you will better understand what is happening in the development process and be able to utilize the development tools more productively.

Some Terms Defined

The following is a list of terms used by Thoroughbred IDOL-IV components with a definition of each term and a short example:

FILE — the term "file" refers both to a physical data file from the operating system's point of view, and to a logical grouping of records related by a common unique identifier. It is similar to, but not as restrictive as, the definition of a relation or table used in Relational Data Base Management theory.

FIELD — "field" refers to a data element within a record. This is usually, but not always, the smallest piece of data with which a program can deal.

SCREEN — a "screen" is a picture that a program uses to display information from one or more files, one or more records at a time. Data can be placed anywhere on a screen, and can constitute fields from several files, computed fields created by the program, and variable or constant data.

FORMAT — a "format" refers to the specification of a record in a file or the fields to be displayed on a screen. In other words, it is the layout of the record or screen defining which fields are included, what type of data each field contains, editing and formatting information, etc.

GLOBAL DICTIONARY — this dictionary stores the default definition information for all system-wide fields. The default information can be changed when the field is used in a format, and changes to the global dictionary do not affect any definitions of fields already included in existing formats.

VIEW — a "view" of a file is a picture that shows several records from a file as rows on the terminal screen. Each field is displayed as one of the columns of a row. Data records can be displayed, maintained, or added using a view, and file-wide commands are available to make "mass" changes to or deletions from the whole file or selected groups of records.

LINK

the term "link" refers to an object that is used by IDOL-IV to relate formats, files, screens, and views. For example, a format can describe several different files; a screen can be used to display/maintain data in several different files/formats, etc. A link is created that relates each of these objects to its counterparts so that the developer can save even more time in designing the various components of his or her application system.

HELP

most development environments today have a "help" facility, and Thoroughbred IDOL-IV is no exception. However, the IDOL-IV help system is somewhat unique in that it is pervasive throughout all components of the system. Help text is named and can be set up at the time the other application objects are being created. This makes documenting the system very easy; descriptive information is written while all aspects of the development process are fresh in the developer's mind. Of course, help is not required, so a certain amount discipline is still necessary. But, creating help text in IDOL-IV is about as easy **to remember** to do as it is ever going to get.

MESSAGES

another of the dictionaries that is available within the IDOL-IV development environment is the "message list" dictionary. This function allows the developer to create and maintain the action and text of all messages needed in an application program or system. Messages can be either simple prompts that require no response or messages that require several different types of responses from the end user. Responses to messages can be alphanumeric entries, function keys, or a highlighted bar selected using cursor control keys.

MENU

a "menu" is a list of options (usually displayed using a "screen") such that when one is selected, an application function is executed or another menu is displayed. IDOL-IV contains a menu system designed to work with all of the various types of application functions that can be developed within the Thoroughbred environment

3 OVERVIEW OF THOROUGHBRED IDOL-IV

(including Thoroughbred BASIC programs). One distinct feature of this menu system is that a menu is not restricted to a **pre-defined** screen layout. In other words, the menu can be made to appear any way the designer wants it to.

LIBRARY — a "library" is a collection of application objects that are related in some fashion. In IDOL-IV a library is designated by the first two characters of the names of all the application objects within it. This helps organize objects together and makes it easier to find them when documentation is required on a system. The scope of a library is determined by the designer/developer, but should comprise a tightly related group of application programs and their respective objects, such as Accounts Receivable or Payroll.

DICTIONARY-IV: IDOL-IV Design Dictionaries

IDOL-IV has a number of jobs to perform, one of which is to act as a repository of information. Through its design dictionaries, it is used by the applications designer to create and store the description of files, screens, menus, the global data element dictionary, help text, and application messages. These dictionaries can also be used to describe the interrelationships among various application objects. It is intended that all information relating to the use of a system's application objects be stored and maintained here.

First, IDOL-IV allows the designer to create and describe a "library" as defined above. A library is identified by a two-character code that must precede the name of each object in that library. This code, then, is used as the first two characters of the name of the objects in each of the other dictionaries (except the Global Dictionary). A brief description of the library and several other statistics can be stored in the library definition.

The Global Dictionary of data elements is the only dictionary that is system-wide, rather than library-wide. And, as such, it is very helpful in maintaining consistency among the uses of the same or like fields. The Global Dictionary can be either created as a first step in database design, or can be created "after the fact" once formats are created. A designer that follows good database design techniques will create the Global Dictionary first, and then refer to fields in the Global Dictionary as he or she creates formats of files. This ensures that fields that should have the same characteristics do, except where specifically required otherwise.

Once the Global Dictionary has been created, the designer may then create the definition of any files required in the application database. This is done by defining formats in the format dictionary of IDOL-IV. Each format must be assigned to a library, and can contain up to 99 fields.[1] Each field must have at least a name[2] and a length specification, but may also contain a number of additional (optional) specifications.

Among these optional specifications are data type (a field defaults to a character string type), data formatting, validation rules, and aids to entry and editing of the data (e.g., prompting message, help text, default values). Of course, these specifications should come from the Global Dictionary definition of the field initially, but can be overridden in a give format. Also, clever design of the Global Dictionary allows the designer to use the same global definition for many copies of the same type of field.

For example, let's say that a format is to contain several groups of three fields as shown in Figure 3.1. This situation could require a large number of different global entries in some systems, but in IDOL-IV it requires only three. The name of the respective global entry is used to "load" the default field specifications into the format, and then the name of the field is changed to the name required in the format for that specific field.

In other words, the global field "school-name" in Figure 3.1 is used as the basis for the "local" fields "high-school", 'undergrad-school", and "graduate-school". (The connection between the other "local" fields and their respective global fields is more easily seen.) It should also be noted that this use of the Global Dictionary is facilitated by defining all of the global data elements **before** defining any formats.

At the time that formats are being created, the designer is offered the opportunity to create help text on any field. In fact, the designer must take specific action to **avoid** being prompted to enter help text. This field help text will be available to a user anytime that field from that format is displayed on a screen.

In addition to the dictionaries mentioned above, the designer is allowed to create and maintain a list of messages that can be used throughout the applications. Two basic types of messages are available — prompt/constant messages that display text but do not require response, and action messages that require some type of response. There are three types of responses to action messages: 1) a yes/no response, 2) a specific list of valid responses, and 3) either the **RETURN** or **END** keys.

3 OVERVIEW OF THOROUGHBRED IDOL-IV

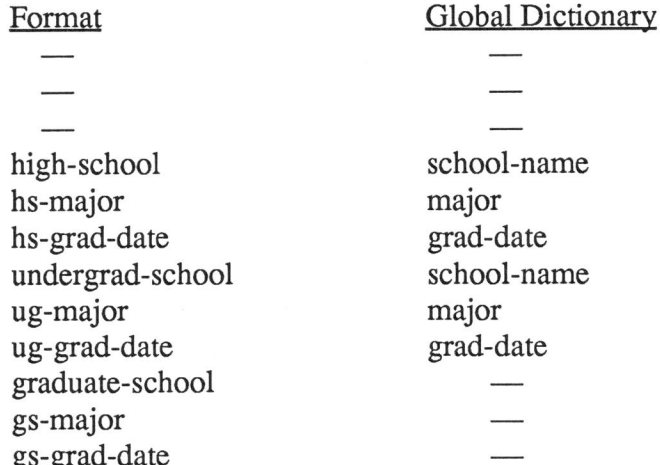

Fig. 3.1 Relationship Between the Global Dictionary and Fields in a Format

Messages stored in the message list dictionary are quite valuable in that they are externalized from each program and can be more easily maintained. This encourages standardization among message text, and promotes the ability to customize the system for a specific user or class of users. It also allows the software system to be quite simply translated to a foreign language. It is curious that more Applications Development Systems do not provide this simple, but very important, function.

IDOL-IV Database Maintenance

As soon as a format has been created, the designer can "test" the record layout and field editing specifications by allowing IDOL-IV to create default screens, views, and links. This **default design** function can also be useful for simple table lookup files that only contain a few data elements, and where screen design is not critical. Important screens in the system, however, should not be created in this default manner, as esthetics for the user are of prime importance in determining user satisfaction.

The designer selects the "Database Maintenance" option by pressing function key **F2** on any IDOL-IV Menu, and the first activity that IDOL-IV completes is to create the physical data file on disk. Then, the default screen is displayed with a number of options: 1) add, 2) change, 3) delete, 4) inquiry, 5) select fields to maintain, and 6) change file. In addition, all of the active function keys are displayed with their current action/result. Within each of these options there are several additional actions available. In essence this is a hierarchical menu system built inside the IDOL-IV Database Maintenance function.

The Database Maintenance (DBM) function also provides an applications developer the ability to create many of his or her data entry functions without writing any "programs" per se. This development function, in conjunction with the IDOL-IV menus, allows a developer to set up formats, paint screens, and allow user access to different screens or views as if each were a separate data entry program. At the most, the developer may have to create some subroutines to accomplish specialized field editing, file/record lookup, etc., within an IDOL-IV DBM screen. Of course, built right into the format definition is the ability to specify a field editing (or other type of) subroutine. Some limitations do exist in IDOL-IV DBM that cause more complex data entry programs to be created with SCRIPT-IV, however, and these will be discussed later in this chapter.

While using the IDOL-IV DBM function, the user may query the file for specific records in one of several ways. The easiest way is to specify some or all of the primary key value in the primary key field and press the **Down Arrow** key. This selects the "starting" record that matches or follows that value and displays it. By pressing the **Down Arrow** key again, the user may display the "next" record, etc., until the end of the file is encountered. At this point the sequence starts over at the first record in the file. The **Up Arrow** key here causes the "previous" record to be displayed.

Records may also be displayed in one of the secondary key sequences by selecting one of the available secondary keys, entering a starting key value and pressing the **Down Arrow** or **Up Arrow** key. Subsequent "next" or "previous" records in that sequence may also be displayed as above.

Screens, Views, and Links

The next step in the design/development process with IDOL-IV is the creation of custom screens, views, and links for data entry programs. An IDOL-IV screen has three aspects to its definition: the list of fields available for display (i.e, the screen's format), parameters that define the characteristics of the screen, and the screen image itself. The screen parameters include the name and a brief description of the screen, its related format, the size and shape of the screen and the size and location of the screen's help window. These parameters can be defined when the screen is initially created, and maintained at any subsequent time.

The screen image is then "painted" on the terminal visually using fairly sophisticated text editing capabilities. The screen image can contain literal text, up to 99 fields from the screen's format, (including fields from lookup files), calculated fields, and highlighting or border areas to aid the user's eye in grouping data elements. The ability to make a screen image pleasing and useful to the user is a significant feature of IDOL-IV.

Another version of a display/maintenance screen for data entry is called a "view" in IDOL-IV. It is a multiple record presentation of records from a single file, and it allows both individual record changes and deletions as well as a number of multiple record functions. These functions include such things as: displaying a list of records that contain specific values in specified fields, counting the number of records in a group, sorting a group of records, changing the value of a field in a group of records, deleting a group of records, copying a group of records to a new file, or moving a group of fields to a new file. The view maintenance function in IDOL-IV is very powerful, and can be extremely useful to a user once he or she understands its capabilities.

A very unique feature of IDOL-IV is the concept of a "link". This is an application object that defines the relationships among files, formats, screens, and views. It also contains information on the security of the associated objects, and allows an applications designer the flexibility of creating several screens for the same format/file, etc. Much more detail on the functioning of links can be found in later chapters.

IDOL-IV Menus

Again, it is amazing how many Applications Development Systems do not provide the relatively simple function of a menu system with which to collect a related group of programs. It is true that it does not take much effort to create a simple menu program, but it is not trivial to create a menu system with built-in security checking, parameter passing, hierarchical processing, and all of the other functions required by today's computer users.

IDOL-IV includes a menu system that provides all of the functions required in an application system created within the Thoroughbred development environment. A menu screen can contain up to 99 selections, and the built-in security system is quite extensive. The designer can create his or her own screen for displaying the menu options and accepting the user's selection, and the selections can be any combination of up to 4 characters or numbers. Also, help text can be created on the menu so that a novice user can get instructions on which option to select to do a specific job. All in all, the menu system is quite sophisticated and promotes the idea of creating a complete system within the development environment.

Special Screen Features

There are four features that IDOL-IV screens contain that should be of special interest to today's applications designers. These are windows, text fields, text editing in all fields, and horizontal scrolling of input fields. Each of these features are described below.

A good example of the use of windows within an IDOL-IV screen is the help system. Each help message is displayed in a variable sized window that may be located anywhere on the terminal screen. Windows can be similarly used in SCRIPT-IV programs to display data requested by the end user.

Text fields are exactly what they sound like — fields that contain lines of text. This is one of the optional field specifications that is available within a format definition, and provides a practically unlimited amount of room for textual data on a record. There can be more than one text field stored per record, and text field maintenance utilizes a window (similar to a help message), which is displayed for entry/viewing/maintenance and then cleared. In fact, help messages are text fields in IDOL-IV system files.

Text fields, as well as all other data fields, allow text editing capabilities during user input and maintenance. These editing functions include inserting and deleting characters and lines, clearing lines, cursor movement within a single field, and many more functions in a multi-line text field. For example, by using the insert line function, a user can maintain a chronological log of activity on a customer, prospect, etc., within a text field with the latest entry always displayed at the "top" of the field.

In addition to the text editing features described, IDOL-IV's various data entry processes provide some standard function keys that react the same everywhere in the system. These are the **END** key, the **HELP** key, and the **GOTO** key. The standard **END** key is Function Key 4 (**F4** or **PF4**); the standard **HELP** key is Function Key 6 (**F6** or **PF6**); the standard **GOTO** key is Function Key 10 (**F10** or **PF10**). At any spot in IDOL-IV where the system is awaiting input, these keys maybe used to "step back one step" (or exit a program, whichever is appropriate), access help data, or skip to a specific field (by number) or record (by key value). This standardization is a feature in many Application Development Systems, and makes the user interface much simpler to learn and remember.

Finally, any data entry field may be defined on a screen as shorter than its defined length in the format. By doing so the designer saves valuable screen space (especially for long character fields), and automatically provides the user the ability to scroll the field horizontally simply by moving the screen cursor toward either end of the field. Additional characters will be displayed one at a time as the cursor is moved with the arrow keys or in groups using the **TAB** and **BACK TAB** keys. This is of significance in almost any screen design, and again, it can promote more effective screen layout resulting in higher user satisfaction.

REPORT-IV

REPORT-IV is a sophisticated report generator that can be used to develop complex as well as simple reports. It is easily used by an applications developer, and may be useful to an advanced computer user. But, it is a little too complicated for the novice user to handle. As a result of this sophistication, REPORT-IV may be able to handle all (or nearly all) of an application's reporting requirements, keeping the developer from having to create "report programs" with SCRIPT-IV.

In general, REPORT-IV can generate a printout of data from one or more files (formats or links) defined in the IDOL-IV Design Dictionaries. It can select any specific group of records, sort these records properly, process each record as needed, calculate subtotals and totals, and print the end results using features such as page breaks, headings, footings, special character styles, boldfacing, and underscoring. Furthermore, the layout of the report is created by "painting" a picture of it similarly to the screen design process mentioned above.

The basic steps used to create reports with REPORT-IV are similar to those used to develop other IDOL-IV application functions. These steps are: 1) conceive the general contents and layout of the report, 2) locate the data elements that are required for the report, 3) create a report draft (manual layout) of the report's contents and form, 4) create and enter the report definition into REPORT-IV, and 5) generate (execute) the report to produce its output. These steps will be accomplished in detail in a subsequent chapter for several sample reports to give you an idea how REPORT-IV actually works.

The definition of a report in REPORT-IV comprises several different sections. First, parameters are entered that define what library the report belongs to, what its name and description are, who owns it, etc. Next, the report layout is entered. This is broken down into Entry, File, Control, and Report sections. The Entry Section is used to specify the definition of any variable data required by the report, and Initialization and Termination routines. The File Section is used to indicate what files are to be used by the report. The Control Section may be used to control the printing of special lines or report components, specify and control totals and subtotals, specify conditional page breaks, etc. And, the Report Section contains the actual specification of the report layout — in other words, the position of data fields, formulas, literal text, etc. Specific examples of these definition details are included in a subsequent chapter.

Once a report definition has been completed, the report may be tested by executing it. This may be done by using REPORT-IV's Print (Display) Report function, by hooking the report up to an IDOL-IV Menu, or by executing it from a SCRIPT-IV script. The Print (Display) Report function allows a single report or a range of report names to be printed to a selected printer or displayed to the terminal screen. Prior to executing the report, data may also be collected from the user via a data entry screen. In essence, all of the various types of printing facilities required for a complete application system are provided within IDOL-IV.

SCRIPT-IV

As stated earlier in this book, SCRIPT-IV is a set of powerful Fourth Generation Language constructs (commands) seamlessly integrated with Thoroughbred Business BASIC. By itself Thoroughbred Business BASIC is itself a very substantial Third Generation Language that has been used to create a huge library of business applications worldwide. This combination results in a full-function 4GL that is second to none (and far superior to many) in capability.

In fact, SCRIPT-IV alone, when combined with the IDOL-IV Design Dictionaries, is suitable for developing complete business application systems. All the necessary data entry, report, menu, and update programs can be created with this language. However, that is not **required** due to the other aspects of the IDOL-IV development environment. Simple data entry functions can be accomplished with IDOL-IV DBM, menus can be defined using IDOL-IV Menus, and almost all reporting functions can be defined using REPORT-IV. The only application functions that **have** to be created with SCRIPT-IV are update functions, and complex or unique data entry and report functions. Therefore, the application designer has a wide range of choices when it comes to the look, feel, and operation of his or her IDOL-IV-based application system.

A related group of SCRIPT-IV commands that accomplishes a specific application function is called a "script" (rather than a program). This is a somewhat arbitrary differentiation, but is important if for no other reason than that both 3GL programs (Business BASIC) and 4GL scripts (SCRIPT-IV) may reside together in an application system. It is, therefore, a good idea to keep the two types of objects separate.

Finally, SCRIPT-IV commands can be grouped into several categories based on their respective function or use. These categories are: Data Declaration, File Control, Record Access, Screen/Printer I/O, Procedural, and Program Control. Data Declaration commands are available to define data variables, formats, links, screens, and views within a 4GL script. To use any of these types of objects in a script, the developer must first declare them.

File Control is accomplished using the **OPEN, CLOSE, LOCK,** and **UNLOCK** commands, functions that are fairly straightforward in most languages. Record Access can be done with **ADD, CHANGE, DELETE,** and **READ**. These functions are more complicated and deserve a closer look, which we will give them in later chapters. Screen/Printer I/O is accomplished using **INPUT** (from screen), **PRINT** (to screen or printer), and **SETTRACE**, which is really a diagnostic command that causes program execution tracing to be displayed on the specified device.

Procedural commands include **LET** (assignment), **IF/THEN/ELSE/ENDIF**, **DIM** (creates arrays of various sizes), **DO** (to execute a particular procedure within a script or a loop containing several commands), **SET** (set formatted date and/or time), and **PRECISION** (used to control the number of decimal places that will be calculated and stored). Also, any of the functions available in Thoroughbred Business BASIC are available within a 4GL script.

Finally, Program Control is accomplished with **CALL, RUN,** and **ENTER** (to execute various program/script segments), **INCLUDE** (to include a copy of an external script into another script at compile time), **TERMINATE** (to end execution of a script or procedure), and **WAIT** (to pause execution). Most of these commands are used in the sample 4GL scripts included in later chapters of this book.

Conclusions

As you can see, the IDOL-IV Design Dictionaries are a very powerful component of Thoroughbred IDOL-IV. They allow an applications designer to create and store the definitions of all of the objects necessary for database and system design — data elements, record formats, screens, menus, help text, messages, and the interrelationships among these objects. IDOL-IV Database Maintenance provides sophisticated capabilities that promote the extremely quick development of simple screen-oriented applications. In addition, REPORT-IV is capable of supporting nearly all of an application system's reporting requirements.

SCRIPT-IV by itself is powerful enough to create complete application systems. When combined with the components mentioned above, it provides even more efficiency and effectiveness by supporting the development of complex data entry and report functions, and all update functions. Once all of these components have been put to use, the application system's functions can be neatly packaged up and presented to the user for access via the IDOL-IV Menu System.

It should be obvious at this point that Thoroughbred IDOL-IV is at least as powerful as any other Applications Development System available on the market today. It can be used to develop new systems that have all the sophistication and utility of "Fourth Generation Language"-based software. And, it can be used to develop new functions within existing Thoroughbred Business BASIC systems, because of the developer's control over the resulting software's appearance, style, and structure. This development system is truly a vehicle to consider seriously as a means of moving a software development enterprise profitably into the next decade.

Notes and References

[1] Most of the limits inherent in the Thoroughbred IDOL-IV development environment are practical rather than physical limits.

[2] A field name CANNOT contain a period (.), but can contain dashes (-) and letters and numbers.

4

THE BUSINESS APPLICATIONS DESIGN PROCESS

In this chapter we will discuss a number of issues relating to the design of business applications software. We will examine a specific application problem and its design solution. In this context we will review in summary the design processes that today's successful business software developers are using. Also, we will discuss specifically how Thoroughbred IDOL-IV aids in these design activities.

The design activities that successful business software developers use today can be divided into two major components: data or database design, and process or procedure design. We will not discuss at length the issues relating, or the processes used, to gather a system's requirements. The assumption made here is that the types of problems you will be solving are not of the nature that require scientific research or other serious analytical efforts. Rather, they are the more traditional business problems that require "good" systems analysis (usually relating to the data requirements of the system) followed by a somewhat informal, but accurate and methodical, system design.

With that in mind, we can relate the two components of systems design mentioned above to two corresponding methodologies that are quite helpful in fulfilling the respective design activities. These methodologies are: data normalization and structured design. This is not to say that other methodologies are unnecessary or that these are the only ones to use. In the situation where most of the system design is inherent in understanding the problem to be solved, these two methodologies are all that is needed to ensure the resultant software system is well designed and functional.

Introduction to Data Normalization

Data normalization[1] is a small subset of the formal process of Data Analysis, which includes a number of additional activities. For relatively small, simple business systems, most of the other activities that comprise Data Analysis are not required. When large, complex, high volume, high transaction rate systems are being designed, the activities of Data Analysis other than data normalization become significant, and should be considered in detail. For the sake of this discussion, however, we will concentrate on data normalization and leave the rest of Data Analysis for another time.

Quite simply, data normalization is the process of grouping data elements into a logical structure of records. It is accomplished for the following reasons:

1) to reduce redundancy that can cause problems with the storage and retrieval of data

2) to identify all dependencies that can cause problems when deleting data elements or changing the data design

3) to simplify the structure and contents of each record

A fully normalized record consists of a unique identifier relating to some system entity, together with a set of fields that describe that entity. For example, a customer file should contain records describing a customer (entity) identified by a unique customer code or number. The process of data normalization, then, is the iterative decomposition of potential groups of data elements into simpler and simpler records. Designing a group of files using data normalization rules will result in a system that is not only logically understandable but also much easier to implement and maintain.

Relational Data Modeling

The concepts of data normalization were originally developed in conjunction with the ideas surrounding the relational approach to data modeling. We will not cover the entire relational theory in this book, but we do need to understand a few of its concepts in order to deal with the issues and procedures of data normalization.

The relational data model has three major components: the data structure, data integrity rules, and data manipulation operators. This data model is based on a mathematical theory that logically describes terms and rules for representing data in a particular fashion. It encompasses the logical representation of data, not its physical storage.

In extremely simplified terms the relational data structure (see Figure 4.2) describes a data model that **appears to the user** as a table (called a 'relation') of rows (called 'tuples', pronounced "tooples") and columns (called 'attributes'). The rows can be thought of as **records** in a file, and the columns as **fields** in a record, each field being defined to take on values from a set or pool (called a 'domain') of possible values.

There are a number of additional details, but the most important ones for this discussion are:

1) each record (tuple) in the file (relation) contains the **exact same fields** (attributes) as all other records, and

2) each field (attribute) is **atomic,** in that it can contain only a single value and not a list of values.

Some Applications Development Systems allow either or both of these rules to be violated (in fact IDOL-IV allows the first rule to be violated for compatibility with existing software), but for our discussion we will assume that these relational data structure rules are followed without fail.

In relational theory, the data manipulation operators are the types of commands that are allowed to be performed on data stored relationally, and are of no interest to us at this point. However, the relational integrity rules introduce some terms that are of use to us in understanding and describing data normalization. These terms include:

PRIMARY KEY   the field (attribute) or combination of fields that **uniquely** identifies each record (tuple) in a file (relation). See Figure 4.1.

FOREIGN KEY   a field (attribute) or combination of fields in a record (tuple) that are the primary key to another file (relation). See Figure 4.4 later in the chapter for an example of a foreign key.

4 THE BUSINESS APPLICATIONS DESIGN PROCESS

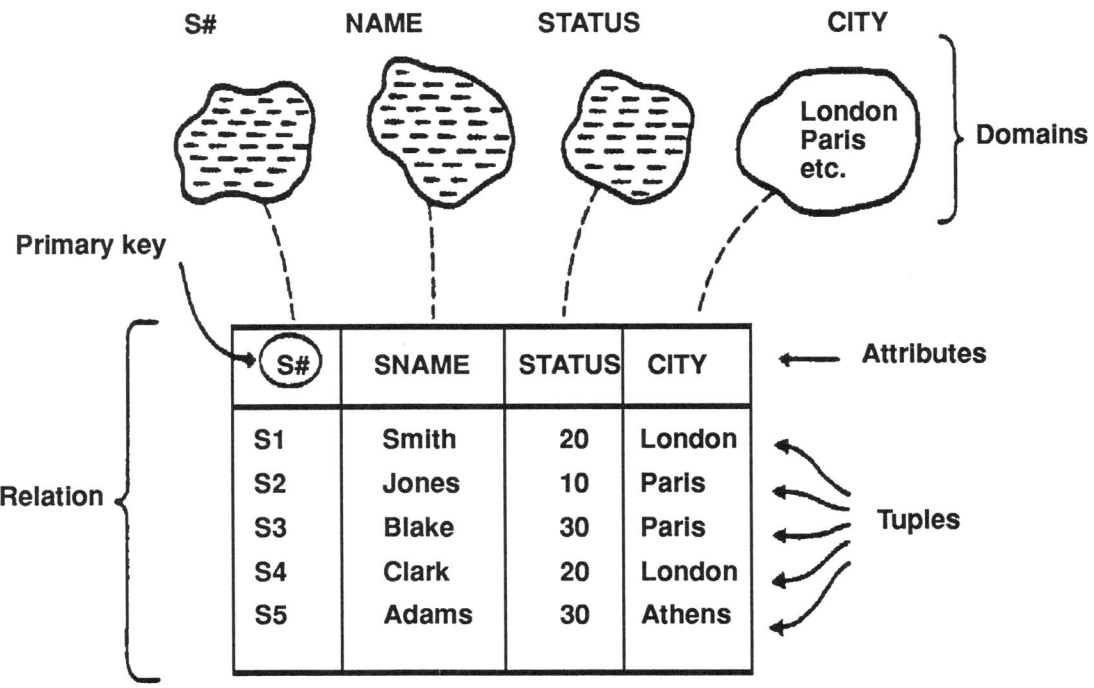

Fig. 4.1 The Relational Data Structure

Again, there are a number of additional details involved in the relational data integrity rules, but these two terms will suffice for this discussion. With these few concepts and terms we can now begin our examination of data normalization.

Data Normalization Rules

The first step in data normalization is to gather all of the potential data elements together that could possibly be associated with each other in describing an entity of the system. This is typically the result of requirements analysis, and can be done in any number of ways. One simple method used quite often is to analyze a company's existing documents and reports as the source of entities and their descriptive attributes.

Irrespective of methodology, what results from this step is an unnormalized file (relation). For example, Figure 4.2 shows a sample form that a company might use to record the personnel requisition for a new employee. (This form is taken from the example application described later in this chapter.)

Figure 4.3 shows the unnormalized file that results from analysis of the Personnel Requisition Form. The **boldfaced** field at the first of the list of fields is the unique identifier (primary key) of the file.

The next step is to convert the unnormalized file into **first normal form**. First normal form requires that **repeating groups** be removed from the unnormalized file and placed into a new file. A "repeating group" is a field or group of fields that can take on more than one value within a record. The key of the new file will most likely be the key of the unnormalized file concatenated with the identifier field (or fields) of the repeating group.

In the Personnel Requisition example above no repeating groups can be found. However, this phenomenon is common in the database design of accounting systems. Figure 4.4 shows an example sales order form that contains just such a situation. The detail line of the sales order is a "repeating group" made up of the fields: item code, item description, unit of measure, quantity ordered, item price and extension in the unnormalized entity, **order** (these are shown underlined in the list of fields in Figure 4.4).

When this entity is placed in first normal form, this group of fields must be removed into a separate file storing order detail lines. The result is two files: **order** records (primary key = order number) and **order line** records (primary key = order number + item code). These two files are shown in Figure 4.5.

At this point we need one additional definition to continue this description of the data normalization rules.

4 THE BUSINESS APPLICATIONS DESIGN PROCESS

PERSONNEL REQUISITION FORM

Requisition No: _____ Date: _____

POSITION INFORMATION:

Job Code: _____ Job Title: _____

Status: (FT/PT): _____ Exempt/Non-Exempt: _____

EEO Code: _____ Salary Grade: _____

Minimum Salary: _____ Maximum Salary: _____

If Part Time, then Part Time Rate: _____

Department: _____ Shift: _____

Primary Work Location: _____

Education Required for Job: _____

Experience Required for Job: _____

_____

_____

REQUISITION APPROVAL:

Approver Name: _____

Title: _____ Date: _____

FOR PERSONNEL DEPARTMENT ONLY:

Person Assigned to Fill Req: _____

Telephone: _____ Billing Rate: _____

New Position? _____ Internal Search? _____

Replacement For: _____ Sched Term Date: _____

Status of Requisition: _____

Disposition Date: _____ Who Filled: _____

Total Costs: _____ No Days to Fill Req: _____

Fig. 4.2 Sample Personnel Requisition Form

Data Normalization Rules

File Name	Field Names
Requisition	**requisition #**, req date, job code, job title, education required, salary grade, minimum salary, maximum salary, department, job status (full time/part time), part time rate, shift, location, EEO code, exempt/non-exempt, prior job experience required, recruiter assigned, recruiter telephone, recruiter rate, internal search?, new position?, replacement for, replacement date, req status, disposition date, total costs, approver, approver title, approval date, no. days to fill position, ident.

Fig. 4.3 Unnormalized Personnel Requisition File

FUNCTIONAL DEPENDENCE — one field (attribute), say A, is functionally dependent on another field, say B, if for each value of A there can be associated with it only one value of B. A is said to be functionally dependent on B; B is said to be a determinant of A.

This is an extremely important part of database design and must be well understood and accurately reflected in your database definition to achieve effective system implementation. On the Personnel Requisition Form, for example, the requisition date, job code, education required, etc., are functionally dependent on the Requisition Number. That is, given a specific Requisition Number, there exists only one value for each of these fields. We will test whether or not this is true for all fields in the Personnel Requisition example later in this section.

Functional dependence can also be applied to files with a compound (multiple field) primary key. In this case, **full** functional dependence requires that each field in the file be dependent on the **combination** of the key fields and **not** on only one of them. (The term, functional dependence, is used throughout this discussion as a synonym for "full functional dependence").

Using this definition, we can now take the next step — to convert the first normal form files into **second normal form**. Second normal form requires that the file be in first normal form and that every non-key field (attribute) be functionally dependent on

4 THE BUSINESS APPLICATIONS DESIGN PROCESS

the entire primary key. Assuming that the data analysis resulted in reasonable and logical unnormalized groupings of fields, any file that has a single-field primary key should be in second normal form.

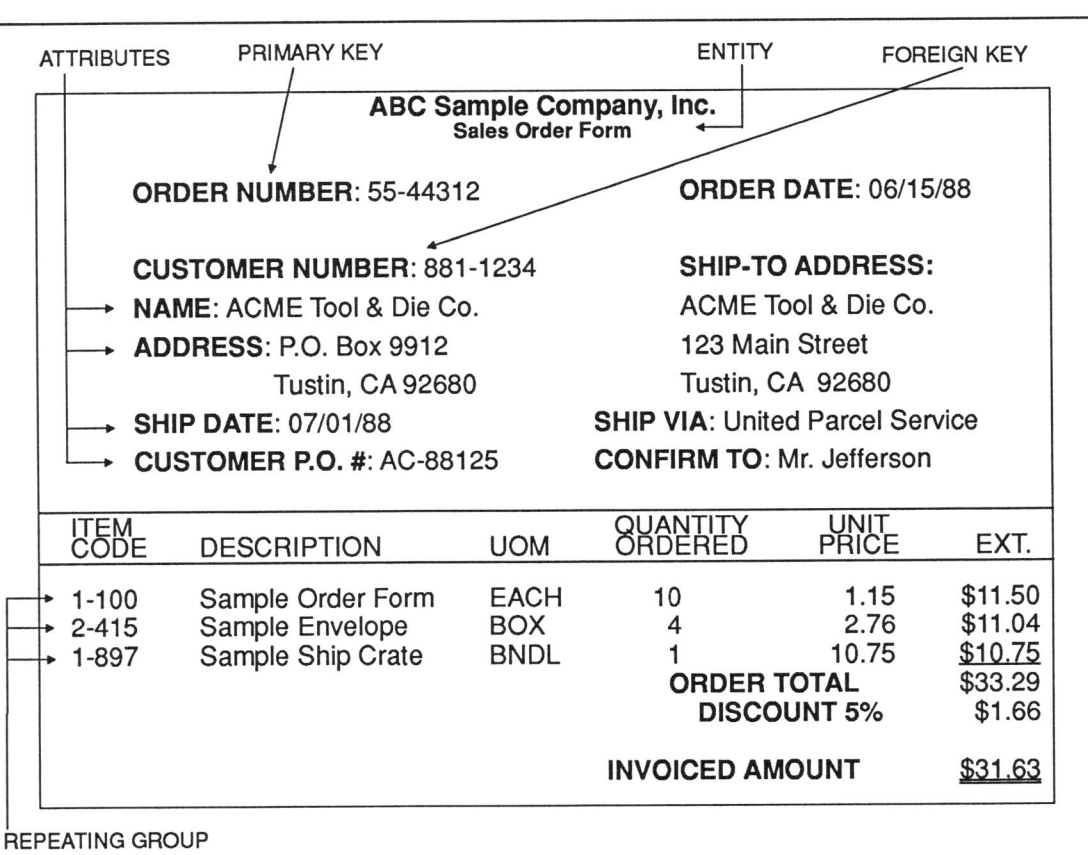

File Name | Field Names

ORDER | (**order #**, customer #, order date, customer name, customer bill-to address, customer ship-to address, ship date, customer p.o. #, ship via, confirm to, total order amount, order discount percent, order discount amount, invoiced amount, <u>item code</u>, <u>item description</u>, <u>unit of measure</u>, <u>quantity ordered</u>, <u>item price</u>, <u>extension</u>)

Fig. 4.4 Sample Sales Order Entity Showing a Repeating Group

File Name	Field Names
ORDER	(**order #**, customer #, order date, customer name, customer bill-to address, customer ship-to address, ship date, customer p.o. #, ship via, confirm to, total order amount, order discount percent, order discount amount, invoiced amount)
ORDER LINE	(**order #, item code**, item description, unit of measure, quantity ordered, item price, extension)

Fig. 4.5 First Normal Form of Sales Order Files

In other words, second normal form conversion only applies to files whose primary keys are made up of more than one field. Fields that are not functionally dependent on the entire primary key of a file with a compound key must be removed into a new file. The key to this new file will be the field that was the "partial key determinant" in the old file.

The Personnel Requisition example has no files that have compound primary keys, so the Personnel Requisition file shown in Figure 4.3 is also in **second normal form**. On the other hand, the sales order example also mentioned above now has a file that is a candidate for second normalization as a result of our first normalization efforts — the order detail line file — since it has a compound primary key.

And, referring once again to Figure 4.5, you will notice that there are three fields in the order detail file that are **not functionally dependent** on the **combination** of order number and item code. These fields are: item description, unit of measure, and item price. They are functionally dependent **solely** on item code (their "partial key determinant"). Therefore, these fields must be removed into another new file, called **product**, let's say, whose key is item code, and whose fields are: item code, item description, unit of measure and item price (among others). The order detail line file is now in second normal form, as are the sales order file and the product file, by virtue of their single-field keys (see Figure 4.6).

File Name	Field Names
ORDER	(**order #**, customer #, order date, customer name, customer bill-to address, customer ship-to address, ship date, customer p.o. #, ship via, confirm to, total order amount, order discount percent, order discount amount, invoiced amount)
ORDER LINE	(**order #, item code**, quantity ordered, item price, extension)
PRODUCT	(**item code**, item description, unit of measure, item price)

Fig. 4.6 Second Normal Form of Sales Order Files

You will note at this point in our discussion of the sales order example, that it is quite likely that item price should also be stored in the order detail line file as well as in the product file. This, at first glance, is a violation of the very data redundancy rules that we are trying to uphold. However, there is a valid operational reason to do this that makes these two fields essentially two **different** data elements.

The item price in the **product** file is a static price, changed periodically as vendor costs dictate. The item price on a detail line of an order may be overridden once it is loaded into the file as the needs of the order, and the sales rules of the company, dictate. In this case, the field, item price, in the order detail line file **is** functionally dependent on the entire compound key.

The last step in the normalization process that we will discuss here is to convert the second normal form files into **third normal form**. Third normal form requires that a file be in second normal form and that each non-key field (attribute) be functionally dependent on the primary key and not dependent on any non-key field. Any fields that fit this criterion are said to have a **transitive dependence** on the primary key of the "old" file, and must be removed into a new file, the key of which is the "field determinant" in the old file. This field determinant will also remain in the old file as a **foreign key**.

In the sales order example shown in Figure 4.4, customer number is indicated as a **foreign key,** and in the Personnel Requisition example shown in Figures 4.2 and 4.3, there are several fields that are candidates for being removed from the Personnel Requisition File. The first group of candidate fields: job title, job status (full time/part time), and exempt/non-exempt are functionally dependent on **job code** and should be removed into a new file, called **job codes**. The next group of candidate fields: minimum salary and maximum salary are functionally dependent on **salary grade** and should be removed into a new file, called **salary grade**. The final group of candidate fields: recruiter telephone and recruiter rate are dependent on **recruiter assigned** and should be removed into a new file, called **recruiter**.

Finally, the Total Recruiting Costs and No. of Days to Fill Requisition fields are more logically stored in a different file, which we will discuss in detail later in the book. Figure 4.7 shows the results of this last normalization step as four files, all in third normal form. Again, the **boldfaced** field at the beginning of the field name list is the primary key, and foreign keys are shown underlined.

File Name	Field Names
Requisition	**requisition #**, req date, job code, education level required, salary grade, department, part time rate, shift, location, EEO code, experience required, recruiter assigned, internal search?, new position?, replacement for, replacement date, req status, disposition date, approver, approver title, approval date, ident.
Job Codes	**job code**, job title, job status, exempt class, EEOC Job Category
Salary Grade	**salary grade**, description, salary minimum, salary maximum
Recruiter	**recruiter id**, name, telephone, rate, internal recruiter
Experience Codes	**experience code**, description (see NOTE)

Fig. 4.7 Personnel Requisition Files in Third Normal Form

NOTE: One additional code file may also be a good design idea although it is not really required by normalization rules. This file is an experience code file, and is useful to ensure that "standard" experience descriptions are entered on each applicant. This will make searching for a given type of experience much easier and more likely to be successful.

This elimination of the transitive dependence of fields during third normal form conversion can have the greatest stabilizing influence on your data design. For example, in the Personnel Requisition example, if all recruiter data elements were stored in the Personnel Requisition file, *the system would not contain any information on recruiters who don't have existing requisition records!* Also, if additional data were required to be kept on recruiters, all personnel requisition records would have to be modified to include the new data elements.

It may appear to you at this point that data normalization is just a "common sense" way to structure files, and that is not too inaccurate at a simple level. However, it is never too late to begin to formalize the processes that you might have been doing in the past "by the seat of your pants." Following these data normalization rules will keep you from designing the database for a system in such a way that future changes will be structurally difficult or impossible. At the same time, the results of data normalization create a very logical grouping of fields into files.

One final note is required for the sake of thoroughness. While it is true that there are further levels of normalization beyond third normal form,[3] those levels are really fine-tuning of the first three normal forms, and are of little interest for us here.

IDOL-IV and Data Normalization

IDOL-IV's Design Dictionaries provide the ability to define a database that has been normalized to third normal form, but allow unnormalized database definitions as well. In other words, nothing is specifically done within IDOL-IV to enforce any database design discipline. It is really up to the application designer to adhere to these rules or not. However, proper use of the Global and Format Dictionaries, which we will discuss in more detail in the next chapter, will aid significantly in this effort.

This approach is understandable for IDOL-IV as it is intended to be used with existing software systems as well as for developing new ones. It is unfortunate, but true, that many existing systems are not well designed from a database (or other) point of view, and IDOL-IV must be able to interface with them as well as newly designed, normalized systems. In any case, proper use of the tools will adequately support a "good" manual database design methodology.

A Quick Overview of Structured Design Issues

This section is not intended to be an introduction to Structured Design Methodology. There are several fine texts[4] on the subject, and this book has a completely different focus. However, a chapter on Applications Design would be incomplete if the subject were not at least mentioned, and there is one fundamental concept in the methodology that is useful within our context here.

The major concept behind Structured Design is the decomposition of the functions of a system into smaller and smaller components of **common functionality** until some basic building blocks are achieved. This process is accomplished using a number of rules and a documentation technique called the "structure chart," and is very conducive to being used with an Applications Development System such as Thoroughbred IDOL-IV. Basically, the bottom level structure chart of a system design reflects the building block modules (or programs), and all higher levels are combinations of these lower level modules (with possibly some additional code as well).

A perfect example of the use of structured design with an Applications Development System such as IDOL-IV can be seen by considering IDOL-IV's Database Maintenance function, which provides data entry/maintenance ability for any file defined within the IDOL-IV dictionaries. This "parameterized data entry subsystem" can be controlled with built-in data element editing and other programming capabilities, and is the equivalent of a very high level symbol on a structure chart.

It is likely that under many circumstances, however, IDOL-IV's built-in facilities may not completely cover all possible field editing requirements. So, you may have to create a SCRIPT-IV script that accomplishes some specific data element editing or calculation. This script would, then, be defined as an individual unit on the lowest level structure chart, and may end up being used in several different places within the system. Structure charting can also be used to describe functionally the various program modules (scripts) that comprise an application process similar to the major data entry functions in the sample application system described below.

4 THE BUSINESS APPLICATIONS DESIGN PROCESS

In other words, by utilizing functional decomposition combined with structure charting techniques that show the various operational modules in the development tool kit that might be used as "black boxes" at a very high level in the chart, you will be able to determine any program modules that need to be created fairly easily. If you follow the other rules of Structured Design, you will also end up with a well designed system that is much easier to maintain and enhance, as specific functionality is defined in a single place.

A Sample Applicant Tracking System (ATS)

Now that we have examined the design issues of critical importance to us in today's software business, let us explore the design of the sample application system that will be the subject of the rest of this book. The example that was chosen is an Applicant Tracking System — one that might be used by an internal Human Resources (Personnel) Department to store and retrieve information on positions that need to be filled within the company, and the potential employees (applicants) who might fill them.

A very similar system might also be used by employment search firms to keep track of requests for specific employees and possible candidates for requested jobs. This particular design is aimed at in-house use, but with very little effort using IDOL-IV, the different terminology and functionality required for a search firm could be implemented.

The business activities that are involved here are:

1) a company finds the need to hire one or more people to do a specific job

2) a requisition is "opened" that describes each job requirement and the attributes of potential candidates

3) the existing database of applicants may be searched to see if any meet the requirements

4) additional applicants are found, entered into the system, and matched against the open requisition(s)

5) eventually an applicant is found that meets the needs of the company, and is hired

6) the open requisition must be updated ("closed"), other potential applicants must be notified, and their records disposed of or kept in the applicant database for possible future employment

7) requisitions that are not filled or otherwise not required anymore must be canceled, placed on hold, etc.

8) several reports are required to analyze the hiring activities

It should be fairly clear that there are two **major** data entry functions (as well as a number of minor ones) required for this system. These major functions are applicant entry and maintenance, and requisition entry and maintenance. Of course, "maintenance" in this case also includes keeping the two databases in "sync" as well as editing their data elements.

The following sections describe the various components of the sample Applicant Tracking System (ATS). Subsequent chapters deal with the details of the development of each system component. Appendices at the end of the book contain IDOL-IV design documentation that may be helpful while you are reviewing this material.

ATS: The Database Design

There are typically two forms in a manual system that support the two major data entry functions mentioned above: the personnel requisition form shown in Figure 4.2, and the employment application form, an example of which is shown in Figure 4.8. The third normalized files that result from an analysis of the employment application form are shown in Figure 4.9.[5]

You will note from Figure 4.9 that there are a fairly large number of fields in the Applicant Masterfile. You will also note that they are all fully dependent on **applicant id**. Good screen design techniques promote the idea that fields on a screen should be kept small in number and should all relate closely in subject matter. Therefore, what you see in Figure 4.9 is really two separate "screen's worth" of data fields. You will find that this idea is followed carefully in later chapters as we discuss screen design for the applicant and requisition files.

4 THE BUSINESS APPLICATIONS DESIGN PROCESS

APPLICATION FOR EMPLOYMENT

Name: _____ Date: _____

Address: _____
_____

Home Telephone: _____ SSN: _____

Highest Education Achieved: _____

Are you a veteran? If so, specify: _____

CURRENT JOB INFORMATION:

Company Name: _____

Address: _____

Telephone: _____ Ext: _____ Start Date: _____

Current Position: _____

Current Salary: _____ Availability Date: _____

Job Experience: _____
_____

PERSONNEL DEPARTMENT INFORMATION:

Source of Applicant: _____ Req No Applied For: _____

Disposition: _____ Date: _____

Recruitment Costs:

Advertising: _____ Agency Fees: _____

Employee Referral: _____ Relocation: _____

Travel/Lodging: _____ Other Costs: _____

Total Recruitment Costs: _____ No Days to Fill: _____

SENSITIVE INFORMATION NOT TO BE USED FOR EMPLOYMENT DECISION:

Sex: _____ EEO Code: _____ Birth Date: _____

Fig. 4.8 Sample Employment Application Form

File Name	Field Names
Applicant	**applicant id**, name, address, city, state, zip, phone, education level achieved, source of applicant, requisition #, comments, current job hire date, availability date, current company name, current address, current city, current state, current zip, current phone, current phone extension, current position, current salary, current experience code, date form completed, disposition code, disposition date, advertisement costs, agency fees, employee referral fee, relocation expenses, travel & lodging expenses, other costs, total costs, number of days to fill job, sex, EEO Code, SSN, birth date, veteran?
Disposition Codes	**disposition code**, description

Fig. 4.9 Applicant Files in Third Normal Form

ATS: A Functional Overview

In addition to the data entry/maintenance functions for the database design described above, there are several other application functions that together make up the sample Applicant Tracking System. These functions are outlined in Figure 4.10.

As with the file design, the reports that have been included in this sample application design are certainly not all that a complete system of this type would require. They are simply representative of the kinds of reports that are possible with REPORT-IV.

The update function, on the other hand, is the major one that an Applicant Tracking System requires. This sample is, however, simplified somewhat so that it can be analyzed in detail without getting bogged down in design logic issues. Finally, the menus were somewhat arbitrarily arrived at, but again show the major capabilities of the IDOL-IV Menu System.

4 THE BUSINESS APPLICATIONS DESIGN PROCESS

Details associated with each of these functions are included in the following chapters. These details include a discussion of how these specific functions work, and how each is designed and implemented using Thoroughbred IDOL-IV. As mentioned previously, detailed design documentation on each application function can be found in the various Appendices.

Code Files & Tables Disposition Codes
Experience Codes
Job Codes
Recruiters
Salary Grades

Views Applicant-Related Views include:
1) View Applicant General Data
2) View Applicant Cost Data

Requisition-Related Views include:
1) View Requisition Records

Reports Applicant-Related Reports include:
1) Applicants by Disposition Code
2) Source Analysis Report

Requisition-Related Reports include:
1) Open Requisitions Summary
2) Recruiter Requisition Assignment
3) Recruiter Analysis Report
4) Recruitment Costs Report

Update Functions Search For Applicants by Req'stn
View Selected Applicants

Menus Applicant Tracking Master Menu
Applicant and Requisitions Reports Menu

Fig. 4.10 Functional Breakdown of Applicant Tracking System

Conclusions

The majority of business applications development is of such a nature that systems analysis is generally accomplished by studying the forms and reports used in a "current" system (either manual or automated) and adjusting them according to new system requirements. The results of this analysis can then be normalized to produce a "good" database design. This design can be thought of as describing "fourth generation data"[6] — the design of which is dictated as much by the use of a 4GL as by a Relational DBMS. The fundamental characteristics of fourth generation data can be summarized as:

1) one fact per field,

2) one entity per file, and

3) all attributes in each record

Adherence to these basic criteria encourages "good" database design as well as "good" system design, and produces systems that are much easier to maintain and enhance.

The functions required to implement the new system can then be enumerated and broken down into their "common functionality" components using structure charts or some similar documentation method. After these two activities, the system is ready to be implemented (at least in a first draft or prototype form).

Utilizing prototyping techniques discussed earlier in this book, the designer/developer can experiment with the system trying various database formats, screen layouts, etc., until a satisfactory result is achieved. As we will see in subsequent chapters, Thoroughbred IDOL-IV makes these activities quite easy and enjoyable to accomplish.

Notes and References

[1]Much of the information in the next few sections has been extracted from two excellent sources on this subject: seminar material on Data Analysis compiled by QED Information Sciences, Inc., Wellesley, MA, and from C.J. Date, <u>An Introduction to Database Systems, Volume I</u>, Fourth Edition, Reading, MA: Addison-Wesley Publishing Company, 1986.

[2]<u>Ibid</u>, (Date), page 233.

[3] Ibid, (Date).

[4] One of the very best is: M. Page-Jones, The Practical Guide to Structured Systems Design, New York, NY: Yourdon Press, 1980.

[5] Of course, the data files in this example have been greatly simplified; in a complete Applicant Tracking System many additional fields would be required in the applicant and requisition files, and additional tables would be needed as well.

[6] Dan Tasker, "In Search of Fourth Generation Data", Datamation, July 1, 1987.

5

IMPLEMENTING THE DATABASE DESIGN

Database design is the most important aspect of system design. All subsequent design and implementation activities are largely dependent on the design of the database for their success. Information cannot be stored or retrieved if it is not defined in the database. Also, many Applications Development Systems (including Thoroughbred IDOL-IV) utilize database design information to validate or verify other design activities.

For example, a portion of screen design entails specifying the locations of database fields into which the user enters data. It is extremely helpful when the screen design utility provides a verification that the database field names used are correctly spelled, are indeed valid database fields, and have special formatting and editing specifications.

This chapter describes the activities that comprise the implementation of a database design using Thoroughbred IDOL-IV. The sample application outlined in the previous chapter has been used for this exercise. Detailed reports on the resulting database layout are included in the appendices at the end of the book.

Global Dictionary

The first step in database implementation should be the specification of the global database dictionary. This dictionary can be as simple as a list of field names and their basic function, or can actually contain data element definitions that are used as defaults when the record layout of a file is created. This latter approach is supported by IDOL-IV's Global Dictionary.

5 IMPLEMENTING THE DATABASE DESIGN

This dictionary allows you to define and store a number of attributes on each "global" data element. It also allows you to create a single "global" data element that can be used as a default for different specific data fields in several formats. This particular feature will be examined in more detail later in this chapter.

Each global data element must have a unique name, and can have any of the following information associated with it (refer to Figure 5.1 for the image of the Global Dictionary Definition Screen). However, the only attributes required for a field definition are name and length; all other attributes are optional. A list of existing global data elements can be displayed as well.

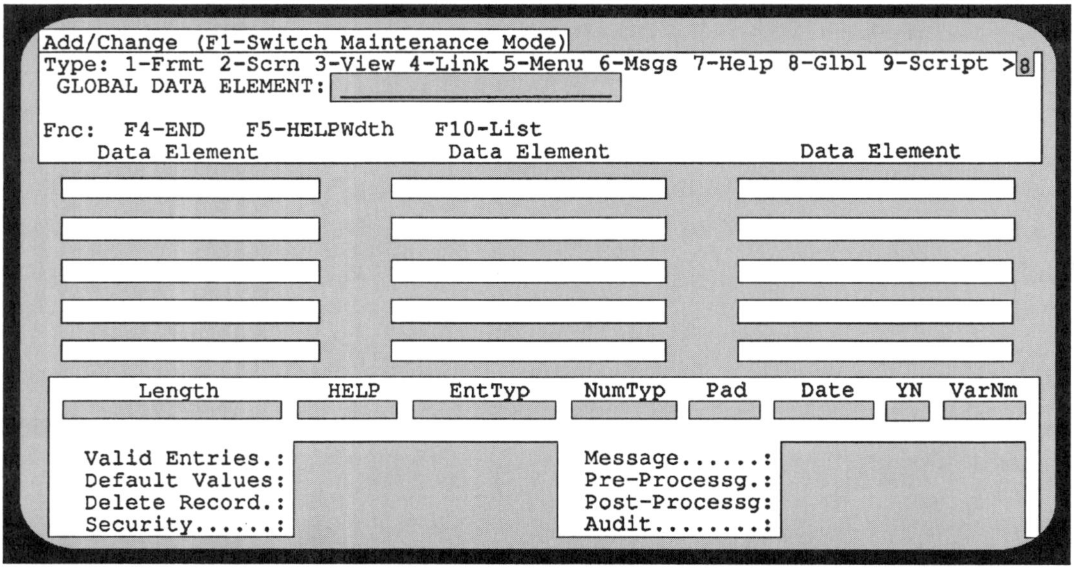

```
Add/Change (F1-Switch Maintenance Mode)
Type: 1-Frmt 2-Scrn 3-View 4-Link 5-Menu 6-Msgs 7-Help 8-Glbl 9-Script >8
GLOBAL DATA ELEMENT:

Fnc:  F4-END    F5-HELPWdth   F10-List
    Data Element              Data Element              Data Element




    Length        HELP      EntTyp    NumTyp   Pad    Date    YN   VarNm


    Valid Entries.:                     Message......:
    Default Values:                     Pre-Processg.:
    Delete Record.:                     Post-Processg:
    Security......:                     Audit........:
```

Fig. 5.1 Global Dictionary Definition Screen

Global Dictionary Attributes:

1) the field's **Length** — This may be either an integer signifying the length of a non-number type field (alphanumeric, date, etc.), or a real number (e.g., 10.2, 4.0, etc.) signifying the length of a number type field. For a real number, the fractional part of the length is the number of decimals

allowed, and the whole number part is the total length of the field. For example, a number field whose length is defined as 10.2 may contain a floating point number up to plus or minus 999999.99. The tenth position is reserved for the sign of the number value. If no fractional part is specified, the field is assumed to be non-numeric.

2) the name of a block of **Help** text — This name identifies a block of help text that can be displayed anytime the field is "touched" by the cursor in Database Maintenance (or within a SCRIPT-IV script) to explain the field's possible values and other information about its use. The help text itself is maintained when the field is defined/maintained in Format Maintenance, or can be maintained separately from the field itself through the Help Dictionary maintenance function (see a later section for more details).

3) the **EntType** (Entry Type) of the field — This attribute specifies whether the field is mandatory or optional, and whether the input will be fixed or variable length.

4) the **NumType** (Number Type) of numeric fields — This attribute specifies what numeric values are allowed in the field. The three choices are: both positive and negative numbers, positive numbers only, and negative numbers only. This attribute combined with the **Length** attribute restricts input values of real numbers and integers to these three categories.

5) **Pad** — This attribute specifies either the padding to be used on a variable length field, or a special format. Padding refers to the "fill" characters that are to be used when the input value is shorter than the **Length** of the field. Fill characters can be either zeros or blanks placed either before or after the input data. Two special formats are also available: a telephone number field, shown as xxx xxx-xxxx but stored internally as 10 digits; and a social security number field, shown as xxx-xx-xxxx and stored as 9 digits.

6) the **Date** type of date fields — This attribute specifies the format of a date field. Four formats are available: MMDDYY, YYMMDD, DDMMYY,

5 IMPLEMENTING THE DATABASE DESIGN

and YYDDD (Julian). Even though dates are stored as character strings in the formats shown here, they are displayed with a delimiter (e.g., 07/24/87) on screens.

7) **YN** — This allows a single character field to be restricted to the values of Y (y) or N (n) only.

8) **VarNm** — This field is not used by IDOL-IV; it is available here simply to be compatible with earlier versions of the IDOL Database Management System.

9) **Valid Entries** — This attribute allows you to restrict the values that can be entered into a field. There are four types of value restrictions: a specific list, one or more ranges, a file lookup validation, and a text field. Several of these validations will be used in the sample application, and will be discussed in detail in later sections of the book.

10) **Default Values** — This attribute allows a preset default value to be specified for a field. This value will be placed into the field before the user enters a value and may be overridden.

11) **Delete Record** — This attribute allows you to define a formula that determines whether or not a record may be deleted from a file. The formula may contain conditional operations and comparisons on the value in this field. This function is only effective in IDOL-IV DBM, and not within a SCRIPT-IV script.

12) **Security** — Field security is made up of three components: the **mode**, which determines the actions that are allowed/restricted (e.g., add and change, add only, change only, or neither); the **display code**, which determines when the value in the field is displayed (e.g., on both input and output, only on input, or only on output); and an optional **password**, a three-character value that can be used to override all field security. This function is only effective in IDOL-IV DBM and not within a SCRIPT-IV script.

13) **Message** — This attribute allows you to set up one of several different types of messages that will be displayed when the user moves the cursor

into this field. You can specify a message from a predefined message list by its number, or set up a specific message for this particular field. The positioning, as well as the display characteristics, of the message are definable also. Further discussion on message lists can be found later in this chapter.

14) **Pre-/Post-Processing** — This attribute allows you to specify the name of a SCRIPT-IV script (or BASIC program) to be executed either before or after a value is entered in the field. Parameters may optionally be passed to the program

15) **Audit** — This attribute allows you to specify transaction auditing to occur on a field. Again, the mode can be defined (add, change, delete, etc.), as well as the name of the file in which the audit records are to be written. This function is effective only in IDOL-IV DBM, and not in a SCRIPT-IV script.

The Global Dictionary may be maintained or created subsequent to the activity described in the next section (Format Definition), or can be implemented entirely in advance (or both). The recommendation here is to do it in advance. In either case, the Global Dictionary **MUST** be kept current and up-to-date for it to be useful. IDOL-IV does not force this to occur, so you must adhere to a certain amount of discipline independent of the development software.

Use and maintenance of the Global Dictionary is only to your benefit. You can actually create an entire software system without making use of the Global Dictionary at all. However, this is downright silly, when it will do so much toward ensuring consistency among the definitions of similar fields, and exact copies of the same field. Even in a third normal form database design, the same field (or field type) may appear a number of times within the files of the database.

Should you not start with the Global Dictionary, and find yourself with several IDOL-IV record formats already defined, you may employ a utility provided with IDOL-IV to create the global data element list from the existing format specifications. This will allow you to convert, again, from a "seat of the pants" approach to a more formal methodology.

5 IMPLEMENTING THE DATABASE DESIGN

The list of global data elements that are used in the sample Applicant Tracking System is shown in Appendix 1. You will note that a number of fields have special validation specifications. For example, values entered into CUR-EXP-CODE and EXP-CODE must be valid in a file called ATEXPCDE; the field EDUC-LEVEL must contain one of a list of valid values (0,1,2,3,4,5, or 6); REQ-STATUS and JOB-STATUS have both a valid list of values and a default value. If you have the sample ATS software available, you might stop here and try several of these fields to understand fully how these validations actually function.

Formats

Once each of the "global" data elements has been defined and assigned its respective attributes, you are ready to define the various data formats (in the Format Dictionary) required for the application system. A format is required in IDOL-IV for two specific reasons: to define a file in the database, and to define a group of fields that are maintained by a "screen" in IDOL-IV DBM or a SCRIPT-IV script. The sample Applicant Tracking System requires both types of formats. We will discuss formats that define files in this chapter, and formats that define screen data in the next chapter.

In addition, when you create your first record format, you will automatically be asked to define the new library to which the format belongs.[1] The library for the sample Applicant Tracking System is "AT", so the names of all application objects (except global data element names) begin with the letters "AT".[2]

The Format Definition Screen (shown in Figure 5.2) has only a few differences from the Global Dictionary Definition screen. Each format is uniquely named (beginning with the library name), and can be described in textual form. Also, IDOL-IV keeps track of the date and time of the latest change to a format (the same is done in all of the other dictionaries as well).

As each data element is entered into the Format Definition Screen, the default field attributes are displayed from the Global Dictionary (assuming a Global Dictionary entry exists). Help text may be entered, and you may alter any attribute that requires changing, **including** the name. In fact, by changing a field's default name you can use the same global data element for several different fields in the same (or different) formats. However, you cannot have two fields with the exact same name in the same format.

Format Definition also allows several functions besides defining fields and their attributes. For example, you may display an alphabetically sorted list of global data elements, you may delete a data element from the format or move it from one place to another[3], and you may change the width of the default help text window. You may also display a list of all other existing format names.

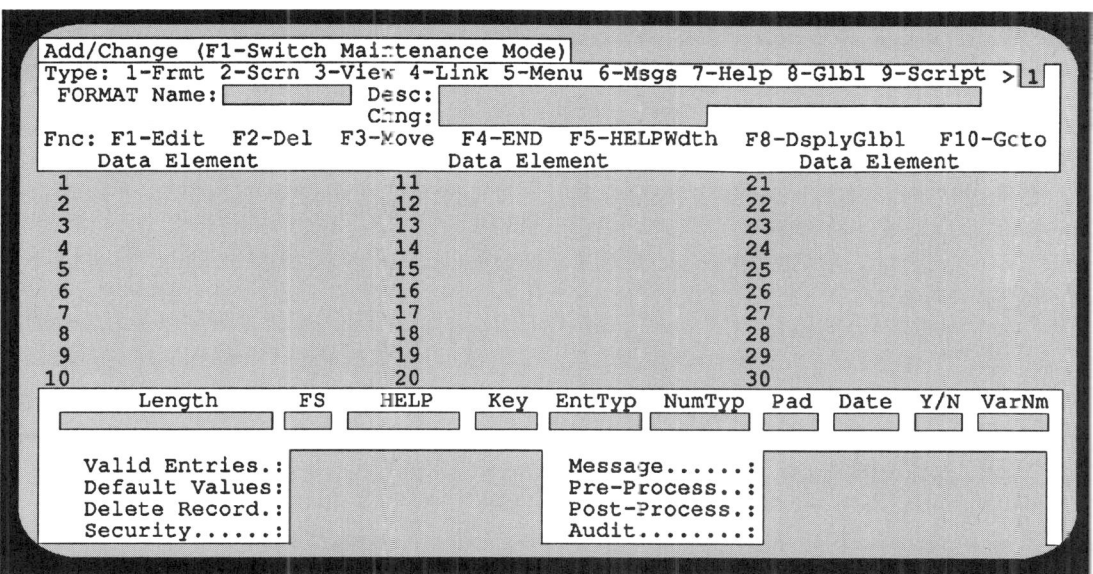

Fig 5.2 Format Definition Screen

Two additional items of information are requested when a field is defined in a format. These are:

1) **FS** — This attribute refers to a "field separator" and may be ignored when defining new formats within IDOL-IV. It allows format definitions to be created for files built using a facility other than IDOL-IV that are allowed with Thoroughbred Business BASIC. If Y is entered, the system automatically places a special character (a field separator) after the data value.

2) **Key** — This attribute allows you to define what field or fields constitute the primary key to the file. The primary key fields MUST be the first fields in the format, and they must be in the proper order for the primary

file sequence. A format with one or more fields specified as key fields defines a keyed (direct) file; a format without any key fields defines either a screen format for a SCRIPT-IV script or a sequential (indexed) file, with records stored in the sequence in which they are entered. Either type of file may have a number of different indexes or keys (see the last section of this chapter for a discussion of secondary indexes).

With these two additional attributes, we can now define all the formats required for the Applicant Tracking System. Refer to Appendix 2 for a listing of each format in the sample application system. From the information contained in the Global Dictionary, it should be fairly obvious what data each format contains, and what restrictions have been placed on a format's fields.

Help Text

The IDOL-IV Help Text Dictionary allows you to add descriptive information to a block of help text, as well as to maintain the help text itself. This is in addition to the maintenance capability built into the other dictionaries where help text is defined. The display parameters for the help text window may also be maintained here, including the window's size, location on the screen, and type of border.

SCRIPT-IV scripts may have uses for blocks of help text that are independent from help defined for fields, formats, screens, menus, etc. That help text can also be added through the use of this dictionary, and accessed by name in the appropriate script. The help text definition screen (not shown here) appears similar to the other definition screens in layout.

Text Fields

A text field is a special, variable-length field that can be used to store large amounts of textual data very efficiently. The **Length** of a text field is specified as "1" in the format. In addition, you can describe the "window" into which the text is entered. You can define the window's size parameters and location on the screen, the display characteristics of the window's border, and an optional heading that will display on the top border of the window.

When the user presses the **ENTER** key in a text field on the screen, the window is displayed with any existing text. When entry/maintenance has been accomplished, the window can be closed and the text window disappears from the screen. (An example of a text field is shown in the Global Dictionary. It is a field called COMMENTS, and the field's attributes can be seen on the report in Appendix 1. The field is defined as field "A", it is 60 characters wide, it is 4 lines deep, its upper left corner is located at column 3 and line 19, its border is reverse video, and the letters "-----APPLICANT COMMENTS-----" are to be displayed on the top border line. Text fields are only allowed in keyed (direct) files, and more than one text field may be defined in a single format (each with a separate letter designation).

Message Lists

IDOL-IV contains a design dictionary that is really a part of all the various system design activities, not just database design. This is the message list dictionary. It contains the definition of the text and action of all messages in an application system. This dictionary is library-specific, but should be thought of as similar in function to the Global Dictionary, in that messages should be defined in this area, and not "hard-coded" inside a format definition or a script. The message list dictionary is introduced here, but is referred to in subsequent sections of the book, as additional messages are required.

Two major kinds of messages are available: messages that require no response and messages that do. A prompting (or constant) message requires no response; it simply displays text in the appropriate location on the screen, whenever the program or script requires it. In addition to the text of the message, you may define the location of the text on the screen, the display characteristics of the text, and the screen clearing parameters.

The screen clearing parameters allow you to control how much of the screen is cleared before and/or after the message text is displayed. The entire screen or just the line containing the message text may be cleared either before or after or both. On the other hand, no clearing at all may be specified.

Three types of messages requiring responses can also be defined: a non-input message, a yes/no message, and an input message. A non-input message differs from a prompting message in that **Help** text may be defined for it, and the user is required to press a key before continuing. The user may press one of three keys as a response to a non-input message: the **ENTER** key, the standard **END** key, and the standard **HELP** key.

A yes/no message is similar to a non-input message, except that the letters Y, y, N, and n are also valid responses besides the **END** and **HELP** keys. The **ENTER** key is not valid for a yes/no message response.

5 IMPLEMENTING THE DATABASE DESIGN

The response to an input message is specific to each input message. Basically, the specification of the response is very similar to defining a field in a format, in that it has a length, entry type, numeric type, padding, etc.

Appendix 3 shows a listing of the messages that were defined for the sample Applicant Tracking System. The messages of interest in this chapter are prompting messages that aid the user in understanding what is required at entry/maintenance of a field value.

Links

IDOL-IV contains one more design dictionary that is of significance for database design activities — the Link Dictionary. Link Definition allows the designer to specify the interrelationships among several application objects (see Figure 5.3), and through clever design, reduce the number of objects that must be created.

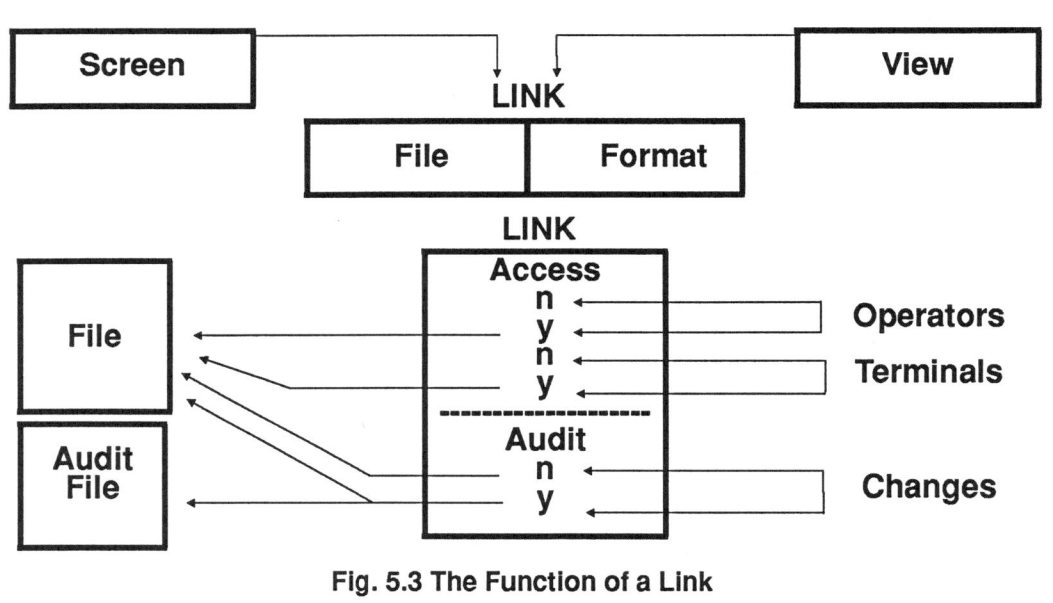

Fig. 5.3 The Function of a Link

For example, let's say that an application we are designing requires a "history" file that contains exactly the same data elements as the "active" file for the same entity. Links can be defined that relate a single format of the two files to two different screens or views so that database maintenance functions may be accomplished using only one format but two separate (and differently laid out) screens.

Link definition is similar to defining other application objects in that the link name is preceded by the library designation, descriptive information may be stored, and the system keeps track of when the link was last changed. Figure 5.4 shows the link definition screen.

```
Add/Change (F1-Switch Maintenance Mode)
Type: 1-Frmt 2-Scrn 3-View 4-Link 5-Menu 6-Msgs 7-Help 8-Glbl 9-Script > 4
 LINK Name:          Desc:
 Password:           Chng:

    Access Codes              File Information         File Maintenance
      Terminal:                  Format...:              Screen:
      Operator:                  Data File:              View..:
                                 Sort File:              Audit.:
```

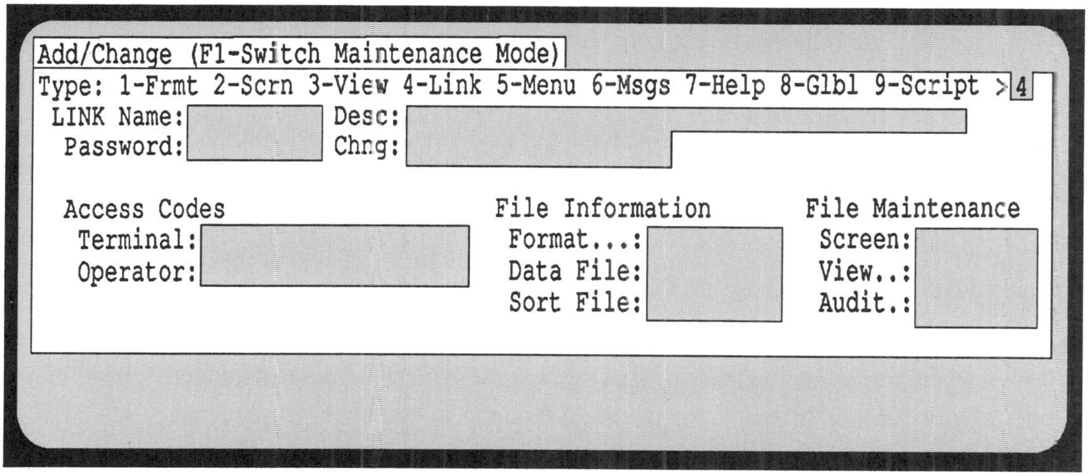

Fig. 5.4 Link Definition Screen

In addition, the object names that this link relates are specified, along with security access control parameters, and whether or not auditing (automatically recording copies of database changes) is desired. Appendix 4 contains listings of the links that have been created to support the sample Applicant Tracking System.

Secondary Keys

Another function of the IDOL-IV Link Dictionary is to store the definition of additional keys (besides the primary key) for a file. In fact, records in a file cannot be sorted any other way than through the use of a primary or secondary[4] key.

5 IMPLEMENTING THE DATABASE DESIGN

After all link fields have been maintained, the secondary keys (sorts) for this link may be defined or displayed and maintained. A secondary key can be created from any field or combination of fields in the format. It may also be created from one or more partial fields (i.e., the first three characters of fieldA plus the second through sixth characters of fieldB plus fieldC). Strictly speaking, this should not be allowed as it implies that fields are not "atomic", as described previously. However, it is allowed in IDOL-IV due to the system's requirement to adapt to existing software and database designs. Finally, each element in the secondary key may be sorted in ascending or descending order and can be made to ignore case or be case sensitive.

Once the secondary keys have been defined or their definitions changed, a function can be executed that will recreate them from the existing data records in the respective file. Secondary keys may be used to access records in database maintenance functions (both IDOL-IV DBM and SCRIPT-IV scripts), and to sort records in a view display or on a report. All of these functions have been included in the sample system, and will be discussed as they are encountered in later chapters.

Conclusions

Implementing a database design using Thoroughbred IDOL-IV is quite easy and enjoyable. Movement among the various design dictionaries is fast and simple — usually one or two keystrokes at the most. Also, recovering from mistakes is always allowed, and backing up to successively previous steps is supported in all logical places.

The ability to store complete field definitions, as well as messages in "global" dictionaries, is also quite helpful in making a system design easy to maintain. Finally, definition reports are provided that allow you to create printed design documentation on the system with very little additional effort.

Notes and References

[1] This will actually occur upon the definition of the first application object other than the Global Dictionary. So, it may not happen at exactly this point, if you have already defined the library elsewhere.

[2] In fact, you can print or display a list of all the AT library objects using the Definition Listing function in IDOL-IV.

[3]These delete and move operations, of course, cannot be done indiscriminately when a file already contains data, as the process that accomplishes database maintenance uses the format to locate individual data items in the record. If changes such as these are required for some reason, the copy or move functions available in View Maintenance (described in a later chapter) may be used to convert the existing records from the original format to the new format. Usually, however, such changes are not required; additional data elements are simply added to the end of the record/format, and unused existing data elements are left alone. Of course, this latter action may waste some disk space, but adequate database design up front should avoid or reduce the occurrences of this situation.

[4]Relational theory calls all keys to a relation (file) "candidate" keys, one being the "primary" key and all others being "alternate" keys. IDOL-IV uses the terms "secondary" key and "sort" key for the relational term "alternate" key.

6

DATABASE MAINTENANCE IMPLEMENTATION AND USE

Once the database design has been implemented, the next step is to create or define the processes required to add data to the database, and retrieve and maintain it. These are generally referred to as "data entry", "file maintenance", or "database maintenance" processes. For the sake of this discussion, all of these terms will be considered synonymous, and we will use the latter as we have in previous chapters.

This chapter continues our discussion of application design implementation with a description of how screens are created and how database maintenance functions are defined. It then describes how a user is expected to accomplish database maintenance using several of the sample Applicant Tracking System (ATS) screens.

First, IDOL-IV's Database Maintenance (DBM) function is used to store and retrieve data in the simple ATS files. Both single-record maintenance (using a screen), and multiple-record maintenance (using a view) are discussed. Detailed examination of the built-in functions available in a view, however, is postponed until the following chapter.

Then, the more complex database maintenance requirements of the Applicant Tracking System are reviewed, and the SCRIPT-IV language is introduced. Both a relatively simple database maintenance function and a more complicated one are discussed and their respective scripts are analyzed. Finally, the functioning of these scripts is described as the user would perceive them.

ATS: Database Maintenance Specifications

Before we embark on an analysis of screen definition, we should review the sample Applicant Tracking System's database maintenance processes. Briefly, ATS database maintenance functions can be divided into two categories: maintenance of simple "lookup" files and maintenance of complex "masterfiles." Lookup files contain only a few fields and require relatively simple field editing; masterfiles contain many fields and require sophisticated field editing and program functions.

The code files in the sample ATS are:

1) the Disposition Code File

2) the Experience Code File

3) the Job Code File

4) the Recruiter Code File

5) the Salary Grade File

The only special field editing required in these five files (other than that which can be specified in the format for each) occurs on the Salary Grade Screen. At entry and maintenance of salary data, it is required that the Maximum Salary Amount be GREATER THAN the Minimum Salary Amount.

Maintenance of data in all code files (except the Salary Grade File) can be done easily with IDOL-IV DBM. The special editing required in the Salary Grade File can be accomplished either by specifying a post-processing script name in the format definition for the Maximum Salary field and using DBM, or by creating a separate database maintenance script for the Salary Grade Code File. In either case, when the user leaves the Maximum Salary field, a post-processing subroutine is initiated, and the two numbers are compared. If the test fails, a message is issued and the user is sent back to the Maximum Salary field (the cursor returns to that field). If the test is okay, the maintenance function continues. More detail on this function is given later in the chapter.

The masterfiles in the sample ATS are:

1) the Applicant Masterfile

2) the Requisition Masterfile

Both of these files require much more in the way of data entry editing and control functions than IDOL-IV DBM offers. Therefore, we must create SCRIPT-IV scripts to accomplish the database maintenance tasks. The functions and editing required for each of these files, and the scripts that support those processes, are described in later sections of this chapter as well.

Creating a Default Screen

The simplest screen to create for use with IDOL-IV DBM is called a default screen. It is created by choosing the Database Maintenance option from the appropriate IDOL-IV menu, and specifying the file (link, screen, or format name) on which to perform maintenance. If no "custom" screen exists for this format, a "default" screen will be created.

```
F4-END   F6-HELP
ATRQMSTR              Employment Requisitions File Link
1)Add  2)Chng  3)Delete  4)Inqry  5)Fields-to-maintain  6)Chng-file  Report: _
REQ-NO............:                  REPLACEMENT-FOR...:
REQ-DATE..........:                  REQ-STATUS........:
JOB-CODE..........:                  REQ-DISP-DATE.....:
JOB-TITLE.........:                  REQ-APPROVER......:
SALARY-GRADE......:                  REQ-APPROVER-TITLE:
PT-RATE...........:                  REQ-APPROVAL-DATE.:
DEPARTMENT........:                  JOB-STATUS........:
SHIFT.............:                  EDUC-LEVEL........:
LOCATION..........:                  IDENT.............:
EEOC-JOB-CAT......:                  PRIM-EXP-CODE.....:
RECRUITER.........:                  SEC-EXP-CODE......:
INTERNAL-SRCH.....:                  EXEMPT-CLASS......:
NEW-POSITION......:                  SALARY-MAX........:
REPLACEMENT-DATE..:                  SALARY-MIN........:
```

Fig. 6.1 Default Screen Layout Example

6 DATABASE MAINTENANCE IMPLEMENTATION AND USE

The default screen layout is very simple. It consists of the fields in the format displayed in columns using the field names as prompts. The default screen for the Requisition Masterfile is shown in Figure 6.1. As you can see, the layout of the screen is not especially creative, but is quite functional for a "quick and dirty" file, or for very simple tables that have only a few fields. It is also quite useful for prototyping format (file) layouts before designing a more permanent screen.

As mentioned earlier in the book, the recommendation here is to use custom screens in all areas of application design; custom screens are easy to create and usually provide a more satisfactory user interface than default screens.

Designing a Custom Screen

Refer to Figure 6.2 for the "custom" version of the Requisition Masterfile Screen, and to Appendix 5 for the screen definition details for this and other screens developed for the sample Applicant Tracking System.

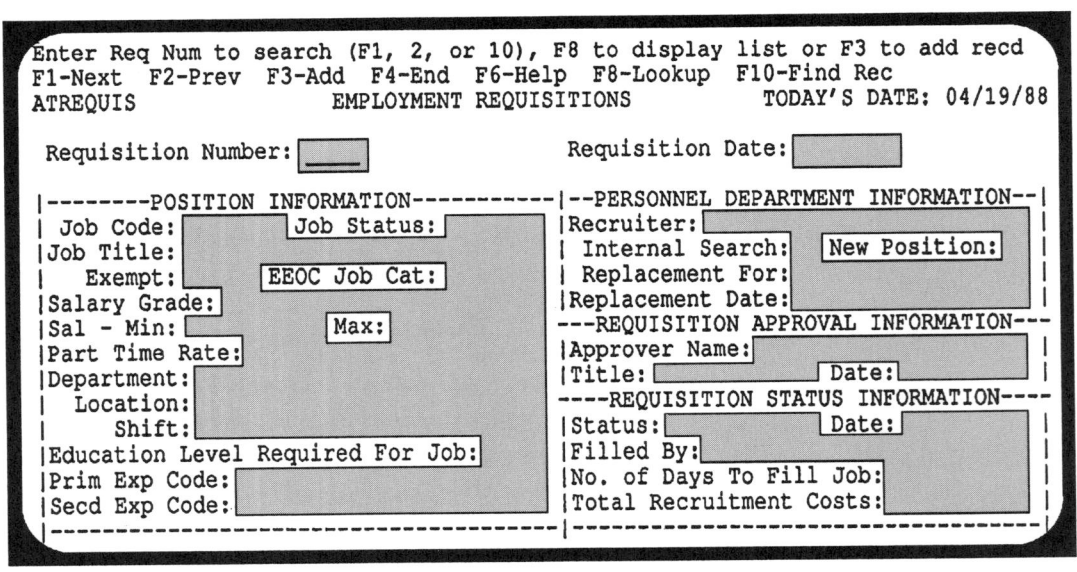

Fig. 6.2 Custom Screen Layout Example

A custom screen layout is "painted" by the applications designer. A number of display mode characteristics are available from which to choose to make the screen layout aesthetically pleasing to the user. Also, any of the following "global" data items may be displayed on the screen to inform the user about the function being performed: system date, terminal date, time, terminal id, operator code, and the name of a menu or the screen itself. Design guidelines for creating screens with data field grouping, borders, and highlighting can all be followed with these basic building blocks.

Each custom screen is assigned a unique name (this name may be the same name as the associated format name or not, as desired), and a textual description is allowed. The link or format that supplies the data fields and their attributes is specified, as well as the screen and help window display parameters. IDOL-IV keeps track of the date and time of the latest change to the screen definition.

Screen display parameters allow you to specify the size of the screen, up to 80 by 24, and the home position of the screen when it is displayed (the column and row of the screen's upper left corner), from 0,0 to 79,24. When multiple screens are displayed simultaneously in an IDOL-IV script, this home position is quite important because it determines where each screen appears and how much of the existing display is altered. Clever use of this feature can create a very effective (and pleasing) interface for the user as he or she moves through the script's various functions.

The help window display parameters allow you to specify the location and size of the help window, and whether the screen should be redisplayed after the user exits from the help window. These parameters override those set up in the help dictionary.

After these parameters are specified, you may "paint" the screen layout. This is done by placing any of the display mode characters, the global data items, or text for labels and prompts on the blank area of the screen. A preview screen function is always available so that you may see just how the system will interpret what you have "painted." All of the text editing functions discussed earlier are available to allow you to manipulate the way the screen appears until it is just what you desire.

Finally, data elements from the specified format (or link) may be placed on the screen using the "formula" function key. Within the formula window, you may also display a list of the data elements available from the associated format and pick one from this list if it has not already been placed elsewhere on the screen. The system places the first character of the field at the cursor position and underscores the field's length. Several other important formula capabilities are available, and are described in the following section, "Screen Formula Capabilities."

The order in which the user encounters the data fields (i.e., the order that the cursor moves through the screen) is controlled by the order of the data elements in the screen definition. This order may be displayed and changed while the screen layout is being created (or afterwards). Data elements are placed in this internal list in the order that they are defined on the screen with the formula function, so the data field order should always be examined and verified after a new data entry field is added to a screen or deleted from one position and added at another.

Screen Formula Capabilities

The formula function has a number of uses other than simply indicating the location of an input field on the screen. For example, one extremely useful feature within IDOL-IV screens is the ability to specify an input field whose screen size is shorter than its length specification in the format. This allows the field to be placed on the screen taking less room than its defined length, but still offers the user the ability to view and maintain the field by horizontal scrolling of the data. The data value in the field can be scrolled left or right by moving the cursor to the respective end of the field and pressing the appropriate arrow key (or by using the **TAB** and **BACK TAB** keys).

The specification of this feature is done within the formula window for the subject field. A sample of this may be found in the Current Employment Address field on the Applicant General Information Screen (refer to the Screen Definition Report in Appendix 5). The CUR-ADDRESS field is defined as 30 characters long, but in this particular case, only 27 characters are physically available on the screen. So, the formula specification for that field appears as /FIELD(27) = CUR-ADDRESS. This tells the system to display 27 characters and allow input of 30 characters (the defined length of the field) automatically turning on the field scrolling features.

Another useful formula function is the ability to specify a mathematical calculation using existing data field values, thereby creating a calculated data field. For example, a column total can be calculated as the sum of the numeric fields that comprise the column and can be displayed below the column as a total data field **without** having to define the total data field in the format.[1] SCRIPT-IV also provides a facility to recalculate all formulas on a screen so that the display of running totals can be kept current.

Finally, many different types of field formatting can be accomplished within the formula window, such as various kinds of display masking. The best examples of this facility can be seen in report definitions shown in Appendix 9. All of these examples can be done within screen formulas as well.

Using IDOL-IV Database Maintenance With a Custom Screen

Once the screen has been developed, the first step in adding data to a file is creating the file on disk. IDOL-IV DBM detects that this must be done and prompts you with default file size information to use. You can create the file exactly as big as it needs to be, or you can add to the record length with the expectation that additional fields will be added to the record format.

It may be a good idea to leave some expansion room when first testing a new database design, as no amount of planning will completely avoid the need to add a field after you have begun screen design and implementation. In fact, this is one very powerful aspect of prototyping that makes using this type of tool all the more productive.

After IDOL-IV has created the file on disk, it will display the appropriate screen layout with its standard Database Maintenance function keys and action prompts (see Figure 6.3). The user may at any point press the **HELP** key to display any available help text or the **END** key to exit the program.

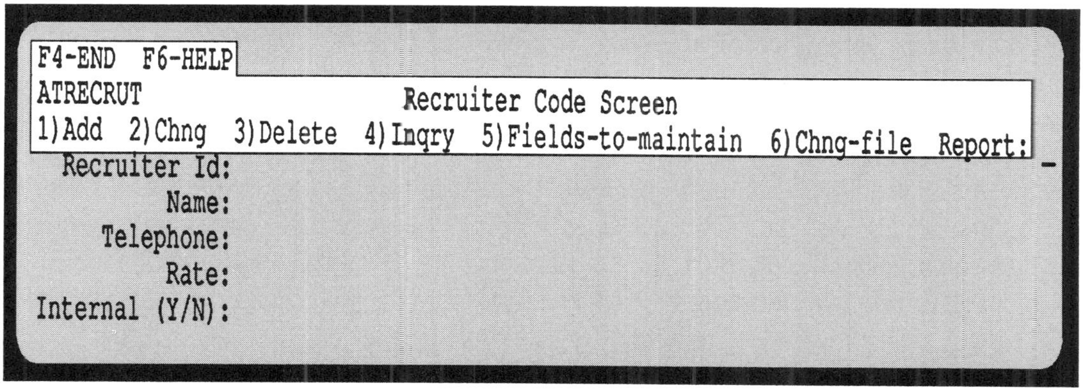

```
F4-END   F6-HELP
ATRECRUT                   Recruiter Code Screen
1)Add  2)Chng  3)Delete  4)Inqry  5)Fields-to-maintain  6)Chng-file  Report:
   Recruiter Id:
           Name:
       Telephone:
            Rate:
   Internal (Y/N):
```

Fig. 6.3 Recruiter Code Screen Showing Mode Selection

Before accessing any records, the user must first choose the action or "mode" he or she wishes to begin. Records may then be added or selected for processing. The basic modes are: Add, Change, Delete, Inquiry, and Select-fields-to-maintain. After a maintenance or inquiry mode has been selected (see Figure 6.4), the records to process are chosen by pressing the "Next Record" key (**Down Arrow**), or by entering a key value and pressing the **RETURN** key. The sequence of record retrieval when using the Next Record function will be in the primary key order unless a secondary key (sort) is specified by using the **SORT** function key (see Figure 6.4).

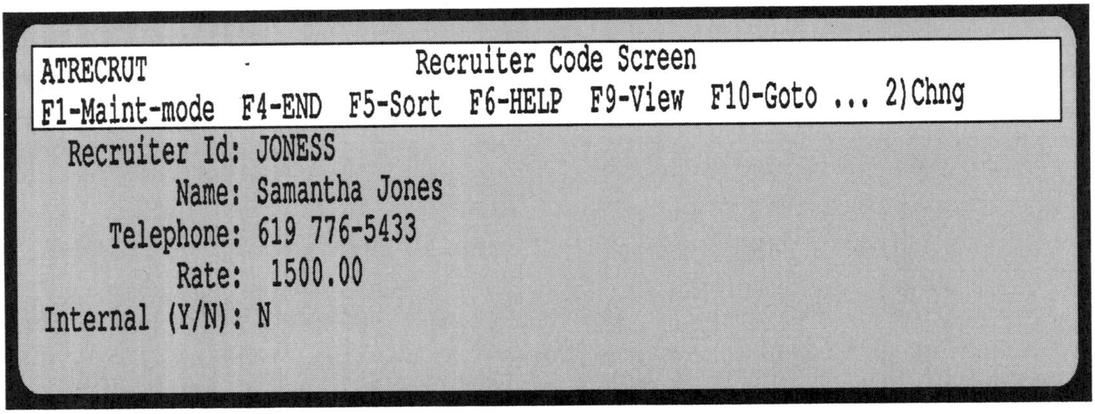

```
ATRECRUT                    Recruiter Code Screen
F1-Maint-mode  F4-END  F5-Sort  F6-HELP  F9-View  F10-Goto ... 2)Chng
    Recruiter Id: JONESS
            Name: Samantha Jones
       Telephone: 619 776-5433
            Rate: 1500.00
 Internal (Y/N): N
```

Fig. 6.4 Recruiter Code Screen After Mode Selection

During maintenance of a specific record, the **PageUp**, **PageDown**, and **GOTO** function keys are always available to skip to a particular data field. The **PageUp** key takes the cursor to the "first" data field on the screen while the **PageDown** key takes the cursor either to the "last" data field on the screen or to the "next" required field. The target field for the **GOTO** key is specified by its number in the screen input order list. Specifying field 99 usually causes the system to terminate maintenance and request to save the changes made or abort the maintenance of that record. Of course, an attempt to skip past a required field using the **GOTO** function will also be ignored, and the cursor will be placed on the "next" required field on the screen.

If only certain fields need to be changed in several records, the Select-fields-to-maintain mode may be chosen. This function allows the user to specify those fields that need maintenance in each record, and then allows record selection to begin. As each record is displayed the cursor will move automatically to the specified fields skipping all others. Rapid maintenance of small groups of fields across a number of records can be facilitated easily in this manner.

When the user has finished filling out a new record or changing the contents of an existing record, a Yes/No message appears asking the user whether or not to add the new record or save the changes to an existing record. This confirmation ensures that any purposeful changes made to existing data are saved, while any inadvertent changes can be canceled. Likewise, in Delete mode, any records selected for deletion will only be deleted after a confirmation message verifying that the user wishes to delete that particular record.

The View Maintenance function[2] is also available when the user is in change or inquiry mode. By selecting the view function, the user causes the maintenance/display action to switch from single-record to multiple-record format (see Figure 6.5). If no view definition exists for this format, the format's fields will be displayed from left to right across the screen. The cursor may be moved to specific fields in any displayed record, and the values in those fields may be changed. Access to editing capabilities with view maintenance is determined by parameters stored within the view definition. These parameters are discussed in more detail in a later chapter.

```
ATRECRUT                Recruiter Code File View
F1)Recover-Column  F2)Del-Column  F3)Chng-Field-Width  F4)End  F5)Select-Sort:
F6)Help  F7)Special-Functions  F8)Commands  F9)Single-Record-Mode  F10)Goto  :
RECRUT                                                       I
ID      RECRUITER NAME                  RATE    TELEPHONE    N
------  ------------------------------  -------- ------------ -
ALLENH  Henry Allen                     1050.00 714 577-9922 Y
ARTHUD  David Arthur                    1250.00 213 987-1234 N
JOHNSL  Lorraine Johnson                1200.00 714 998-7763 Y
JONESS  Samantha Jones                  1500.00 619 776-5433 N
SMITHK  Ken Smith                       1000.00 213 123-4561 N
SULLIJ  John Sullivan                   1100.00 714 876-5433 Y
```

Fig. 6.5 Recruiter Code File Displayed as a View

Within View Maintenance, records may be scrolled left and right if more **fields** exist than can fit across the screen. If more **records** exist than can be displayed on the screen, these records may be scrolled onto the screen as well. With the cursor resting on a particular record, the user can press the View function key again and return to single-record maintenance mode on that record.

Types of SCRIPT-IV Scripts

Since IDOL-IV DBM is somewhat limited in its ability to support complex database maintenance tasks, IDOL-IV contains a complete, very high-level (i.e., fourth generation) development language, called SCRIPT-IV. This language can be used in conjunction with the IDOL-IV Design Dictionaries to develop database maintenance functions of varying complexity. And, as we will see in later chapters, SCRIPT-IV can be used for all the other types of data processing functions as well.

One of the ways some Fourth Generation Languages greatly improve the efficiency of systems development is to accomplish the various types of programming functions using "program types" that are specifically designed for this purpose. IDOL-IV is one of those 4GLs. Within SCRIPT-IV there are six different **types** of scripts that can be created, depending upon the requirements of the system design and the design and development methodologies being used.

As mentioned previously, an IDOL-IV script contains a Data Declaration section where all data objects required by the procedure are predefined. This is to provide explicit data-type checking, and to facilitate the creation of bug-free, accurate, application functions. In addition, IDOL-IV scripts execute in a relatively small amount of computer memory. The combination of these two features with the need to support many kinds of design and development methodologies creates the need for different types of 4GL scripts. The wide variety of scripts available with IDOL-IV not only makes it possible to create virtually every type of commercial application but also promotes the efficient utilization of available computer resources.

The first type of script is called a primary script and usually contains the initialization of the data environment and other setup functions. Any previously defined data environment is cleared at the beginning of a primary script. If the functional requirement is small (or limited in scope) enough, a single primary script may be all that comprises an application process (see the simple data entry script example later in this chapter).

For many application functions, however, a single primary script will not be able to (or should not be designed to) accomplish the entire task. This is where the other types of scripts will need to be used. For example, some application functions require a large number of sequential steps that may or may not be repeated through several repetitions. In this case, a primary script followed by one or more continuation scripts may accomplish the required task.

A continuation script is similar to a primary script except that it does not clear the data environment. Also, it **must** contain the **exact same** data declaration section as its primary script. This allows the continuation script to refer to the value of any of the definitions and to change those values. The entire data environment and its "current" values are available to the primary and all continuation scripts. Furthermore, any continuation (or the primary) script may be executed from any other continuation (or the primary) script depending, of course, on the logic within the particular function.

To add further capabilities to this process while still remaining within the memory limits required for IDOL-IV application functions requires another type of script. This type of script facilitates the creation of a series of program steps that need to be executed at a specific location (or several such locations) within the process. In other words, control would be passed to this new type of script, its steps executed, and control passed back to the **exact same location** from which the original script was exited.

This type of script is called an overlay script, and again must contain the same data declaration as the "calling" script (i.e., the script that executes the overlay). The entire data environment is passed to the overlay script and passed back to the "calling" script when control is returned. Thus, all data values can be referred to or modified in the overlay script and passed back to the "calling" script without concern as to whether or not the data exists at this point in the logic of the process. Overlay scripts are perfect for external subroutines (not in-line) that are associated with a specific series of scripts (i.e., those that all have the same data declaration section).

Your first question at this point should be "Do I really have to enter even a simple data declaration section into several different scripts?" The second should be "What if I change my mind; do I have to make the changes in several scripts?" The answer to both questions, of course, is no. A type of script called a copy script is used for this purpose. A copy script is one whose commands are merged into and become a part of another script at compile time. The spot where the merge occurs is indicated by an **INCLUDE** command followed by the copy script name. It should be obvious that this offers the powerful capability of creating a specific block of commands once (e.g., a data declaration section) and having it included in as many other scripts as is required.

Of course, Data Declaration commands are not the only candidates for a copy script. Any group of commands that execute a specific, common function may be set aside into a copy script and included into scripts where they are needed. In other words, copy scripts are ideal for common in-line subroutines.

One of the most efficient ways to ensure bug-free applications is to create a system by constructing small, relatively simple blocks of commands that are tested and proven reliable, and then combining these building blocks into more and more complicated functions. This idea is inherent in all structured design methodologies. The copy script, and the public script described below, are both integral parts of the tool set required to accomplish this type of system implementation.

A public script is similar to an overlay script **except** that a public script has **its own separate data environment**. Therefore, any data values that are required in the public script from the "calling" script must be specifically passed into the public script as parameters. Also, any data values that the public script must return to the "calling" script must be set up as parameters and passed back out. In this way a public script is very useful as a means of creating **common** external subroutines that can be used anywhere they are needed within a system regardless of predefined data definitions. We will not examine the use of a public script in this chapter.

The final type of script is a pre/post process script used within IDOL-IV DBM. This type of script allows you to create sophisticated field editing procedures (similar to those discussed in an earlier section of this chapter) using SCRIPT-IV without having to create an entire database maintenance script. The pre/post process script's name is placed in the format definition and executed by IDOL-IV DBM either as the cursor enters the data field ("pre-process") or leaves the data field ("post-process"). This type of script is not examined in detail in this chapter either.

A Simple SCRIPT-IV Data Entry Script: Its Operation

We are now ready to discuss a simple SCRIPT-IV database maintenance script in detail. The script's name is ATSGMM0, and its function is to allow maintenance of Salary Grade records stored in the ATSALGRD code file. This script was designed to duplicate as many of the functions offered in IDOL-IV DBM as possible. Therefore, its operation is very similar to that found in DBM. In fact, the main ATS menu (see Figure 9.1) includes two entries for maintaining Salary Grade records: option 10, which uses DBM and a custom screen (ATSALGRD), and option 11, which uses the ATSGMM0 script. This has been done so that you can compare the user interface and operation of the predefined IDOL-IV DBM functions to a custom-designed script.

When the script ATSGMM0 is executed, you will see a screen display that is quite similar to the one seen using option 10 (see Figure 6.6). The main difference is that no mode selection is required by the user before records can be added or selected for modification. The function keys available are **F4-End** (which terminates the script), **F6-Help** (which can be pressed while in any data field), and **F8-View Records** (which displays a list of salary grade records in a window and allows one to be selected for maintenance). Pressing the **F6-Help** key causes a help window to be displayed on the terminal below the ATSALGRD screen. The location and size of the help window are defined and stored with the screen definition, but can be overridden within a script (not done here). Also, the help window may be left showing on the screen or "closed" and removed from the terminal display after use.

```
F4-End  F6-Help  F8-View Records
ATS - Salary Grade Masterfile Maintenance
Salary Grade: __
 Description:
 Min. Salary:
 Max. Salary:
```

Fig. 6.6 Salary Grade Record Selection

The **UpArrow** and **DownArrow** keys are used to select the "previous" and "next" record in the file, respectively, for viewing or modification. If the beginning or end of the file is reached, a message to that effect is displayed on the top line of the terminal screen. An existing record may also be selected by entering a Salary Grade code and pressing the **RETURN** key. If a code is entered in this fashion that does not belong to an existing record, the script asks if you are entering a new record (rather than saying that the record does not exist). A positive response to this question places you in "add mode" and you are allowed to enter data into the data fields on the screen. When you are done, the script asks whether or not you wish to add the record to the file. A negative response to this question causes the data that was entered to be thrown away (as does **F4-End** while filling out the data fields).

Once an existing record is displayed (see Figure 6.7), you may edit its data fields simply by moving through the screen making the appropriate changes. An error message is displayed if you enter a Maximum Salary Amount that is less than or equal to the Minimum Salary Amount. If any changes are made to a selected record, the script asks if you want to save them before going on to another record. A negative response causes the changes that were made to be abandoned and leaves the record unchanged on the disk.

```
F3-Delete Record  F4-End  F6-Help  F10-GoTo Field
ATS - Salary Grade Masterfile Maintenance
Salary Grade: 01
 Description: Grade 1
 Min. Salary:     8425.00
 Max. Salary:    13520.00
```

Fig. 6.7 Salary Grade Record Editing

You may also delete an existing record after it has been selected (i.e., displayed) by pressing the **F3-Delete** key. A message is then displayed asking you to confirm the delete request. As in DBM, the **F10** key may also be used during record editing to **GOTO** the specific field (by its number). Pressing **F4-End** during record editing takes you back to record selection, again abandoning any changes you might have made to the record before pressing the **F4** key.

A Simple SCRIPT-IV Data Entry Script: Main Procedure

Let us now examine the script code to see how these functions have been accomplished. Figure 6.8 shows the main body of script ATSGMM0.[3] Since this database maintenance function is accomplished using a single primary script, the data declaration section has been placed within the script, and not stored in a copy script. The first four lines of Figure 6.8 show the data declarations for ATSGMM0: a screen definition, a link definition, a view definition, and three temporary script data fields or variables.

Data Declaration commands and procedure names are left justified within a script; all other commands are indented at least to the first tab position. Other indenting is allowed by the script editor to make a script easier to read (by humans), but it is not required. The MAIN-PROCEDURE procedure name indicates the start of the script, and this procedure usually ends with either a **TERMINATE** or a command to execute the next script in a series. Again, ATSGMM0 is a single script, so its MAIN-PROCEDURE ends with a **TERMINATE**, returning control to the IDOL-IV menu system from where the script was executed.

The first few commands in the MAIN-PROCEDURE accomplish setup functions. An **OPEN SCREEN** command is used to load the screen attributes into program memory, and an **OPEN (link)** command is used to connect the script to the data file ATSALGRD. A **PRINT SCREEN** command causes the screen ATSALGRD to be displayed on the terminal (no data, just the screen layout), and a **PRINT MESSAGE** command causes Prompt (P) message #30 from the Message List ATMSGS to be displayed[4]. You will notice that no positioning data is included in these display commands whatsoever. All of this information has been included in the definition of these application objects and is external to the script.

Most of the rest of the MAIN-PROCEDURE procedure is a **DO LOOP** command that encompasses everything up to the matching **ENDLOOP** command, and is executed UNTIL the script variable, MODE-FLAG, contains the value "DONE". Since MODE-FLAG is not set to any value before the **DO LOOP**, it contains no value at the start of the first time through the loop (i.e., it was initialized with the rest of the data environment in this primary script). Therefore, the loop of commands will execute AT LEAST once.

The first command inside the **DO LOOP** is a **LET** command that assigns the value "INIT " to the script variable, MODE-FLAG. This serves to set the loop to continue execution. A **PRINT MESSAGE** (prompt message #32) is then executed which places the list of function keys on the screen (the first line shown in Figure 6.6), followed by an **INPUT SCREEN** command. The **INPUT SCREEN** and **INPUT MESSAGE** commands (shown later) are the only two SCRIPT-IV commands that allow the user to enter data into the screen.

```
Script: AT SGMM0    Type: 1
Desc: Salary Grade Masterfile Mx                          Page: 1
Last Change Date: 06/18/88    Last Compile Date: 06/17/88
          Time: 08:34:19               Time: 10:55:21    Date: 06/20/88
================================================================================
    SN   ATSALGRD
    LN   ATSALGRD
    VN   ATSALLVW
    DN   MODE-FLAG (5), MSG-RESP (1), OLD-SALGRD (2)

    MAIN-PROCEDURE
        OPEN SCREEN ATSALGRD
        OPEN VIEW ATSALLVW
        OPEN ATSALGRD
        PRINT SCREEN ATSALGRD
        PRINT MESSAGE "P,30" USING "ATMSGS"
        DO LOOP UNTIL MODE-FLAG = "DONE "
           LET MODE-FLAG = "INIT "
           PRINT MESSAGE "P,32" USING "ATMSGS"
           INPUT SCREEN ATSALGRD CLEAR KEY
           IF TERM-KEY = 4 THEN LET MODE-FLAG = "DONE " ENDIF
           IF TERM-KEY = 8 THEN DO LOOKUP-RECORDS ENDIF
           IF TERM-KEY < 0 OR (TERM-KEY = 0 AND SALARY-GRADE <> "  ") THEN
               DO GET-RECORD
           ENDIF
           IF MODE-FLAG = "DELET" THEN DO DELETE-RECORD ENDIF
        ENDLOOP
        TERMINATE

    LOOKUP-RECORDS
        LET K9$ = SALARY-GRADE
        PRINT MESSAGE "P,27,,,,Sal Grade" USING "ATMSGS"
        PRINT VIEW ATSALLVW USING KEY RANGE FROM "" TO "zz"
           KEY INTO K9$
           WINDOW LINE IS 12
                  COLUMN IS 3
                  NUMBER LINES ARE 10
                  CHARACTERS ARE 50
                  BORDER IS "R"
                  HEADING IS "Y"
        IF TERM-KEY = 1 THEN LET SALARY-GRADE = K9$, TERM-KEY = 0 ENDIF
```

Fig. 6.8 Main Body of ATSGMM0 Script

This **INPUT SCREEN** command causes all screen data to be cleared (**CLEAR** option specified) and requests data be entered only in the Key field of the ATSALGRD screen. The effect here is to clear the screen of any displayed data, but have the existing key value displayed as soon as the screen cursor enters the SALARY-GRADE field. Accepting data only from the key field is quite useful when retrieving a record's key value prior to looking for that record in the file. No matter what the user enters into the key field (SALARY-GRADE) and no matter what key he or she may then press, the **INPUT SCREEN** command is terminated.

Both **INPUT** (**SCREEN** and **MESSAGE**) commands set a system variable, called TERM-KEY, to a number based upon which key on the keyboard was last pressed during the **INPUT** (for example, Function Key 4 will set TERM-KEY to a value of 4; see the IDOL-IV documentation for details on TERM-KEY values and how they function). This system variable is tested in the next three commands in the **DO LOOP**. The first **IF/THEN/ENDIF** command tests for the entry of Function Key 4 (**F4-End**); if it was pressed, the variable, MODE-FLAG, is set to "DONE ", eventually ending the **DO LOOP** and terminating the script. If TERM-KEY contains any other numeric value, this command does nothing.

The second **IF/THEN/ENDIF** command checks for a TERM-KEY value of 8 (i.e., **F8-View Records** was pressed). If this is the case, the LOOKUP-RECORDS procedure is executed (see Figure 6.8). This procedure places a new function key message on the screen (prompt message #27) and then executes a **PRINT VIEW** command. This command causes a list of records to be displayed in a window. The records come from the file for which the view was defined. The window parameters are specified in the **PRINT VIEW** command along with the border type and whether or not the view headings are to be displayed. The **KEY INTO** clause allows a starting display value to be passed to the **PRINT VIEW** and collects the user's selection (the key value of the chosen record) when the window is closed. The BASIC variable, K9$, is used here to implement this function.

Rather than using the BASIC variable, the SALARY-GRADE field could have been used in both the first and last commands of the procedure, except that no selection value is to be passed back to the MAIN-PROCEDURE unless **Function Key 1** is pressed (see the text of prompt message #27). If SALARY-GRADE were used, its original value would be lost if where the user presses any key other than **Function Key 1**. Using the BASIC variable, or another data name (e.g., OLD-SALGRD), keeps this from happening.

The third **IF/THEN/ENDIF** command checks for either a TERM-KEY value less than zero (the specific negative values that are of interest are explained in the following section) or a TERM-KEY value of zero (the **RETURN** key) and a SALARY-GRADE value that is not blank.[5] If either of these two conditions are true, the procedure, GET-RECORD, is executed. If both are false, this command does nothing. Finally, the last command in the **DO LOOP** (another **IF/THEN/ENDIF**) checks for a MODE-FLAG value of "DELET", and if it finds it, the procedure, DELETE-RECORD, is executed.

If, at this point in the script, the value of MODE-FLAG is "DONE ", the loop ends and the **TERMINATE** command is executed. If MODE-FLAG contains any other value, the loop begins again with the first command in the loop (**LET**). It should be fairly clear that the only way to end the loop is to have the user press the **F4** key. Entry of a negative value function key (e.g., **UpArrow** or **DownArrow**), or the **RETURN** key (TERM-KEY = 0) causes other things to happen, but does not end the **DO LOOP**.

A Simple SCRIPT-IV Data Entry Script: Get Record Procedure

Let us now examine how a record is retrieved from the ATSALGRD file for display or editing. This is accomplished in the two procedures, GET-RECORD and SET-FILE-KEY (see Figure 6.9). Again, the GET-RECORD procedure is executed from the MAIN-PROCEDURE when the user presses the **RETURN** key or a TERM-KEY with a negative value.

From Figure 6.9 you can see that GET-RECORD is a compound **IF/THEN/ENDIF** command with three main components. The first component checks TERM-KEY for a value of zero, and executes a **CHANGE** command. The second component checks for a value of minus three (**DownArrow** key in IDOL-IV), and the third checks for a value of minus four (**UpArrow** key in IDOL-IV). In the second and third components, the SET-FILE-KEY procedure is executed before the **CHANGE** command. This procedure simply executes a **READ** with a key value of whatever is in the SALARY-GRADE field and returns.

READ and **CHANGE** are the SCRIPT-IV commands used to retrieve a record from a file. A record retrieved with **READ** can be displayed but not modified, and any number of users on multiple terminals can access the same record simultaneously. A record retrieved with **CHANGE** can be displayed and modified (any changes made to its fields will automatically be written back into the file at the end of the **CHANGE** command), but only one user may **CHANGE** a record at a time. In other words, a **CHANGE** com-

```
Script: AT SGMM0    Type: 1
Desc: Salary Grade Masterfile Mx                         Page: 2
Last Change Date: 06/18/88   Last Compile Date: 06/17/88
         Time: 08:34:19             Time: 10:55:21    Date: 06/20/88
================================================================================

    GET-RECORD
        IF TERM-KEY = 0 THEN
           CHANGE ATSALGRD USING KEY SALARY-GRADE
              PROCESSING  IS DISPLAY-RECORD
              MISSING KEY IS ADD-RECORD
              BUSY        IS BUSY-RECORD
              END         IS END-OF-FILE
        ELSE
           IF TERM-KEY = -3 THEN
              DO SET-FILE-KEY
              CHANGE ATSALGRD USING KEY NEXT
                 PROCESSING  IS DISPLAY-RECORD
                 BUSY        IS BUSY-RECORD
                 END         IS END-OF-FILE
           ELSE
              IF TERM-KEY = -4 THEN
                 DO SET-FILE-KEY
                 CHANGE ATSALGRD USING KEY PREVIOUS
                    PROCESSING  IS DISPLAY-RECORD
                    BUSY        IS BUSY-RECORD
                    END         IS BEGINNING-OF-FILE
              ENDIF
           ENDIF
        ENDIF

    SET-FILE-KEY
        READ ATSALGRD USING KEY SALARY-GRADE

    BUSY-RECORD
        INPUT MESSAGE "N,5,,,,Salary Grade" INTO MSG-RESP USING "ATMSGS"

    END-OF-FILE
        INPUT MESSAGE "N,2,,,,Salary Grade" INTO MSG-RESP USING "ATMSGS"

    BEGINNING-OF-FILE
        INPUT MESSAGE "N,9,,,,Salary Grade" INTO MSG-RESP USING "ATMSGS"
```

Fig. 6.9 GET-RECORD, SET-FILE-KEY and Error Procedures

6 DATABASE MAINTENANCE IMPLEMENTATION AND USE

mand automatically locks the record when it is retrieved and releases the lock when the record has been written. No other code must be written to accomplish multi-user concurrency control (record locking).

The design idea implemented in GET-RECORD is: if a user enters a SALARY-GRADE and presses **RETURN**, try to get that specific record; if the user presses the **DownArrow**, get the record whose key is **immediately after** the value in SALARY-GRADE; if the user presses **UpArrow**, get the record whose key is **immediately before** the value in SALARY-GRADE. Therefore, the first component of GET-RECORD tries to retrieve a specific record with a **CHANGE** command. The other two components position the file pointer (cursor) at the record whose key value is stored in SALARY-GRADE, and then retrieve the "next" or "previous" record, as required, using a **CHANGE** command.

It might appear at first that we are doing extra work by executing the SET-FILE-KEY procedure **each time** a "next" or "previous" record is requested by the user. However, the obvious advantage of using the SET-FILE-KEY procedure in this way is that the user can browse from one record to another for a time, and then easily reset the starting point of the browse and begin again from that new record. Also, removing the SET-FILE-KEY procedure does not speed up the data entry process noticeably.

A number of possible error conditions may result from either a **READ** or a **CHANGE** command. Several of these are evident in the GET-RECORD procedure and are shown in Figure 6.9.[6] A BUSY error means that another user has locked the record for editing (issued a **CHANGE**) and we cannot get to it at this moment. This is usually handled by a message to the "locked out" user, followed by a retry to get the record. In most multi-user systems, records undergoing a **CHANGE** are not kept locked for long, so this is a workable solution.[7]

The other typical error conditions occur when the user encounters the beginning or end of a file while using the "next" or "previous" functions. These errors are again handled with messages presented to the user. After the message, the user is allowed to try any record retrieval command available, and can continue to do so until the desired record is retrieved.[8]

For each one of the error conditions mentioned above, an error message has been defined in the message dictionary (stored in the ATMSGS message list). All of these messages are "non-input" type messages: ones that display text and wait for the user to press the **RETURN** key in acknowledgement, but do not require any other response. These messages are displayed from their particular error procedure (e.g., BUSY-RECORD, END-OF-FILE, etc.)

In addition to standard message text, variable data has been designed into these messages so that more specific information can be displayed to the user. In the examples mentioned above, the name of the file is specified in the **INPUT MESSAGE** command along with the message type and number.[9] This makes it appear to the user as though each different file has its own set of messages, while allowing the designer to set up and maintain only one set for the entire system.

A Simple SCRIPT-IV Data Entry Script: Add Record Procedure

The ADD-RECORD procedure (see Figure 6.10) is executed when a SALARY-GRADE value is entered by the user, the **RETURN** key is pressed, and no record is found. Rather than issue a "record not found" message, this script has been designed to ask the user if he or she is adding a new record (an input type message that requires a Yes or No response). The response to the **INPUT MESSAGE** command is stored in the script variable, MSG-RESP, which is used to determine if any of the rest of the procedure is to be executed. In other words, if the response is "N", the rest of the procedure is skipped.

Three **LET** commands are then used to clear data (except the key value) from the screen format before allowing the user to enter the new record's data field values. This is required because even though the screen display is cleared in the MAIN-PROCEDURE using the **CLEAR** option on the **INPUT SCREEN** command, the data in the screen format (and therefore the file format) is never cleared in this script once a record is retrieved. So, the key value in SALARY-GRADE is saved, the rest of the data fields in the screen format are cleared (the second **LET**), and the key value is replaced in the screen data field, SALARY-GRADE.

We are now ready for the user to enter the new record's data field values. This is done with an **INPUT SCREEN** command. This particular example only allows data to be entered into three of the four fields on the screen. Thus, the user cannot change the key value that brought him or her to this part of the script.[10] This **INPUT SCREEN** command also includes a POST PROCESS option that causes a procedure called CK-SALARY-AMOUNTS to be executed upon leaving the SALARY-MAX field (see Figure 6.10).

6 DATABASE MAINTENANCE IMPLEMENTATION AND USE

```
Script: AT SGMM0    Type: 1
Desc: Salary Grade Masterfile Mx - Primary            Page: 3
Last Change Date: 04/18/88    Last Compile Date: 04/18/88
            Time: 11:47:13                    Time: 11:48:48    Date: 04/19/88
==============================================================================
    ADD-RECORD
        INPUT MESSAGE "Y,6,,,,Salary Grade" INTO MSG-RESP USING "ATMSGS"
        IF MSG-RESP = "Y" THEN
            LET OLD-SALGRD = SALARY-GRADE
            LET ATSALGRD = ""
            LET SALARY-GRADE = OLD-SALGRD
            INPUT SCREEN ATSALGRD DATA-NAME LIST SALARY-DESC, SALARY-MIN,
                                                 SALARY-MAX
                POST PROCESS SALARY-MAX, CK-SALARY-AMOUNTS
            INPUT MESSAGE "Y,3" INTO MSG-RESP USING "ATMSGS"
            IF MSG-RESP = "Y" THEN
                ADD ATSALGRD USING KEY SALARY-GRADE
            ENDIF
        ENDIF
```

Fig. 6.10 ADD-RECORD Procedure

CK-SALARY-AMOUNTS is the procedure that compares the two salary values and issues an error message (non-input message) if the Maximum Salary amount is less than or equal to the Minimum Salary amount. After the end of the POST PROCESS procedure, the LET ATSALGRD.FIELD = 0 statement causes the cursor to return to the same field rather than moving to the next field.[11]

An **INPUT SCREEN** command takes the user through the input fields once and then terminates. If your system design requires you to go back to the **INPUT SCREEN** command after it terminates, you must surround the **INPUT SCREEN** command with a **DO LOOP/ENDLOOP** command (see the other database maintenance scripts in the appendix for examples of this approach).

So far all we have done is collect data from the screen. After the **INPUT SCREEN** command executes once, an **INPUT MESSAGE** command displays a message and waits for a "yes" or "no" response. The message asks the user whether or not to add the new record to the file. If the response (returned in MSG-RESP) is "Y", the new record is added with the key value that was entered in the SALARY-GRADE field. Finally, the main **IF/THEN/ENDIF** command is closed.

It may not be totally obvious at this point where the script execution continues after the ADD-RECORD procedure has been completed. By reviewing Figures 6.8 and 6.9, you will see that ADD-RECORD is executed as a result of the first portion of the main **IF/THEN/ENDIF** in GET-RECORD. Control first returns to the **CHANGE** command which executed the ADD-RECORD procedure. None of the rest of the commands in GET-RECORD are executed, so control then returns to the **DO LOOP** in the MAIN-PROCEDURE, within the second **IF/THEN/ENDIF** command. This is the end of that command, so the next command executed is the **IF/THEN/ENDIF** that checks for a MODE-FLAG value of "DELET". The **ENDLOOP** command marks the end of the commands performed in the **DO LOOP**.

A Simple SCRIPT-IV Data Entry Script: Display Record Procedure

If a record is found by one of the three **CHANGE** commands in the GET-RECORD procedure, the DISPLAY-RECORD procedure is executed (see Figure 6.11). This procedure contains another **DO LOOP/ENDLOOP** command that allows the user to see the data in the chosen record, modify it, and selectively update it to the file.

The first two commands within the **DO LOOP** cause the screen display to change from "record selection or browse mode" (Figure 6.6) to "record editing mode" (Figure 6.7). Again, positioning and other parameters are inherent in the definitions of the screen and message, and not included in the script. Prompt message #31 displays the edit function keys, and the DATA option on the **PRINT SCREEN** command causes the data values in the fields of the screen to be printed in their respective locations.

Next, the MODE-FLAG script variable is set to "EDIT ", and the data in the screen format is copied into a BASIC variable, S$, to be used later in the **DO LOOP**[12] to determine whether or not the user changed any data on the screen. The user is then prompted to enter data in three of the four data fields on the ATSALGRD screen with the INPUT SCREEN command. This use of the **INPUT SCREEN** command is exactly the same as the one in the ADD-RECORD procedure, except that it contains two data names having a POST PROCESS rather than one.

The post processing procedure on the SALARY-MAX field is the same one that was used in the **INPUT SCREEN** command in the ADD-RECORD procedure. The other post processing procedure, CK-TERM-KEY, occurs when the screen cursor leaves the SALARY-DESC field. This procedure is used to detect which function key the user presses (other than **RETURN** or **DownArrow**) while sitting on the SALARY-DESC field. Since this is the first field where the cursor stops when a record is displayed, it is the most likely field from which the user may wish to select another record or delete the displayed record (the only two functional choices other than **End**).

```
Script: AT SGMM0    Type: 1
Desc: Salary Grade Masterfile Mx - Primary                    Page: 4
Last Change Date: 04/18/88    Last Compile Date: 04/18/88
              Time: 11:47:13                Time: 11:48:48    Date: 04/19/88
================================================================================
    DISPLAY-RECORD
        DO LOOP UNTIL MODE-FLAG = "EDONE" OR MODE-FLAG = "DELET"
            PRINT MESSAGE "P,31" USING "ATMSGS"
            PRINT SCREEN ATSALGRD DATA
            LET MODE-FLAG = "EDIT "
            LET S$ = ATSALGRD
            INPUT SCREEN ATSALGRD DATA-NAME LIST SALARY-DESC, SALARY-MIN,
                                                SALARY-MAX
                POST PROCESS SALARY-DESC, CK-TERM-KEY,
                             SALARY-MAX, CK-SALARY-AMOUNTS
            IF TERM-KEY = 4 THEN
                LET MODE-FLAG = "EDONE"
                LET ATSALGRD = S$
            ENDIF
            IF MODE-FLAG = "EDIT " AND S$ <> ATSALGRD THEN
                INPUT MESSAGE "Y,1" INTO MSG-RESP USING "ATMSGS"
                IF MSG-RESP <> "Y" THEN LET ATSALGRD = S$ ENDIF
                LET MODE-FLAG = "EDONE"
            ENDIF
        ENDLOOP

    CK-TERM-KEY
        IF TERM-KEY = -4 THEN
            LET MODE-FLAG = "EDONE", ATSALGRD.FIELD = 99
        ELSE
            IF TERM-KEY = 3 THEN
                LET MODE-FLAG = "DELET", ATSALGRD.FIELD = 99
            ENDIF
        ENDIF

    CK-SALARY-AMOUNTS
        IF SALARY-MAX <= SALARY-MIN THEN
            INPUT MESSAGE "N,16" INTO MSG-RESP USING "ATMSGS"
            LET ATSALGRD.FIELD = 0
        ENDIF
```

Fig. 6.11 DISPLAY-RECORD and Other Edit Mode Procedures

A Simple SCRIPT-IV Data Entry Script: Display Record Procedure

The CK-TERM-KEY procedure contains a compound **IF/THEN/ENDIF** command that checks specifically for the **UpArrow** (TERM-KEY = -4) and **Function Key 3**. Any other function key (TERM-KEY value) is ignored. The **UpArrow** key would be pressed when the user wishes to return the cursor to the key field (SALARY-GRADE) and retrieve another record. **Function Key 3** would be pressed when the user wishes to delete the displayed record. In either case, MODE-FLAG is set to the appropriate value and the ATSALGRD.FIELD system variable is set to 99. As stated above, the screenname.FIELD variable controls the field to which the cursor returns after a post processing procedure. Setting this variable to 99 causes the entire **INPUT SCREEN** command to be terminated upon return from the post-processing procedure. Therefore, what is happening here is that the script is checking to see whether the user wants to continue to edit the record or not.

Function Key 4 (F4) is treated differently from the other function keys by the **INPUT SCREEN** command. F4 immediately terminates the **INPUT SCREEN** command without proceeding through any POST PROCESSing procedure. Thus, checking for a TERM-KEY value of 4 does not do us any good in the CK-TERM-KEY procedure, but must be done immediately after the **INPUT SCREEN** command (before TERM-KEY can be changed by another **INPUT** or a **PRINT** command). If **F4** is pressed (while the cursor is in on any screen field), the **IF/THEN/ENDIF** command following the **INPUT SCREEN** command will be executed, setting MODE-FLAG to "EDONE" (editing done) and the screen format, ATSALGRD, back to its original value (stored in S$). In other words, we are using this function key as an abort key that interrupts editing and discards any changes to the screen's fields that might have occurred before the function key was pressed.

If the user did not abort, we next want to determine whether or not the user made any changes that we need to save. This is done with another **IF/THEN/ENDIF** command. If MODE-FLAG still contains the value "EDIT ", and the screen format contains different data from the "saved copy" in S$, we issue a message asking the user whether or not to save the changes detected. If the response is not "Y", we replace the changed screen format with the saved copy. In either case we set MODE-FLAG to "EDONE' to terminate the **DO LOOP** and return through the GET-RECORD procedure (where we write the record back to the file via the **CHANGE** command) to the MAIN-PROCEDURE.

A Simple SCRIPT-IV Data Entry Script: Delete Record Procedure

Finally, if **Function Key 3** is pressed in the DISPLAY-RECORD procedure and MODE-FLAG is set to "DELET", this also terminates the **DO LOOP** and returns control back to the MAIN-PROCEDURE. The DELETE-RECORD procedure is then invoked to delete the record from the file (see Figure 6.12).

```
Script: AT SGMM0    Type: 1
Desc: Salary Grade Masterfile Mx - Primary              Page: 5
Last Change Date: 04/19/88    Last Compile Date: 04/18/88
            Time: 12:14:50                Time: 11:48:48    Date: 04/19/88
=============================================================================
     DELETE-RECORD
          INPUT MESSAGE "Y,2" INTO MSG-RESP USING "ATMSGS"
          IF MSG-RESP ="Y" THEN
              DELETE ATSALGRD USING KEY SALARY-GRADE
                 BUSY IS BUSY-RECORD
              PRINT SCREEN ATSALGRD CLEAR DATA-NAME LIST SALARY-DESC,
                                                        SALARY-MIN,
                                                        SALARY-MAX
          ENDIF

     END-SCRIPT
```

Fig. 6.12 DELETE-RECORD Procedure

To ensure that we do not delete a record unless the user really wants us to, we confirm that he or she pressed the correct function key by issuing a Yes/No message to that effect. If a positive response is received from this confirmation message, we proceed with the **DELETE** command, once again checking to see that no other user is editing the record we are trying to delete. We use the same BUSY-RECORD procedure that was shown in Figure 6.9 to accomplish this busy record check. Upon return to the MAIN-PROCEDURE, the deleted record's data is cleared from the screen but its key value is still displayed (as a result of the **INPUT SCREEN** command's options). Other records may be displayed or added at this point.

More Complex SCRIPT-IV Data Entry Scripts: Organization

The sample ATS contains several more complex data entry processes that we, unfortunately, do not have enough space to examine in as much detail as we did the simple script above. Instead, in this section we will review some of the additional capabilities of SCRIPT-IV and leave the detailed examination of the associated scripts as an exercise for those readers who wish to do so.[13]

Options 1 and 4 on the main ATS menu (again see Figure 9.1) allow the user access to data entry processes that are more complex both in operation and in implementation than the script we reviewed in the previous sections. Each of these processes is implemented using a series of scripts that include a primary, a continuation, several overlay, and several copy scripts.[14]

The primary script contains the set up functions required for the process, such as opening files (links) and screens, displaying initial messages and screens, initializing script variables, etc. In addition it handles any errors that occur in trying to **OPEN** files, and executes the continuation script when it is done.

The continuation script contains the main processing loop (similar to the MAIN-PROCEDURE in the ATSGMM0 script) for browsing, adding, or editing records. When its execution is complete, it returns to the IDOL-IV menu system using a **TERMINATE** command. The overlay scripts each accomplish some specific function within this main loop, such as adding a record, copying a record, deleting a record, editing a record, validating a data field value in a "code" file, etc. These major overlay scripts are executed from the continuation script; the other overlay scripts are executed from one of these major overlay scripts.[15]

The Data Definition section for each process is stored in a copy script (ending with the letters "DS"), and each script in the series contains an **INCLUDE** command at the very beginning that specifies this copy script name. This guarantees that each script in the series has exactly the same data environment as all the others.[16]

More Complex SCRIPT-IV Data Entry Scripts: Operation

The operation of these scripts is similar in many ways to that of the simple data entry script described above, but does differ in several important aspects. In this section we briefly review the operation of one of the more complex data entry processes (Applicant Masterfile Maintenance), and then examine some of the SCRIPT-IV capabilities used to create this process.

First, let us take a quick trip through the process from the user's point of view. The next few figures (Figures 6.13 through 6.19) show the screen images at various stages in the maintenance or data entry process. Figure 6.13 depicts the screen image as it appears immediately after the user presses Option 1 on the ATS menu. You will note that the user may still enter an Applicant ID (the key field of the file being maintained) and attempt to retrieve a record (using either **Function Key 10** or **RETURN**). Also, you will

6 DATABASE MAINTENANCE IMPLEMENTATION AND USE

notice that the "next record" and "previous record" functions are activated using **Function Key 1** and **Function Key 2**, respectively, rather than with the **DownArrow** and **UpArrow** keys.

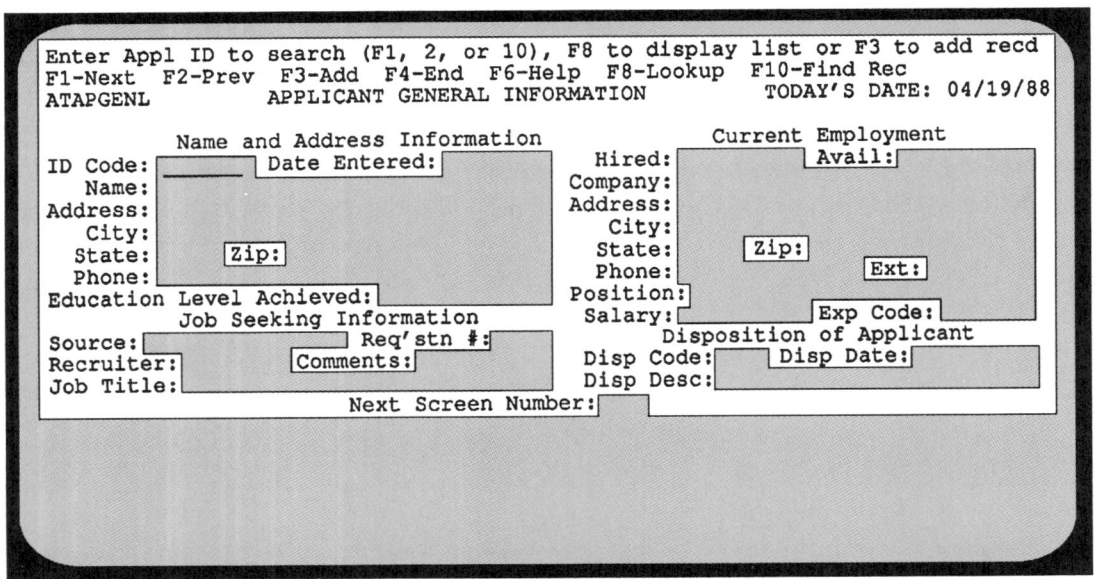

Fig. 6.13 Applicant Masterfile Maintenance Browse/Add Screen

If **Function Key 10** (or **RETURN**) is pressed and the record does not already exist, however, the user receives a message to that effect, rather than being asked if he or she is adding a new entry. In this process the user must enter a new key value and press a specific function key to enter "add mode" (in this case **Function Key 3**) from "browse mode." These are simply two different approaches to this part of the user interface; one is not necessarily better than the other.

Since the two masterfiles, ATAPMSTR and ATRQMSTR, are more complex in their data structures than the code file maintained by ATSGMM0, some additional functions are required in the data entry processes. For instance, both masterfiles contain fields whose values are constrained to be an existing key value in one of the code files.[17] To make it easier to enter a valid code value, a "lookup" function has been provided that allows the user to display a list of the possible code records. This list can be displayed using **Function Key 8** while the screen cursor is in the code field. After a choice is made from the list using **Function Key 1**, the key of the selected record is retrieved from the list and placed in the code field.

This lookup function is also available to provide a list of the masterfile records while the screen cursor is in the masterfile key field (Figure 6.14 shows the screen image of the Applicant Masterfile Maintenance process with the "main lookup" window displayed). While any of the lookup windows are displayed, the records within the window can be scrolled up and down by using the **Arrow** keys, the **PageUp** and **PageDown** keys, and the **Home** key. As the prompting messages in Figure 6.14 state, **Function Key 1** can be used to retrieve the record we wish to maintain, or we can close the window with **Function Key 4**. Figure 6.15 shows a screen display of a record that has been chosen using one of the several browse and retrieve methods described above.

The script code that implements the "main lookup" function can be found in the "1L" scripts, and the "code lookup" function can be found in most of the overlay scripts whose names end with a lowercase letter (e.g., ATAPMM1a). The "lookup" function is accomplished with a **PRINT VIEW** command that allows the script designer to create a "lookup window" anywhere on the terminal screen, draw a border around the window (if desired), and display a list of records within the border. The beginning and ending key values of the list are specified as well as the starting point for the display (i.e., the starting point does not have to be the beginning key value of the list). The script designer also controls which function keys are used to return a valid code value (if any), and whether or not the window is cleared from the screen after its use. The script designer must also take care to "refresh" whatever portion of the original screen was "displayed over" when the **PRINT VIEW** was executed.[18]

Figures 6.16 and 6.17 show additional examples of "lookup windows" that are available within Applicant Masterfile Maintenance. Figure 6.16 shows the "code lookup" window for the **Exp Code** (Experience Code) field. It is displayed by moving the cursor to the **Exp Code** field and pressing **Function Key 8**. You will notice that this window has been placed in the lower left corner of the screen, and does not cover up the **Exp Code** field. This approach has been used, where possible, so that the user can maintain visual contact with the field that corresponds with the lookup window being displayed. This aids the user in "keeping his or her place" within the large amount of data displayed on these types of screens.

6 DATABASE MAINTENANCE IMPLEMENTATION AND USE

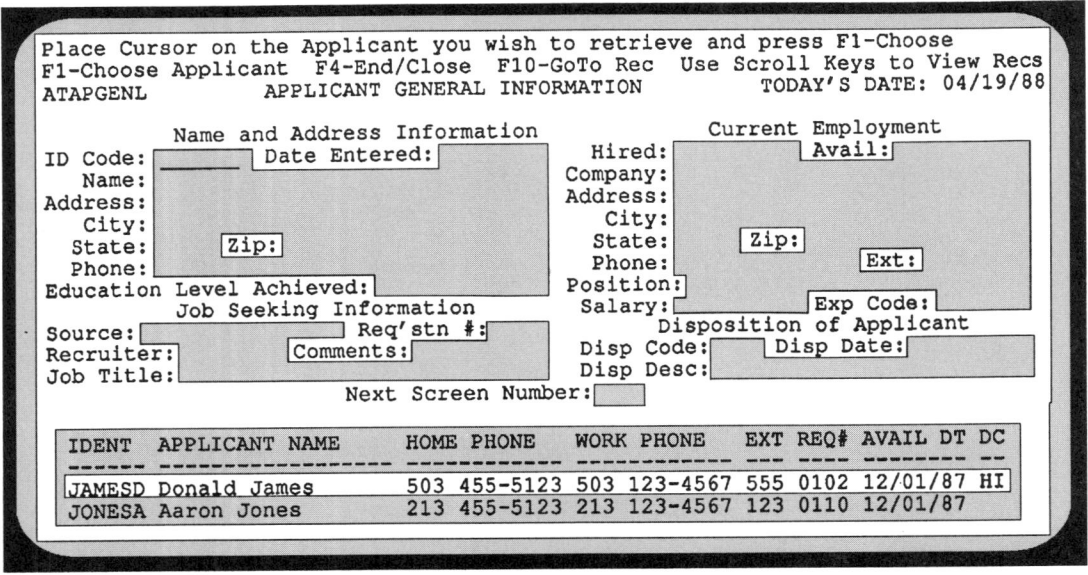

Fig. 6.14 Applicant Masterfile Maintenance Main Lookup Window

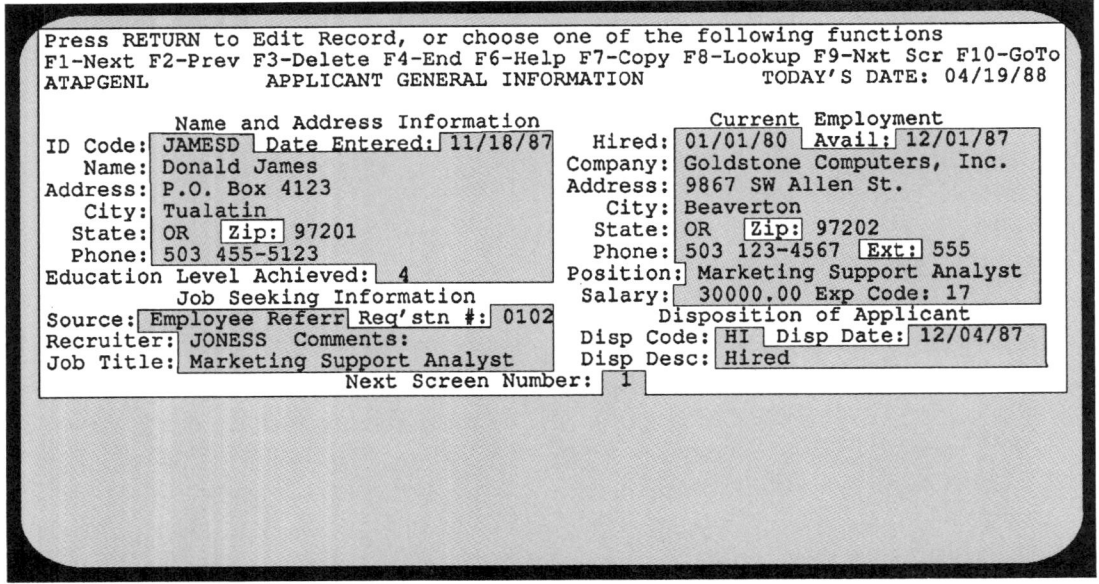

Fig. 6.15 Applicant Masterfile Maintenance Retrieved Record

More Complex SCRIPT-IV Data Entry Scripts: Operation

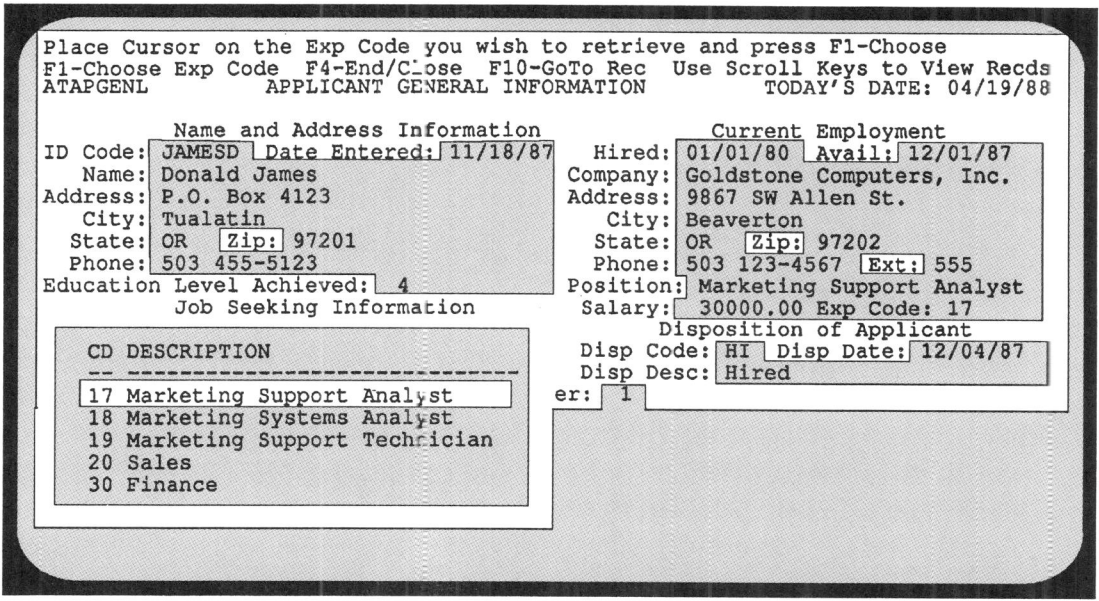

Fig. 6.16 Applicant Masterfile Maintenance with Experience Code Lookup Window

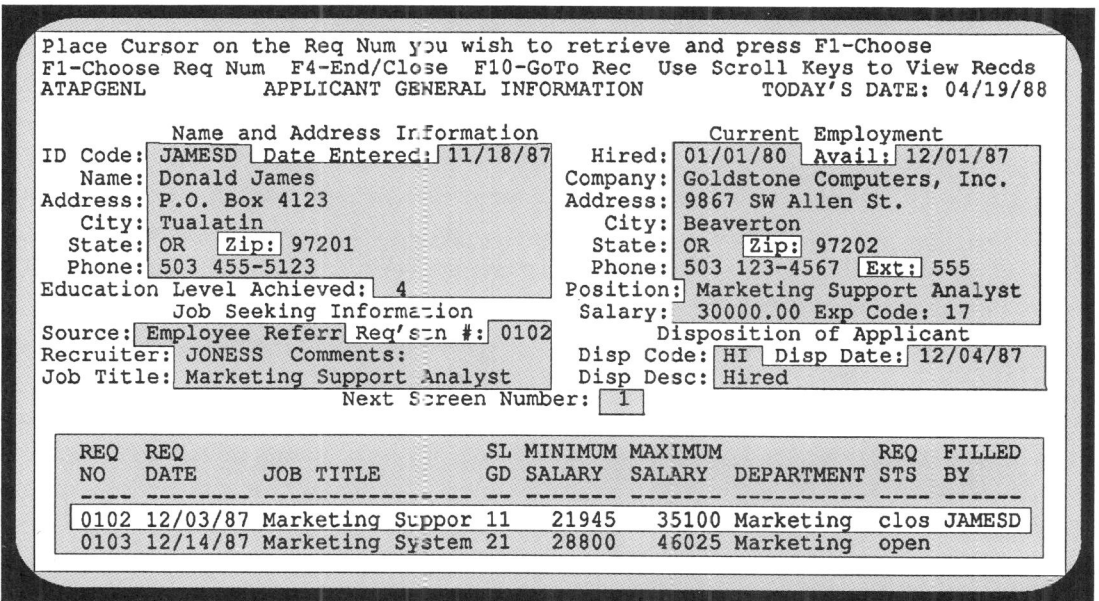

Fig. 6.17 Applicant Masterfile Maintenance with Requisition Number Lookup Window

103

6 DATABASE MAINTENANCE IMPLEMENTATION AND USE

Figure 6.17 shows the "code lookup" window for the **Req'stn #** (Requisition Number) field. This **PRINT VIEW** is similar to the previous one except that it takes the entire screen width to display all the necessary data. Also, you will note that Requisition #102 contains a reference to the Applicant record we are maintaining in the FILLED BY field. You will find more on the cross-referencing of these two files later in this section.

One of the major differences that you will find between the Applicant Masterfile Maintenance and all other database maintenance functions in the sample ATS is that the Applicant Masterfile contains too many fields to fit on one screen. Therefore, two screens have been created to display and allow maintenance of Applicant data. You may notice in Figure 6.15 that **Function Key 9** is used for "Nxt Scr", which means "Next Screen," and that the last field at the bottom of each screen is Next Screen Number.

Both of these items allow the user to move from one Applicant data screen to the other, and Figure 6.18 shows the message (on the first line of the figure) that is displayed when the user presses **Function Key 9**. This message is called a "select" message, and operates the same as a "ring menu" in many PC software packages. The user moves a "highlight bar" on top of the option that is to be selected, and presses the **RETURN** key to pick it. The script designer can also pick which option the highlight bar starts on. In this case, since we are on screen 1, the highlight bar automatically starts on top of **Recruitment Costs — Screen 2**. We simply press the **RETURN** key and screen 2 is displayed (see Figure 6.19). When we press **Function Key 9** on screen 2, the highlight bar automatically starts on top of **General Data — Screen 1**.

Figures 6.15 and 6.19 indicate another major difference between the more complex database maintenance scripts and the simple one we reviewed previously. This difference lies in the fact that when the user browses through Applicant records (or Requisitions) he or she does not "lock" each record that is displayed (i.e., the script is using **READ** commands rather than **CHANGE** commands). Compare the top lines of the screens on these two figures, and you will see that when a record is displayed, the message in Figure 6.15 is displayed. The user must press the **RETURN** key "to reserve the record for editing", or in SCRIPT-IV terms, to issue a **CHANGE** command that locks other users out until the **CHANGE** is completed. This approach makes it much easier for multiple users to view existing database records without constantly stumbling over each other's "locks".

More Complex SCRIPT-IV Data Entry Scripts: Operation

Fig. 6.18 Applicant Masterfile Maintenance Select Message

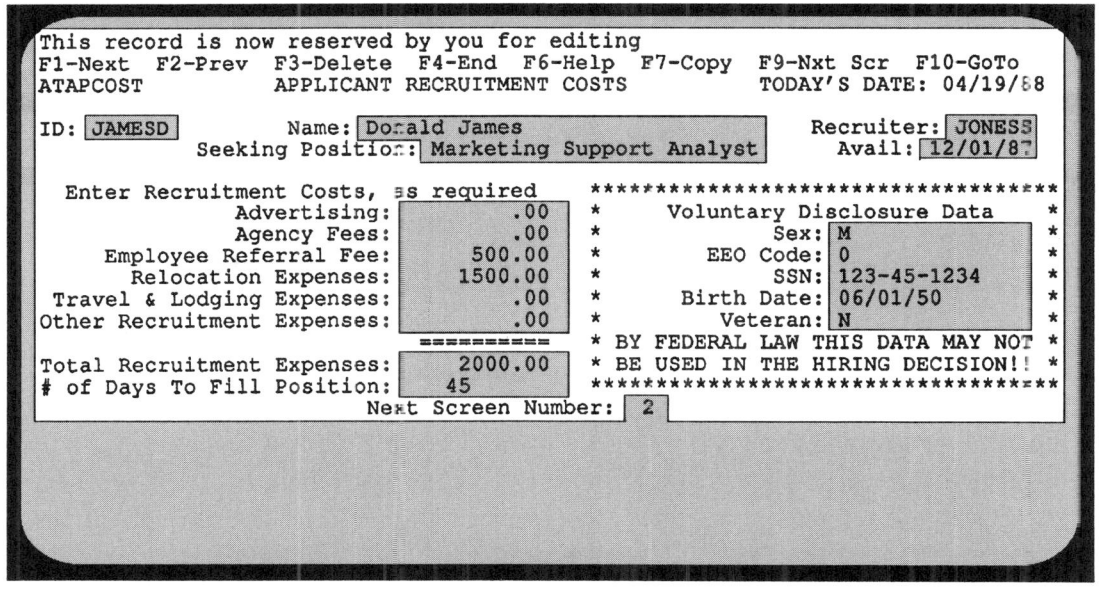

Fig. 6.19 Applicant Masterfile Maintenance Screen 2

6 DATABASE MAINTENANCE IMPLEMENTATION AND USE

Another function that has been included in these complex scripts (and would have been included in scripts that maintain the code files if these had been written) is "**referential integrity**." This concept comes from the relational theory of data modeling, and states (paraphrased from relational terminology):

If a field in a record is supposed to contain a value that is a foreign key reference to a record in another (or the same file), the value of that field MUST be valid or the field must not contain a value at all.

At first this does not sound too difficult to accomplish. In fact, following the **PRINT VIEW**, the rest of the script code in the "lookup" overlays mentioned above accomplishes half of this function. In other words, values entered into code fields are checked against records in the code file, and invalid entries are not allowed. However, what would happen if the key to one of the code records were changed from, say, "ABC" to "XYZ"? Any file whose records contained the original code value would no longer meet the referential integrity rule. And the same problem would occur should a code record in use be deleted from the code file.

The vast majority of designers neglect to solve this part of the problem and basically ignore referential integrity in their software design. However, because of the facilities available with IDOL-IV, we have implemented a solution in the ATS.

The only realistic solution to this half of the problem is to provide checks against this situation occurring during maintenance of the keys to the code files. Within the sample ATS, you will find these checks between the Applicant and Requisition masterfiles. This has been done because each of these files may refer to a valid record in the other: an applicant may be interviewing for a specific job (requisition number), and eventually a requisition is filled by an applicant.

The implementation of this rule is not really difficult, but its execution may take some time in a database with a large number of records. What you will find in the sample ATS are checks in three scripts to prevent a violation of referential integrity. In the "1E" script a check is made toward the end of the MAIN-PROCEDURE to determine if the key value of the record being maintained has been changed; if so, the CHANGE-KEY-VALUE procedure is executed. This procedure executes the "1K" overlay, which checks for the use of the old key value in the other masterfile, and changes all occurrences of it to the new key value. A similar check is done when an attempt is made to delete a masterfile record. In this case, however, the delete request is rejected if the key of the masterfile record being deleted is "in use" in the other masterfile.[19]

The other major difference between the simple script and these masterfile maintenance scripts centers around the fact that in the masterfile maintenance scripts, the screen formats and the file (link) formats are not the same (i.e., do not contain exactly the same fields). This results primarily from the fact that data from the code file is displayed on the masterfile maintenance screen along with the validated code. This is typically done as a visual verification to the user that the correct code was chosen, but can also aid significantly in completing the "picture" of the automated "record" being maintained. Another use of this approach might be a calculated field that is not stored in the file (although this has not been included in the sample ATS design).

As a result of these data differences, you will find additional script code in the "1A' and "1E" and "2E" overlays that move data from format to format using **LET** commands.[20] This facility, of course, makes it very easy to display data from many files on the terminal screen at the same time, and even maintain data in multiple files from one screen (although creating a simple user interface to accomplish this latter function can sometimes be a little difficult).

Conclusions

Data entry (database maintenance) processes are the part of a system where the user usually spends the most time and has the most problems. Therefore, it is extremely important that application designers take this into account and spend extra time and effort to make these functions easy for a new user to master. It is equally as important that an Applications Development System (4GL) offer the capabilities and features that are necessary to support this requirement.

It should be evident from the material in this chapter that IDOL-IV offers ample facilities for maintaining data in an application system's database. Of more significance, however, is the fact that very sophisticated database maintenance processes can be created and packaged using IDOL-IV, so that the least experienced operator can quickly and easily become an effective system user.

Simple data entry tasks can be created as easily as "painting" a screen and defining a format. Complex tasks can be created by adding to these objects a Fourth Generation Language script of powerful, high-level commands that control every aspect of the screen and its data. All of the functions that might be required in a data entry and maintenance process are available in either type of task.

6 DATABASE MAINTENANCE IMPLEMENTATION AND USE

If IDOL-IV DBM is used as part of the database maintenance facilities within an application system, it is important that the application designer make all SCRIPT-IV scripts for data entry act similarly to IDOL-IV DBM. This is required so that the user is not confused by moving back and forth between two differently designed data entry processes. And, as seen in this chapter, this can be easily done with SCRIPT-IV. Of course, this requirement can be avoided by creating all of a system's data entry processes with SCRIPT-IV, and not allowing the user access to IDOL-IV DBM, but that decision is up to the application designer.

In either case, IDOL-IV is robust in the database maintenance area. But, unlike many other Applications Development Systems, it has substantial capabilities in the other areas of applications systems implementation as well. In subsequent chapters we will examine these other areas to complete the picture of a real, full-function Fourth Generation Language.

Notes and References

[1] One caution should be noted here. A "calculated data field" cannot be stored in the file from which the total is calculated. It is a display-only field. Therefore, if this facility is used, the total must be recalculated every time it is needed (e.g., in reports on the same data, other screens, etc.)

[2] The View Maintenance function is discussed in more detail in a later chapter.

[3] The various logical segments of an IDOL-IV script are called "procedures", and each is assigned a procedure name. These names can be seen left-justified throughout the script code. Any of these procedures may be executed by placing their name after a **DO** command (as we will see later in this chapter).

[4] The **PRINT SCREEN** command causes the last four lines of Figure 6.6 to be displayed; the **PRINT MESSAGE** command causes the second line to be displayed.

[5] Note the parentheses in the **IF/THEN/ENDIF** command. Complex conditions can be combined using the logical operators: AND and OR.

[6] Error handling procedures of this type may also be placed all together at the end of the script for easy location (see other sample ATS scripts). These three have been grouped with the GET-RECORD procedure in this sample script for convenience of presentation.

Notes and References

[7] Another part of this solution is to provide a database maintenance process that does not lock records that are merely being "browsed". The more complex scripts in the ATS use this approach where the browse functions issue **READ** commands, and only issue a **CHANGE** command when the user indicates that he or she wants to edit the record.

[8] An alternative to this error message approach is to proceed automatically to the first record in the file when the end-of-file is encountered (and vice versa). This allows a user to browse "forever" without getting an error message. This approach, however, is not used in the sample ATS scripts.

[9] Three additional, optional parameters may be specified in an **INPUT MESSAGE** command: display mode, line clearing parameters, and positioning parameters. These have not been included in the **INPUT MESSAGE** commands in this script, requiring the extra commas between the message number and the first piece of variable data.

[10] If this were allowed, the user could end up trying to add a "duplicate record" to the ATSALGRD file. Duplicate primary keys are not allowed in IDOL-IV files.

[11] The normal value of the screen-name.FIELD system variable is 1, causing the cursor to move from one field to the next. Controlling this system variable allows the designer to have complete control over the movement of the cursor on the screen. In other words, fields can be skipped depending upon other field values, or fields can be added but not edited, and so on.

[12] Business BASIC variables can be used within scripts whenever desired. In this case, it is easier to store a copy of the screen in a BASIC variable than in a script variable, since the length of a BASIC variable does not have to be predefined. Also, to reduce memory usage, BASIC variables may be selectively cleared from memory after use (set equal to 0 or ""), while predefined script variables cannot.

[13] These scripts are very well "commented" so that someone with an introductory understanding of SCRIPT-IV can follow their logic fairly easily.

[14] The script naming convention adopted for this application is described below. The names of the Option 1 scripts start with "ATAPMM" and the Option 2 scripts start with "ATRQMM". "AT" is the library, "AP" stands for Applicant,

and "RQ" stands for Requisition. The "MM" stands for Masterfile Maintenance. The "0" script (as in ATAPMM0) is the primary script, the "1" script is the continuation script, and the "1X", "2X", or "1x" are overlay scripts (where "X" or "x" is an alphabetic character). Any script that ends with two alphabetic characters is a "copy" script (as in ATAPMMDS). The uppercase ending alphabetic characters are somewhat indicative of the function of the script (e.g., "1A" = add, "1C" = copy, "DS" = data section). The lowercase ending alphabetic characters are simply used in sequence to indicate re-usable external subroutines within a series (e.g., "1a" = the first subroutine, "1b" = the second).

[15]In fact, this distinction is also evident in the naming conventions mentioned earlier. Names of overlay scripts ending with an uppercase character indicate "major" overlays executed from the continuation script. Names of overlay scripts ending with a lowercase character indicate those executed from one or more of the "major" overlays rather than from the continuation script. PLEASE NOTE that the rules defining what types of scripts can be executed from what other types are not as restrictive as these examples might indicate. You should refer to the IDOL-IV documentation for a complete description of these and other script structure rules.

[16]Regardless of whether the data declaration for the script series is maintained in one common copy script or whether it is maintained in each script within the series, if the data definition for the script series is changed, any change must be made effective by recompiling the **entire series** of scripts after the change is made.

[17]This is an implementation of the concept of a "foreign key", as discussed in an earlier chapter.

[18]For this reason you will note that all of the code lookup windows are displayed in one of two spots on the screen so that the same "refresh screen image" can be used repeatedly to return the screen display to its original condition. Also, a copy script is used to "merge in" the standard "refresh screen" logic where necessary. Note also that this same approach is used to refresh the screen following the display of the help window.

[19]It is possible to argue that the delete check should remove the old key value from the records in which it is "in use," thus maintaining referential integrity. However, this can be a very dangerous decision for a computer program to

Notes and References

make. The suggestion here is to disallow the delete, and require the user to make the decision regarding removing the obstruction by changing the values in the other masterfile and then retrying the delete.

[20]The SCRIPT-IV syntax for copying values from one format to another is quite simple: **LET** format-name1 = format-name2. This will cause all the values in fields that exist in **both** formats to be copied from format-name2 to format-name1. Of course, this same result can be achieved by copying each individual field one at a time, but the former approach takes a lot less script code, and possibly less time to execute.

7

DESIGNING AND USING A VIEW OF A FILE

While more traditional data entry processing is typically done one record at a time, it is often quite helpful to be able to display and maintain a **list** of records on the screen simultaneously. Comparisons of data values among records aids analytical tasks and promotes better decision making. Being able to display a report on the screen is definitely helpful; being able to display **and** maintain a list of records is a real plus. Finally, with the incredible proliferation of the "spreadsheet metaphor" more and more computer users desire (and expect) to see "records" of information (from the same file) as "rows" on the screen.

All of this leads to what in IDOL-IV is called a "view". A view is a way of displaying and maintaining a list of records from a file. View maintenance can be very simple or can take on significant complexity. This chapter presents the activities a developer undergoes to create a view definition, followed by a brief description of some of the functions available to the user of a view. One thing that will become evident as you proceed through the latter part of this chapter is that some parts of view maintenance are really for sophisticated users only, and should not be attempted by (or accessible to) the novice user.

Creating and Saving the View Definition

View maintenance can actually be done at any time on any format, link, or screen defined in the IDOL-IV Design Dictionaries. A specific view definition does not have to be created first. As mentioned in the previous chapter, access to view processing is also available through IDOL-IV DBM when the user is inquiring into or changing existing records.

7 DESIGNING AND USING A VIEW OF A FILE

However, for formats that have more than just a few fields, it is a good design rule to create specific view definitions for particular uses and have them accessible to the appropriate users directly from an IDOL-IV menu. This is the approach described here, and is the approach that was taken in designing and implementing the sample Applicant Tracking System. Both the requisition and applicant files have specifically defined view maintenance processes available from the main ATS menu (see Figure 9.1). The Requisition Records View is the one used in this chapter to highlight the functions of view processing.

The first step in creating a view definition, once the view specifications have been developed, is to access IDOL-IV DBM. Then, select **2-View**, and enter the format (or link) name to be used as the basis for the view (in this case, we use the link named ATRQMSTR). The fields in the format will be displayed across the screen (indicated by dashes showing the size of each field). If any records exist in the file associated with the format, they will be displayed as well (see Figure 7.1).[1]

```
REQ-NO
ATRQMSTR              Employment Requisitions File Link
F1)Recover-Column  F2)Del-Column  F3)Chng-Field-Width  F4)End  F5)Select-Sort:
F6)Help  F7)Special-Functions  F8)Commands  F9)Single-Record-Mode  F10)Goto  :
---- -------- ---- -------------------------- -- ---------- --------------
0100 12/03/87 0110 Dir, Product Marketing     24    .00 Marketing
0101 12/04/87 0142 Sr. Technical Writer       16    .00 Documentation
0102 12/03/87 0154 Marketing Support Analyst  11    .00 Marketing
0103 12/14/87 0152 Marketing Systems Analyst  21    .00 Marketing
0110 12/03/87 0154 Marketing Support Analyst  11    .00 Marketing
0123 12/04/87 0142 Sr. Technical Writer       16    .00 Documentation
0151 01/15/88 0102 V.P., Marketing Oper.      30    .00 Sales
```

Fig. 7.1 First Step in View Definition

From this point you can make changes to this default view so that you end up with the view definition that meets your specifications. These changes comprise selecting the columns to be displayed, adjusting displayed column width, adding titles to displayed columns, and setting overall view parameters.

Creating and Saving the View Definition

The Requisition Records View specification developed for the sample ATS required that the following fields be displayed:

> REQ-NO
> REQ-DATE
> JOB-TITLE (15)
> SALARY-GRADE
> SALARY-MAX
> SALARY-MIN
> DEPARTMENT (10)
> REQ-STATUS (4)
> TOTAL-REC-EXP
> NO-DAYS-TO-FILL
> IDENT

Three fields are to be displayed in columns smaller than the field length (JOB-TITLE, DEPARTMENT, and REQ-STATUS), and the column width is shown in the list above next to the field name. Also, the fields are to be displayed in the order shown in the list, regardless of their sequence in the format.

Three functions are available to the developer to accomplish these tasks: **Del-Column**, **Recover-Column**, and **Chng-Field-Width**. First, all unwanted columns can be deleted. This leaves the fields listed in the specification, but not necessarily in the correct order. In the Requisition Records example, SALARY-MAX and SALARY-MIN are both out of order. This can be rectified by first deleting a column, and then recovering it in the "correct" position in the display (this latter function is accomplished by placing the cursor in the target position and pressing the **Recover-Column** key; a list of columns that can be recovered is displayed for your selection).

Once all columns are in their correct position, field width can be adjusted according to specification. The three fields mentioned above required this process in the Requisition Records example.

To finish the view layout, column titles can be placed above the dashes that indicate each field. Two lines are available within which to describe each column. These two lines are accessible by pressing the **Special-Functions** key and selecting "H" for (column) headings. After entering these headings it is a good idea to save this new view definition. Again, the **Special-Functions** key is used, and "S" is selected to save the view. The format (or link) name that was used as its basis is displayed as a default name,

7 DESIGNING AND USING A VIEW OF A FILE

but can be changed before the view is saved (in fact, this view was renamed to ATREQSVW). Now, every time this view is accessed, either directly from a menu entry or via IDOL-IV DBM, the specific columns and their respective titles will be displayed (see Figure 7.2).[2]

```
REQ-NO
 ATREQSVW              Employment Requisition View
 F1)Recover-Column  F2)Del-Column  F3)Chng-Field-Width  F4)End  F5)Select-Sort:
 F6)Help  F7)Special-Functions  F8)Commands  F9)Single-Record-Mode  F10)Goto  :
REQ  REQ                       SL MAXIMUM MINIMUM              REQ  FILLED
NO   DATE     JOB TITLE        GD SALARY  SALARY  DEPARTMENT   STS  BY
---- -------- ---------------- -- ------- ------- ----------   ---- ------
0100 12/03/87 Dir, Product Ma  24  59850   37450  Marketing    open
0101 12/04/87 Sr. Technical W  16  29650   18565  Documentat   clos LOGANL
0102 12/03/87 Marketing Suppo  11  35100   21945  Marketing    clos JAMESD
0103 12/14/87 Marketing Syste  21  46025   28800  Marketing    open
0110 12/03/87 Marketing Suppo  11  35100   21945  Marketing    re-o
0123 12/04/87 Sr. Technical W  16  29650   18565  Documentat   open
0151 01/15/88 V.P., Marketing  30 120000   60000  Sales        open
```

Fig. 7.2 Completed View Definition

Three additional **Special-Functions** are available to control certain actions during view processing. The "D" function allows the designer to determine whether or not field names are displayed on the top line of the screen as the cursor is moved from one field to another. This is a toggle switch, and can be changed from "on" to "off" to "on" as desired.

The "R" function allows the designer to determine the movement of the cursor as it leaves a field after maintenance. To maintain data in a field displayed in a view, the user must press the **ENTER** key while the cursor is resting in the target field. This will highlight the field and allow maintenance. Another **ENTER** after the value in the field is changed will exit maintenance mode. The direction the cursor moves from the maintained field is determined by this **Special-Functions** switch — either Down (default), Left or Right. Again, this may be changed at will as maintenance requirements change.

The "L" function allows the designer to "lock" columns so that they remain displayed when horizontal scrolling occurs. These columns are typically the key and descriptive fields in the record and aid in identifying the remaining data displayed in the view. The applicant views in the sample ATS all have the IDENT and APPLICANT NAME fields locked. This is indicated by a "V" displayed on the top terminal line at the position where scrolling occurs. Every character to the left of the "V" remains "locked" on the display.

View Display and Record Selection Functions

Filling the screen with as many records from the file as will physically fit, and displaying them in the primary key sequence, is not the only alternative in view display. One function and four Commands are available to modify this situation: the **SORT** function, and the **SET**, **LIST**, **SORT**, and **COUNT** Commands. The **SORT** function is available throughout view display and maintenance, and allows you to select which of the secondary keys to use to sequence the displayed records in the view. The **SET** Command allows you to specify the number of lines (heading+records) which are to be displayed on the screen (from 4 to 20 with 20 as the default). For example, the command **SET LINES=15** causes only 12 records (and 3 heading lines) to be displayed.

The **LIST** Command allows you to specify which records from the file you wish to be displayed. It also allows this list of records to be printed to a printer, rather than displayed on the screen. Options include specifying a key (primary or secondary) range, one or more conditions that must be true, and printer control options (if required). This Command is very helpful when only selected records are of interest for analysis or maintenance.

When a **LIST** Command is specified for selecting records, a **SORT** Command may also be specified to cause the selected records to be displayed in a particular order. One of the secondary keys is chosen, and any records that match the **LIST** criteria are displayed/printed in the **SORT** order. Also, restriction criteria can be added to the **LIST** command to cause only certain records to be displayed. The results from the **LIST** command may be sent to the terminal screen or to a valid printer designation. If printed, a heading for the listing may be specified.[3]

Finally, the **COUNT** Command can be issued to return the number of records in the file that meet certain criteria. In this case, the number of records is the important piece of information, rather than seeing the records themselves.

7 DESIGNING AND USING A VIEW OF A FILE

Mass (Groups of Records) Functions

Another set of Commands is available with which to accomplish "mass changes" to the records in a file. These commands include: **CHANGE, DELETE, COPY,** and **MOVE**. With these Commands the sophisticated user can, in effect, create and execute any number of ad hoc update processes that would all together take a significant amount of program development time. However, as mentioned earlier in this chapter, these Commands are not for the novice user. Serious havoc can be created by someone who does not really understand what he or she is doing.

The **CHANGE** and **DELETE** Commands allow the user to select specific records that match certain criteria, and either change the value in particular fields or delete the records from the file. Of course, all Delete Record specifications in the appropriate format must also be met for records to be deleted.

The **COPY** and **MOVE** Commands allow the user to select a group of records to be duplicated in another format (or link) or moved to another format (or link). The major difference between **COPY** and **MOVE** is that **COPY** leaves the original records and **MOVE** does not. Since it is possible to duplicate existing unique keys with these Commands, the user must also specify what action to take should a duplicate key be encountered. The choices are: ask whether or not to replace, replace without asking, or skip the new record entirely. This provides complete control to the user during the processing of the Command.

Also, as mentioned earlier, these two commands offer the capability of "converting" records from an old format to a new one with added or dropped fields. **COPY**ing the old records to the new format causes the system to copy data in like-named fields. Any "old" fields missing from the new format will be ignored, and new fields will be left blank.

Parameterization of View Functions

To protect the data in existing records from being changed (or destroyed), while still providing the display capability of view processing, IDOL-IV View Definition includes two parameters for the designer to use. These are the **Change** parameters: Key and Data.

By setting both of these parameters to "Y", the designer activates all of the capabilities described above for designing and redesigning the view definition, manipulating data records displayed in a view, and adding or deleting records in a view. Setting both parameters to "N" restricts a view user to display and scrolling capabilities only, which can be important for the novice user.

Turning either parameter "on" by itself allows the respective portion of data records to be changed but still restricts view definition activities. The IDOL-IV documentation should be checked for more details on the functioning of the individual parameters by themselves.

Conclusions

The use of IDOL-IV Views can be a very powerful addition to the traditional types of database maintenance processing available in most application systems. They can also be a significant enhancement to the inquiry and listing capabilities of such a system. Because Views utilize the popular and pervasive "spreadsheet metaphor", they are immediately recognizable to the user. This recognition combined with the substantial functionality of IDOL-IV view processing make this type of multiple-record database maintenance function a must for the business applications systems of the '90s.

Notes and References

[1] Views can display more data than fits on the terminal screen. Records in the view can be scrolled horizontally using the standard IDOL-IV scrolling keys (**Arrow** keys, **TAB**, **BACK TAB**, and **HOME**).

[2] You may note that this view is defined as less than 80 characters in length. This was done specifically so that it could also be used in a **PRINT VIEW** command in a SCRIPT-IV script (see previous chapter). The applicant views, on the other hand, are all defined greater than 80 characters in length.

[3] In fact, the Code File Listings shown in Appendix 7 were all produced using the **LIST** command in View Maintenance.

8

DESIGNING AND IMPLEMENTING REPORTS

Report creation with a 4GL can take one of several forms. Some 4GLs contain commands that are designed specifically for output production. Others contain a separate software component that is intended to create application output, but is not necessarily a part of the "language." Still others depend on a "foreign" (or add-on) product to provide report production capability to their Applications Development System.

As do many full-function 4GLs, IDOL-IV offers more than one alternative for designing and implementing reports; these include 1) IDOL-IV Query — a component of IDOL-IV that allows simple listings and reports with simple totalling to be produced; 2) REPORT-IV — a component of IDOL-IV that has built-in report creation capabilities for designing and generating both simple listings and complex reports; and 3) SCRIPT-IV output commands — a subset of SCRIPT-IV that can be used in scripts to produce output.

In this chapter we will discuss REPORT-IV, as it is the way that most application system output will be generated with IDOL-IV. In fact, it is the only way output in the sample Applicant Tracking System is produced (other than by using the **LIST** command in View processing discussed in the previous chapter). The capabilities in SCRIPT-IV are only required for those reports that are very complicated or that require logical functioning other than just producing output (e.g., updating records, creating temporary or other files, etc.). And, IDOL-IV Query is really designed as an end-user tool for producing simple reports and lists, and will not be discussed in this book.

8 DESIGNING AND IMPLEMENTING REPORTS

ATS: Report Specifications

In a previous chapter we listed six reports that are a part of the sample Applicant Tracking System. Two of these six reports are described in detail in this chapter. Their description comprises the report's specification (a brief outline of the report's function, the selection criteria for choosing records to print on the report, the report's sequence, the fields that are to be printed on the report and any totalling that is required), followed by the report definition and some sample report output. Complete specifications for all six reports, and sample output from each report can be found in Appendices 8 and 9 at the end of the book.

The first report that we will examine is a simple listing of records from the requisition file summarizing "open" requisitions, that can be used to analyze existing job openings. The report's specification is shown in Figure 8.1 below:

Report #3. **Open Requisitions Summary Report (ATOPNRQR)** - prints a list of all "open" requisitions grouped by department. Selection is for all reqisitions with a requisition status (REQ-STATUS) of "open". The report is sequenced by requisition number (REQ-NO).

The data fields printed are:

Req No
Req Date
Department
Job Title
Salary Grade
Min Salary
Max Salary
Primary Experience Code
Recruiter ID

Fig. 8.1 Report Specification for Report #3

Creating a Simple Report Definition

The second report is somewhat more complicated in that it prints data from several files and subtotals several fields. Its "primary" records are from the Requisition file and are grouped by Department. This report can be used to analyze recruitment costs that have been accrued by department in hiring employees. The report's specification is shown in Figure 8.2.

Report #6. **Recruitment Costs Report (ATRECCSR)** - prints a list of closed reqisitions by Department showing recruitment costs. Selection is for all closed requisitions. The report is sequenced by Req No within Department.

The data fields printed are:

Department (once for each group)
Req No
Req Date
Job Title
Salary Grade
Min Salary
Max Salary
Primary Experience Code and Description
Recruiter ID and Name

Subtotals By Department include:

applicants hired
Total Recruiting Expenses
Avg No Days To Fill Positions

Fig. 8.2 Report Specification for Report #6

Creating a Simple Report Definition

Before defining your first report in REPORT-IV, you must define the Library within which that report belongs. This is done in exactly the same manner as defining the IDOL-IV Design Dictionaries library. Once this is done, you may begin to create a report definition.

8 DESIGNING AND IMPLEMENTING REPORTS

The first step in defining a report in REPORT-IV is naming the report and setting the report parameters, such as report title, owner, report width, etc. One of these parameters is of some interest at this point. It is the Report Definition Type, and can be set either to **R** for report, or **F** for a file (format) definition. This latter setting is available so that a REPORT-IV definition can be created and used to generate output from files that are NOT a part of the IDOL-IV Design Dictionaries. In other words, you may define files here that are a part of an existing system, without going to the IDOL-IV Format Dictionary, and create reports from those files. For our purposes here, this parameter will not be used.

It is now possible to enter the report layout and other information regarding source of report records, subtotals, and so forth. Figure 8.3 shows the Report Definition screen and the various sections of a report definition.

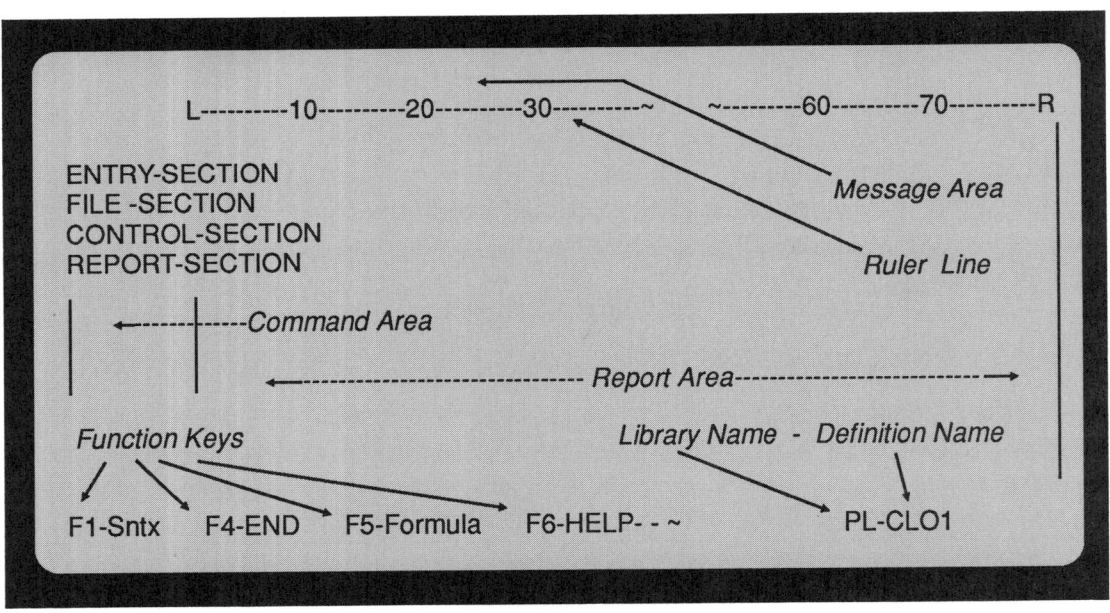

Fig. 8.3 Report Definition Screen

You will notice from the previous figure that each REPORT-IV Definition is made up of four separate sections: the ENTRY, FILE, CONTROL, and REPORT sections. For Report #3 we do not need to enter something in every section of the report definition.

Creating a Simple Report Definition

In fact, we will only need the FILE and REPORT Sections for this report. In the FILE Section we enter a File Definition (**FD**) for each file from which data will be extracted. In the REPORT section we define the layout of each report line, including the placement of headings and data elements. Note that we can also place comments or remarks in the report definition to make it easier for others to figure out what the report is supposed to be doing. Refer to Figure 8.4 below for the definition of the Open Requisitions Summary Report.

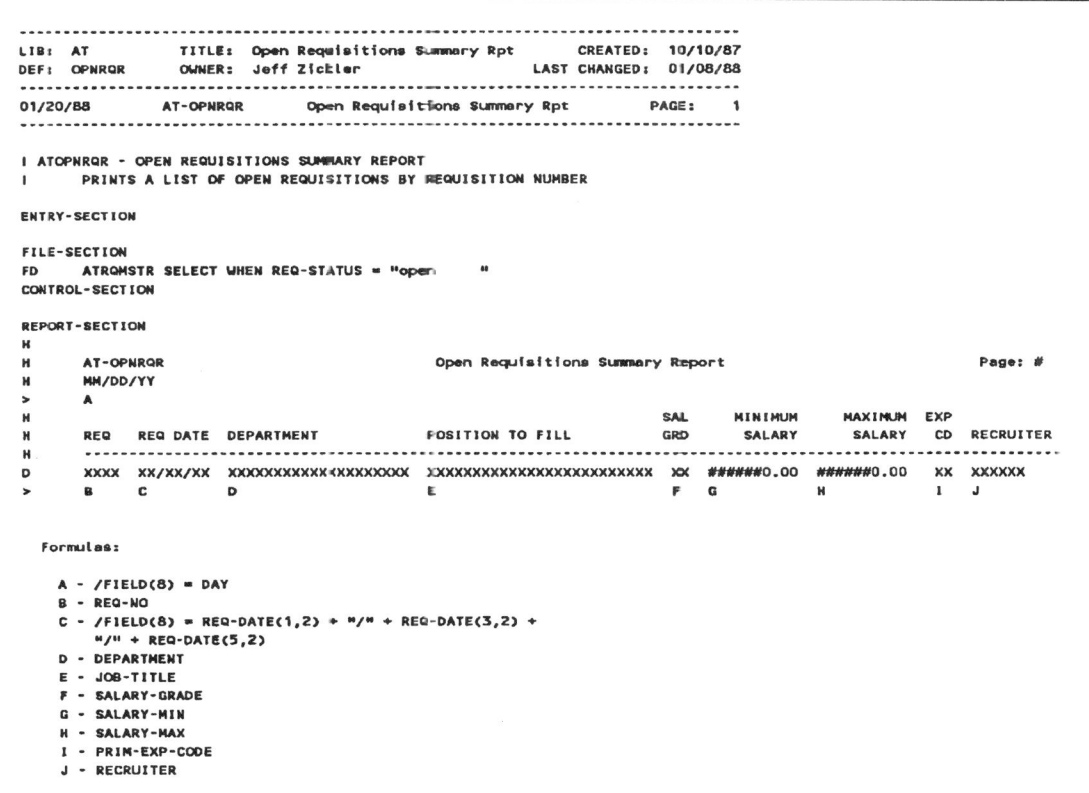

Fig. 8.4 Report Definition of Open Requisitions Summary Report

For this simple report all we have to define is the file from which records are to be selected, what records to select, and the physical layout of the report output. A File Definition (**FD**) is placed in the FILE section of the report with the appropriate IDOL-IV Link name specified. In this case ATRQMSTR is the Requisitions Masterfile link name. In addition, we add a **SELECT WHEN** clause to the **FD** that tells REPORT-IV which records to retrieve when the report is executed. As specified above, we only want requisitions with a status of "open".[1]

Once the File Definition and **SELECT WHEN** clause have been entered, you should press the **F1-Sntx** (Syntax Check) key to ensure that REPORT-IV understands what you have entered. This also causes the list of fields in the **FD**(s) to be loaded into the report definition. This list is useful in laying out the report detail lines (see the following paragraphs).

Creating the report layout in the REPORT section is done in exactly the same manner as "painting" a screen in the IDOL-IV Screen Dictionary. The letter **H** is placed in the first position of each heading line (lines printed once per page), and the letter **D** is placed in the first position of each detail line (lines printed once per record). Literal text is simply typed on the report definition screen wherever appropriate. Then, the **F5-Formula** key is used to place data fields in the report definition. At any time during report creation the **F10-DspDN** key can be used to display the list of fields (Data Names) that are currently defined for the report.

Several items should be noted regarding the formulas in the Open Requisition Summary Report. First, we have used two built-in functions to aid us in printing all the information we desire — the page number is placed on the report definition using the special character "#",[2] and the date is placed on the format using the function **DAY** within a formula (A). You should also note that the Requisition Date field had to be formatted for the report (see formula C). This is because the date is stored as 6 characters (MMDDYY or in several other forms depending on your choice of date types in the file's format) rather than as a date with delimiters. Other than these items, the REPORT section of this sample report is quite simple. Some sample output from the report is shown in Figure 8.5.

Creating a More Complex Report Definition

The more complex report example requires us to use all four report definition sections in order to produce the output that we desire. Refer to Figure 8.6 for the report definition for the Recruitment Costs Report.

Creating a More Complex Report Definition

```
AT-OPNRQR                       Open Requisitions Summary Report                           Page: 1
05/26/88
                                                    SAL   MINIMUM    MAXIMUM   EXP
 REQ   REQ DATE  DEPARTMENT     POSITION TO FILL    GRD   SALARY     SALARY    CD   RECRUITER
 ........................................................................................
 0100  12/03/87  Marketing      Dir, Product Marketing    24   37450.00   59850.00   13   SMITHK
 0123  12/04/87  Documentation  Sr. Technical Writer      16   18565.00   29650.00   19   JONESS
 0151  01/15/88  Sales          V.P., Marketing Oper.     30   60000.00  120000.00   11   SMITHK
 0288  02/16/88  Marketing      Dir, Product Marketing    24   37450.00   59850.00   10   JONESS
 0600  04/21/88  Marketing      Mgr, Product Marketing    12   24125.00   38585.00   16   ARTHUD
 0812  04/21/88  Marketing      Spvr, Marketing Support   10   19915.00   31875.00   17   JOHNSL
 2010  04/20/88  Marketing      Prin. Technical Writer    09   18150.00   29015.00   10   SULLIJ
 2100  04/20/88  Marketing      V.P., Marketing Oper.     25   40825.00   65315.00   11   ALLENH
 3000  04/20/88  Marketing      Prin. Mktng Systems Anlst 09   18150.00   29015.00   18   JONESS
 3050  04/21/88  Marketing      V.P., Marketing           25   40825.00   65315.00   11   JONESS
 9013  04/21/88  Marketing      Sr. Mktng Support Analyst 15   16950.00   27175.00   17   ALLENH
```

Fig. 8.5 Sample Output from Open Requisitions Summary Report

The ENTRY section allows us (among other things) to define and initialize "temporary" data elements or variables that we need in the report. For this report we need two counter fields — one to count the number of requisitions in a department, and the other to use as the denominator in an average calculation, as we shall see later. These are defined and set to zero in the ENTRY section of the report definition.

In the FILE section we again specify the file(s) from which the report will retrieve records for printing. For this report we have a much more complex set of files with which to deal. If you refer to the report's specification earlier in this chapter, you will note that we desire to print data not from a single file, but from a group of **related** files.

The main file is still the Requisition Masterfile, but we also need the Recruiter Name (stored in the Recruiter Code File), the Total Recruiting Expenses and No. of Days to Fill the Job (stored in the Applicant Masterfile), and the Primary Experience Code Description (stored in the Experience Code File). The appropriate record from each of these "related" files may be found using a field in the Requisition Masterfile: RECRUITER, IDENT, and PRIM-EXP-CODE, respectively. (These fields are called **foreign keys**, introduced in Chapter 4.)

8 DESIGNING AND IMPLEMENTING REPORTS

```
------------------------------------------------------------
LIB:  AT          TITLE:  Recruitment Costs Report    CREATED:      10/10/87
DEF:  RECCSR      OWNER:  Jeff Zickler                LAST CHANGED: 11/25/87
------------------------------------------------------------
01/20/88         AT-RECCSR      Recruitment Costs Report         PAGE:   1
------------------------------------------------------------

I  ATRECCSR - RECRUITMENT COSTS REPORT
I      PRINTS A LIST OF CLOSED REQUISITIONS GROUPED BY DEPARTMENT
I      SORT3 OF ATRQMSTR IS DEPARTMENT + REQ-NO

ENTRY-SECTION
DD     COUNT(3.0)
DD     COUNT1(3.0)
I101   COUNT = 0; COUNT1 = 0

FILE-SECTION
FD     ATRQMSTR SORT BY SORT3
:           SELECT WHEN REQ-STATUS(1,6) = "closed"
FD     ATRECRUT
FD     ATAPMSTR
FD     ATEXPCDP

CONTROL-SECTION
CB1    WHEN REQ-NO CHANGES
CB2    WHEN DEPARTMENT CHANGES
ST1    WHEN DEPARTMENT CHANGES; TOTAL-REC-EXP; NO-DAYS-TO-FILL

REPORT-SECTION
H
H      AT-RECCSR                      Recruitment Costs Report                           Page: #
H      MM/DD/YY
>      A
H      REQ                      SAL    MINIMUM   MAXIMUM  PRIMARY EXPERIENCE
H      NO.   REQ DATE  JOB TITLE  GRD    SALARY    SALARY   CODE AND DESCRIPTION           RECRUITER
H      ------------------------------------------------------------------------------------------
CB1C   COUNT = COUNT + 1
CB1C   COUNT1 = COUNT
CB2    **** DEPARTMENT: XXXXXXXXXXXXXXXXXX  ****
>                      B
CB2
D      XXXX  XX/XX/XX  XXXXXXXXXXXXXXXXXXXXX  XX  ######0.00  ######0.00  XX  XXXXXXXXXXXXXXXXXXXXXXXXXXX  XXXXXX
>       C    D         E                       F    G           H          I   J                             K
D              TOTAL RECRUITING EXPENSES: ######0.00   NUMBER OF DAYS TO FILL POSITION: ###0
>                                         L                                             M
D
ST1C   IF COUNT = 0 THEN COUNT1 = 1
ST1              TOTAL RECRUITING EXPENSES:$######0.00   AVG. NO. OF DAYS TO FILL POSITIONS: ###0   NO. OF HIRED APPLICANTS: ##0
>                                          N                                              O                                  P
ST1

Formulas:

   A - /FIELD(B) = DAY                     C - REQ-NO
   B - DEPARTMENT                          D - /FIELD(8) = REQ-DATE(1,2) + "/" + REQ-DATE(3,2) +
                                                "/" + REQ-DATE(5,2)
                                           E - JOB-TITLE
                                           F - SALARY-GRADE
                                           G - SALARY-MIN
                                           H - SALARY-MAX
                                           I - PRIM-EXP-CODE
                                           J - EXPER-DESC
                                           K - RECRUITER
                                           L - TOTAL-REC-EXP
                                           M - NO-DAYS-TO-FILL
                                           N - ST1(1):"$######0.00"
                                           O - ST1(2) / COUNT1:"###0"
                                           P - COUNT:"##0"; COUNT = 0
```

Fig. 8.6 Report Definition of Recruitment Costs Report

This relationship among the files in the FILE section is determined automatically by REPORT-IV from the **sequence** of the file definitions in the section and the names of the fields. In other words, the system can recognize this foreign key relationship and create the necessary file access commands without the designer having to specify any more details than the order of the files.[3]

In the FILE section we also specify the **SELECT WHEN** clause, and for this report we specify the sequence or secondary key to use with the **SORT BY** clause and the IDOL-IV key number associated with the sequence. We have placed a comment at the top of the report definition spelling out the sequence associated with the key number (SORT3) used in the **SORT BY** clause so that others can better visualize the report's specification.

The CONTROL section of a report definition is used to specify when Control Breaks, Subtotals, and Totals should occur. The Recruitment Costs Report requires two Control Breaks and one Subtotal — the Control Breaks (**CB1** and **CB2**) are required to count the number of requisitions printed within a department and to print the department "subheading" data, respectively, and the Subtotal is required to specify which fields are to be printed as the department subtotal data. In the CONTROL section we simply state when the Control Break is required, for example **WHEN REQ-NO CHANGES**, and the system does the rest. For Subtotals we specify when the Subtotal is required and which fields are to be added up for subtotal printing.

Finally, in the REPORT section we again "paint" the layout of the report. However, for this more complex report we have a number of additional items to specify in this section. The letters **H** and **D** are again used to indicate the heading and detail lines of the report, but two additional "line types" are required as well. The letters **CB** are used to indicate a Control Break line and **ST** for Subtotal lines. The additional **C** on the **CB1** lines in the REPORT section indicate "calculations" rather than printing lines.

To summarize the Recruitment Costs Report definition, we can state it in English as follows:

1. For each Requisition Number printed, add 1 to COUNT, and set COUNT1 to COUNT.

2. When the value in the DEPARTMENT field changes, print the Department Name and skip a line.

8 DESIGNING AND IMPLEMENTING REPORTS

3. For each Requisition, print the fields specified.

4. When DEPARTMENT changes, set COUNT1 to 1 if it is still 0, and print the subtotals specified; skip a line after the subtotal fields. Set COUNT back to zero after printing (see Formula P as described below).

A few details are contained in the formulae for this report as well. For example, Formula N contains the specification for the subtotal of the field TOTAL-REC-EXP as ST1(1):"$######0.00". The ST1(1) indicates the first field in the list of fields being subtotaled as defined on the **ST1** line in the CONTROL section of the report. The latter portion of this formula is the numeric print mask showing a floating "$" before the amount, a maximum of 9,999,999 dollars and 99 cents.

Formula O indicates a similar situation, except that the resulting subtotal is divided by the number of records printed in the subtotal to show the "average" Number of Days to Fill each job in the department list. This formula is the reason that we need two counters — if the number of records were zero, this formula would cause an error as IDOL-IV does not allow division by zero. Therefore, we must ensure that the denominator is never zero by placing the **ST1C** line above the **ST1** printing lines.

Finally, Formula P prints one of the counter fields (COUNT) and then sets it to zero for the next subtotal group (please note the sequence within Formula P, as we don't want to set COUNT to zero **before** printing it). Figure 8.7 shows report output from the Recruitment Costs Report.

Other Reporting Capabilities

In addition to the more traditional reports, with IDOL-IV you have the capability to create reporting functions that accomplish more than just printing or displaying information. For example, many application systems have the requirement to contain reports that are not "fixed" in specification as the ones in the sample ATS are. These "variable specification" reports must obtain information from the user as the report is executed that determines selection criteria, processing statements, etc.

In fact, many reports that are "fixed" really should be "variable." Selection criteria (at least) should be set at execution time rather than at development time. A small library of "variable" reports tends to provide much more flexibility and usable information to the user of a system than a much larger library of "fixed" reports.

```
AT-RECCSR                              Recruitment Costs Report                                Page: 1
05/26/88
REQ                             SAL    MINIMUM    MAXIMUM  PRIMARY EXPERIENCE
NO.   REQ DATE  JOB TITLE       GRD    SALARY     SALARY   CODE AND DESCRIPTION                RECRUITER
----------------------------------------------------------------------------------------------------
**** DEPARTMENT: Documentation  ****

0101  12/04/87  Sr. Technical Writer   16   18565.00   29650.00  19 Marketing Support Technician   JONESS
          TOTAL RECRUITING EXPENSES:    150.00   NUMBER OF DAYS TO FILL POSITION:  101

          TOTAL RECRUITING EXPENSES:   $150.00   AVG. NO. OF DAYS TO FILL POSITIONS:  101   NO. OF HIRED APPLICANTS:  1

**** DEPARTMENT: Marketing      ****

0102  12/03/87  Marketing Support Analyst  11   21945.00   35100.00  10 Marketing                   JONESS
          TOTAL RECRUITING EXPENSES:    2000.00  NUMBER OF DAYS TO FILL POSITION:   45

0103  12/14/87  Marketing Systems Analyst  21   28800.00   46025.00  17 Marketing Support Analyst   SMITHK
          TOTAL RECRUITING EXPENSES:    800.00   NUMBER OF DAYS TO FILL POSITION:   63

          TOTAL RECRUITING EXPENSES:  $2800.00   AVG. NO. OF DAYS TO FILL POSITIONS:   54   NO. OF HIRED APPLICANTS:  2
```

Fig. 8.7 Sample Output from Recruitment Costs Report

Another "reporting plus" function is a report with embedded updating or a report followed by an update. Both of these types of functions are found in most application systems, as they are quite useful. IDOL-IV, again, has more than one way to accomplish the creation of these types of functions. SCRIPT-IV has commands that make it easy to design and implement either of these types of application processes. Also, REPORT-IV contains the capability to collect data from a data entry screen before the report is executed and use it in creating the report output.

Conclusions

Creating report output (either printed or displayed) should be one of the easiest and least complicated system implementation tasks when a 4GL is used. It should be addressed as a different type of system development task from the other types of application functions (e.g., screens, menus, etc.). At the same time, it is certainly not the only system implementation task that a 4GL should address.

8 DESIGNING AND IMPLEMENTING REPORTS

Unfortunately, many 4GL vendors have missed these important points. A number of 4GLs (of limited function) do reports very well but not much else, while others do not address report creation as a separate style of application development at all. In these latter 4GLs, a reporting function is looked at as another kind of screen function, and this is simply not the case.

Report functions have a number of requirements that screen-oriented functions do not, and vice versa. What is required is a 4GL that approaches this issue head-on, and provides a coherent and coordinated set of tools that addresses each type of application function with capabilities that are required to accomplish that function. At the same time, where capabilities overlap there must be consistency of syntax and equivalency of function.

IDOL-IV takes just this approach. As you can see by comparing the syntax and function of the SCRIPT-IV commands described in Chapters 6 and 10 with the REPORT-IV commands described in this chapter, the two are very similar and even overlap in several areas. At the same time, REPORT-IV provides capabilities that are not available (or needed) in SCRIPT-IV, and vice versa. In addition, both tools allow you to create all the various types of reporting functions required by a complete business application system.

It is very easy for a developer/designer to move from one IDOL-IV tool to the other and back without having to adjust his or her thinking processes. This is of great significance, as the application design process is not a simple linear procedure, but rather one of trial and adjustment, rework, and trial again. Tools that foster the ability to move freely among the various portions of an Application Development System making changes, trying different things, and finally settling on a finished product are truly invaluable to today's applications designer.

Notes and References

[1] You will note in the report definition that the **SELECT WHEN** clause is shown as REQ-STATUS = "open   ". The five extra spaces are required because the REQ-STATUS field is 9 characters long. An alternative syntax is available that does not require you to know how long a field is, and this syntax can be found in the definition of Report #6 in Figure 8.6.

Notes and References

[2]Be sure not to use this character in a title or heading (e.g., "Req #"), as it will be replaced with the "current" page number when the report is printed.

[3]You should note here that the field name PRIM-EXP-CODE does not match the name of the key field to the Experience Code file (EXPER-CODE). This was done intentionally during system design, but causes us a little extra work here. In order for REPORT-IV to find the primary Experience Code record for each Requisition, we must provide a link for the Experience Code file with the key field named PRIM-EXP-CODE. We do this by defining a new link in the IDOL-IV Format and Link Dictionaries (called ATEXPCDP) that is "linked" to the physical data file containing Experience Code records (ATEXPCDE). We then place that new link name in the report definition, and now REPORT-IV has no trouble "connecting up" all the specified files.

9

DESIGNING AND IMPLEMENTING MENUS

A "menu" can have a simple function or can take on very complex characteristics, but it is undoubtedly required in any business application system. However, an astounding number of Application Development Systems provide no way to create even a simple menu application. Recently the developers of some of the more "popular" systems have caught on, but some of these products still have a distinct shortcoming in this area.

In its simplest form a menu is a collection of related application functions from which the user may select one or more functions to process. As well, much complexity may be added to menus, such as security checking, access control, database control, parameter collection and passing, etc. Any full-function 4GL must provide some mechanism with which to create these essential application functions, whether it be through language commands or through some predefined, parameterizable system. In addition, all of the comments made in earlier chapters regarding the control of the screen and its layout also apply to menus. Menu design and functioning is a critical part of the user interface of any application system, and **must** be under the control of the system designer.

IDOL-IV, as this chapter relates, contains a sophisticated menu system that can be used simply to allow access to related application functions. Or, it can be used to provide access control and security as well as pass parameters to programs and handle "conflict processing" in a multi-user system. In the following sections, the menus required for the sample Applicant Tracking System are described, and then the various capabilities of the IDOL-IV Menu System are examined in detail.

9 DESIGNING AND IMPLEMENTING MENUS

ATS: Menu Specification

The primary use of a menu is to collect together various application functions so that the user may access them in some logical manner without having to know detailed information about them, such as their names, what parameters they might require, how to start their execution, etc. The sample Applicant Tracking System requires at least one menu to fulfill this need.

In IDOL-IV a menu may contain up to 99 entries. The sample ATS does not have anywhere near that many functions, so all of its functions could be placed on a single menu. However, one simple aid to helping the user learn an application system is the logical and simple arrangement of its functions. Therefore, the sample ATS functions should be arranged on **at least** two menus — one for data entry or screen-oriented processes, and one for reports. Some argument might be made to break down the screen functions into two or more menus (e.g., masterfiles and code files), but too many menus can be just as confusing as a few illogically arranged ones.

Figures 9.1 and 9.2 show the two menus included in the sample ATS. Appendix 10 at the end of the book contains the definition reports for these two menus. ATMENU01, the main menu, contains the screen-oriented functions and access to ATMENU02, which contains the report functions. The next two sections will describe in some detail how these two menus were created.

Designing and Implementing a Menu Screen

Each IDOL-IV menu includes two components — a menu screen and a menu definition. The screen is displayed on the terminal to prompt the user for his or her selection request. The menu definition, while invisible to the user, provides the IDOL-IV Menu System with information on how to interpret user requests. These two components are described in this and the following section.

Designing a menu screen is done in exactly the same manner as any other screen. As well, implementing a menu screen in IDOL-IV is accomplished with the same tool as other screens. Using the Screen Painter in the IDOL-IV Screen Dictionary, you can sketch the menu screen easily and quickly, placing functions wherever they may logically belong, and trying out several different approaches before finalizing the screen layout. The same built-in functions are available for placing the date, time, operator initials, etc., on the menu screen, and highlighting and other screen attributes may also be useful in creating the style of menu you desire. User input for a given application func-

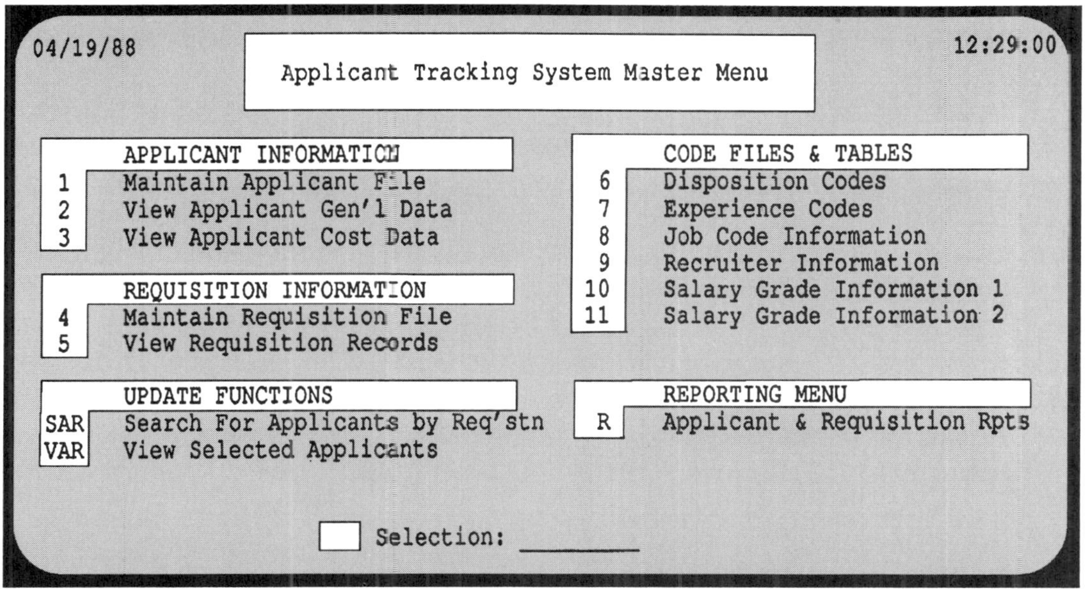

Designing and Implementing a Menu Screen

```
04/19/88                                                    12:29:00
           Applicant Tracking System Master Menu

      APPLICANT INFORMATION              CODE FILES & TABLES
   1  Maintain Applicant File       6  Disposition Codes
   2  View Applicant Gen'l Data     7  Experience Codes
   3  View Applicant Cost Data      8  Job Code Information
                                    9  Recruiter Information
      REQUISITION INFORMATION      10  Salary Grade Information 1
   4  Maintain Requisition File    11  Salary Grade Information 2
   5  View Requisition Records

      UPDATE FUNCTIONS                   REPORTING MENU
  SAR Search For Applicants by Req'stn   R  Applicant & Requisition Rpts
  VAR View Selected Applicants

                        Selection: ____
```

Fig. 9.1 Main Applicant Tracking System Menu Screen

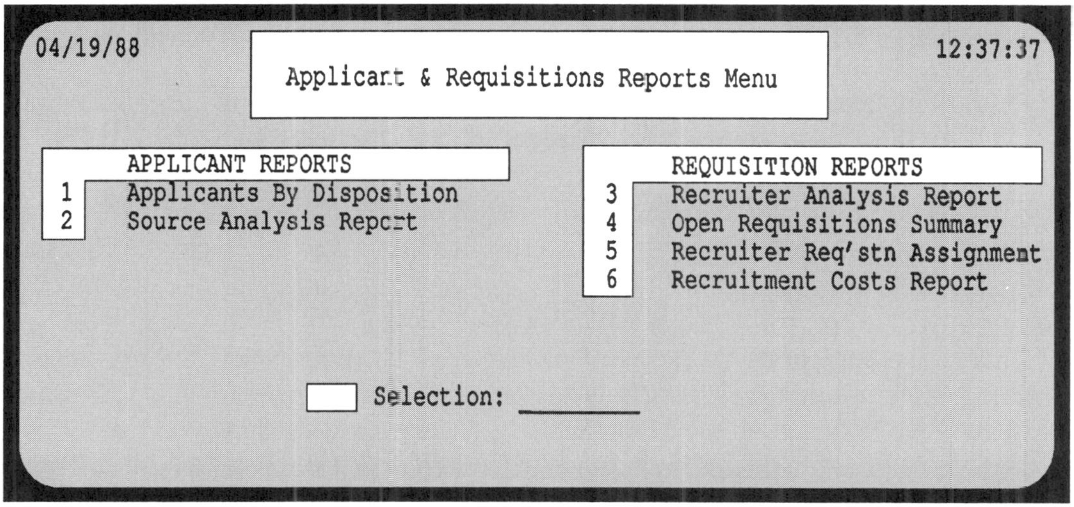

```
04/19/88                                                    12:37:37
           Applicant & Requisitions Reports Menu

      APPLICANT REPORTS                  REQUISITION REPORTS
   1  Applicants By Disposition    3  Recruiter Analysis Report
   2  Source Analysis Report       4  Open Requisitions Summary
                                    5  Recruiter Req'stn Assignment
                                    6  Recruitment Costs Report

                        Selection: ____
```

Fig. 9.2 Applicant Tracking System Reports Menu Screen

137

tion may be specified as one to four characters (or numbers), which gives you a lot of flexibility in creating the type of response required from the user for a given function to be executed.

The only additional detail required to complete the menu screen design is the formula (field name) into which the operator input is to be placed. This field name must be located in the Link/Format specified in the menu definition. The simplest choice is to use the existing link that all IDOL-IV menus use. So, when you create your menu screen entry, you should enter the link, IDMENUIN, in the Link/Format field of the screen dictionary, and the data-name MENU-SELECTION in the formula window of the entry field on the screen. If you forget this, you may go back and edit the screen definition at a later time, but don't forget to do so or the menu will not work.

You are now ready to create a menu definition that will execute the appropriate application functions based on user input to match the menu screen designed above.

Creating the Menu Definition

Each menu definition is placed in the IDOL-IV Menu Dictionary and includes: the name of the menu definition (not necessarily the same as the menu screen name, but that is helpful), the name of the menu screen from the Screen Dictionary, some descriptive data, a help text block describing the functioning of this menu to the user, and a password that may be optionally required for access to this menu when called from another menu.

Once this information is entered, you may enter the descriptions of the menu options. Each of these descriptions includes at a minimum the "user input" required for executing the option, the type of option, and the "action" name of the option. For example, a SCRIPT-IV script would be defined with some user input (e.g., "1", as the first entry on the menu), a type of "P" for program, and an "action" name of the appropriate script name (e.g., ATAPMM0).

There are a number of option types, each with its own notion of "action" name appropriate to its functioning. This information is well described in the IDOL-IV documentation and in the help text on the Menu Dictionary screen and will not be repeated in its entirety here. However, from the menu definition reports in Appendix 10, you will notice the following types: P (SCRIPT-IV script or BASIC program), F (View Maintenance using the IDOL-IV Database View Maintenance function), f (Single Record Screen Maintenance using the IDOL-IV Database Maintenance function), M (used for calling another IDOL-IV menu), and R (used for calling a report function defined in REPORT-IV). The "action" name for each of these types should be fairly obvious from this brief description of their use.

Some Special Menu Features

In addition to the basic functions that a menu system provides, IDOL-IV's Menu System contains a number of other capabilities that are required for designers of multi-user business applications. This section reviews some of these features briefly, even though none of them have been used in the sample Applicant Tracking System demonstration software.

Several additional attributes may be specified on each menu option. Among these items are parameter values to be passed to the called application function (again, each IDOL-IV application function that can be called from a menu has a specific list of possible parameters that can be passed to it), a help text block that can be used to describe the functioning of the menu option, and a password that may be required for the user to have access to the option. Also, each menu option can be associated with a specific list of Terminal IDs and Operator IDs that are allowed to access it.

If a particular type of menu option is used, a message can be set up to be displayed on the screen after the option is chosen but before the action is taken. Also, for certain types of application program design, the menu may be used to open data files required by the function. The names of these data files may be specified on the menu option as well.

Finally, the IDOL-IV Menu System contains the ability to define a sophisticated "conflict processing" setup that, through the menus of an application system, can be used to control when and if a particular function should be processed. This capability comprises both the setting of "conflict flags" as well as the checking of these flags all at the menu level. No additional programming is required to implement this facility in an application system. This does not replace the more traditional record and file locking processes that multi-user systems require, but is intended to supplement these mechanisms for more sophisticated systems that require specific processing sequences.

Conclusions

Menus are usually considered an insignificant part of a business application system, and many times little thought is given to them. Usually the development effort required to create a menu application is relatively small compared to other application functions. And, as a result many designers ignore the importance of menus as a necessary part of any software system. However, well designed menus with capabilities to control access and security, to allow the user to move easily throughout the system, and to execute the functions he or she requires without having to worry about others on the system, are what buyers of multi-user software systems are coming to expect.

IDOL-IV's Menu System provides these capabilities in a fashion that allows the application designer to integrate the results of the various IDOL-IV tools into a consistent whole. The user of an IDOL-IV-based application system will be unable to detect where one tool leaves off and the next begins. He or she will also be able to access those application functions that are necessary to do his or her job in a simple and expeditious manner. Application system menus, if well designed and organized, will make an impressive facade for the application software behind them, and can significantly enhance the effectiveness of the business solution being provided.

10

DESIGNING AND IMPLEMENTING UPDATE PROGRAMS

This class of application functions is not as clearly distinguished from the ones that have been previously discussed as, say, reports are distinguished from data entry functions. As a result many 4GLs do a poor job of supporting an application that is purely an "**update function**". For the purposes of this discussion, an "update" is defined as an application process whose **primary objective** is to retrieve data from one or more existing database files, manipulate that data into other data, and place the results in one or more existing (or new) database files.

Reports, menus, and data entry functions may also contain updating activities; however, their **primary** objective is something else. An update function's objective is to **update** data. It may also contain data entry or the display of data on a terminal or a printer, but it certainly does not have to, and should not have to just because the 4GL supplier designed its language that way! An update function should be able to be created to update data only and nothing else.

Another term commonly associated with "pure" update applications is "batch" — a process that accomplishes application functions without operator intervention. While this describes the essence of an update function, the term "batch" usually connotes other issues that will not be dealt with in this book. Therefore, the processes described in this chapter are labeled "update" functions rather than "batch" functions.

ATS: Update Specifications

The update function (refer to Figure 10.1 for the detailed specifications of this application process) chosen as an example in the sample Applicant Tracking System is a relatively simple one that shows many of the features of SCRIPT-IV useful in update

10 DESIGNING AND IMPLEMENTING UPDATE PROGRAMS

The specification of the Search for Applicants By Requisition function can be stated as follows:

1. Get valid Requisition No from user as target for search

2. Clear existing records from temporary Applicant file

3. Find all Applicant records where the following conditions are true —

               Requisition's Job Title = Applicant's Current Position

    OR   Requisition's Primary Experience Code = Applicant's Current Experience Code

    AND Applicant's Current Salary is in the range of the Requisition's Minimum and Maximum Salaries (inclusive)

    AND Requisition's Education Level <= Applicant's Education Level Achieved

    AND Applicant's Disposition Code is not HI (for hired)

    OR   Applicant's Requisiton No = the Target Requisition No

4. Add selected records to the temporary Applicant file

5. Issue a message to the user stating how many matching Applicant records were found

6. Offer the selected Applicant records, if any, in a view to the user

Fig. 10.1 Specification of Search for Applicants by Requisition

scripts. Its stated objective is to "match available applicants to the characteristics specified in an employment requisition". It does this by searching the applicant file for records with specific field values that match field values in the requisition record identified as the target.[1] Records that match the selection criteria are copied into a temporary file that the user may peruse using an IDOL-IV View.

In order to initiate the update process, the application requires the identity of the target requisition record, and this is collected from the user via a simple data entry script. Thus, this example update function has two major programming aspects — the data collection function and the update function. From the following discussion you will note that the design of the function closely follows this logical breakdown.

The primary script sets up the data environment and opens the appropriate links, screens, and views. It also requests a requisition number from the user and handles all the data entry processing. The continuation script takes the selected requisition record and proceeds to find any applicant records that match. It then copies them into the temporary file, after emptying it of any existing records. The subsequent sections of this chapter examine these scripts in detail. (Both scripts use the **INCLUDE** command to share the data declaration section shown in Figure 10.2.)

Collecting the Target Requisition

The first portion of the sample ATS update function is a simple data entry task, with the requirement to "get a valid requisition record that the user wants to use as a target to find applicant records". First, the record must be a valid requisition, and second it must be the one the user wants to use. These two requirements are fulfilled with the SCRIPT-IV primary script called ATSRCH0. This is the script that is executed when you chose the "Search for Applicants By Req'stn" option from the main ATS menu. After reviewing the script (see Figure 10.3 for the MAIN-PROCEDURE of this script), you will notice that it appears very similar to the data entry scripts discussed in Chapter 6. Since the design and requirements are very similar, you would expect that the commands used to implement the various scripts would be much the same.

After the data declaration section, the script opens the required screens, the two main links, and the view. Then, it starts a **DO LOOP** that is used to collect data from the screen. This loop continues until the user presses the **F4-End** key or the program determines that the user wants to begin the search (i.e., the script variable MODE-FLAG is set to "SERCH").

10 DESIGNING AND IMPLEMENTING UPDATE PROGRAMS

```
Script: AT SRCHDS   Type: 5
Desc: Search for Appl By Req - Data Sectn                   Page: 1
Last Change Date: 05/20/88    Last Compile Date:
           Time: 22:29:32              Time:           Date: 05/31/88
==============================================================================
     * THIS INCLUDE SCRIPT IS USED BY THE ATSRCHnn SCRIPTS THAT SEARCH
     *    FOR APPLICANT RECORDS THAT MATCH A REQUISITION
     SN    ATREQNM1, ATREQNM2
     LN    ATRQMSTR, ATAPMSTR, ATAPTEMP
     VN    ATAPTEMP
     DN    MODE-FLAG (5), MSG-RESP (1), NO-RECORDS (5.0)
```

Fig 10.2 Data Declaration for the Update Scripts

```
Script: AT SRCH0    Type: 1
Desc: Search for Appl By Req - Setup (Prim)                 Page: 1
Last Change Date: 04/19/88    Last Compile Date: 04/13/88
           Time: 12:41:32              Time: 18:09:03   Date: 04/19/88
==============================================================================
     * THIS IS THE PRIMARY SCRIPT FOR THE SEARCH FOR APPL BY REQ FUNCTION
     * THE FOLLOWING INCLUDE SCRIPT CONTAINS THE REQUIRED DATA DEFINITIONS
           INCLUDE ATSRCHDS

     MAIN-PROCEDURE
     * OPEN SCREENS, VIEWS, AND LINKS
           OPEN SCREEN ATREQNM1
           OPEN SCREEN ATREQNM2
           OPEN VIEW ATATMPVW
           OPEN ATRQMSTR
           OPEN ATAPMSTR
     * MAIN INPUT LOOP
           DO LOOP UNTIL TERM-KEY = 4 OR MODE-FLAG = "SERCH"
               LET MODE-FLAG = "INIT "
               PRINT SCREEN ATREQNM1
               PRINT MESSAGE "P,16" USING "ATMSGS"
               PRINT MESSAGE "P,19" USING "ATMSGS"
               INPUT SCREEN ATREQNM1 CLEAR KEY
                   POST-HELP PROCESS REDO-SCREEN-INIT
     * RETRIEVE REQUESTED REQUISITION RECORD
               IF TERM-KEY = 1 THEN
                   READ ATRQMSTR USING KEY REQ-NO
                       PROCESSING  IS EDIT-RECORD
                       MISSING KEY IS MISSING-RECORD
                       BUSY        IS BUSY-RECORD
                       END         IS END-OF-MAIN-FILE
               ENDIF
           ENDLOOP
     * RUN SECOND HALF OF SCRIPT
           IF MODE-FLAG = "SERCH" THEN
               RUN "ATSRCH1"
           ENDIF
           TERMINATE
```

Fig. 10.3 Main Procedure from ATSRCH0

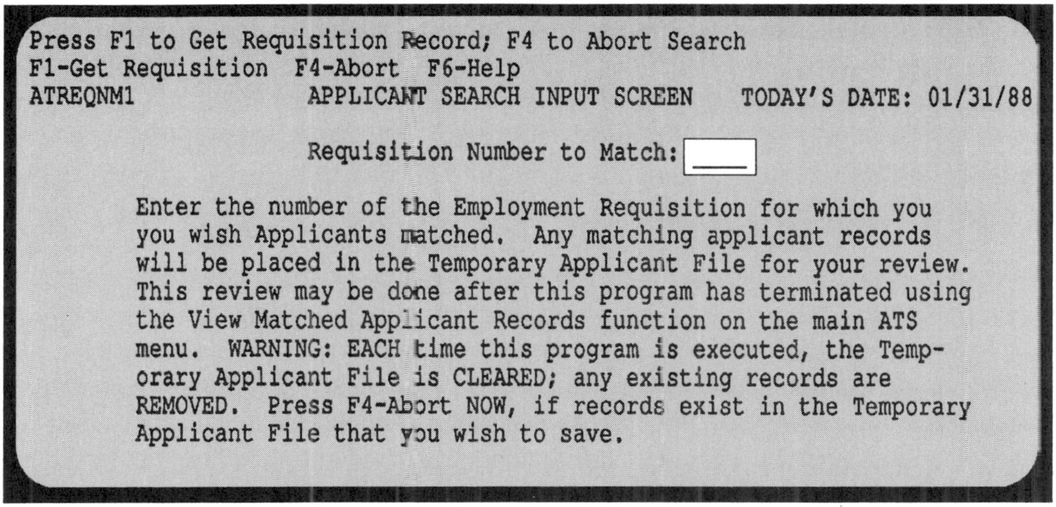

Collecting the Target Requisition

```
Press F1 to Get Requisition Record; F4 to Abort Search
F1-Get Requisition  F4-Abort  F6-Help
ATREQNM1              APPLICANT SEARCH INPUT SCREEN    TODAY'S DATE: 01/31/88

               Requisition Number to Match: [____]

       Enter the number of the Employment Requisition for which you
       you wish Applicants matched. Any matching applicant records
       will be placed in the Temporary Applicant File for your review.
       This review may be done after this program has terminated using
       the View Matched Applicant Records function on the main ATS
       menu. WARNING: EACH time this program is executed, the Temp-
       orary Applicant File is CLEARED; any existing records are
       REMOVED. Press F4-Abort NOW, if records exist in the Temporary
       Applicant File that you wish to save.
```

Fig. 10.4 Requisition Number Entry Screen

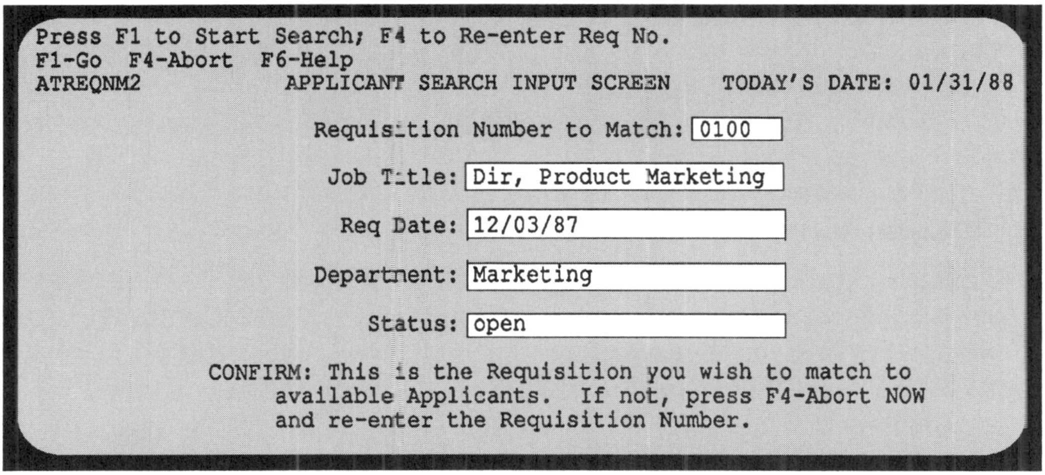

```
Press F1 to Start Search; F4 to Re-enter Req No.
F1-Go  F4-Abort  F6-Help
ATREQNM2              APPLICANT SEARCH INPUT SCREEN    TODAY'S DATE: 01/31/88

               Requisition Number to Match: [0100]
                             Job Title: [Dir, Product Marketing]
                              Req Date: [12/03/87]
                            Department: [Marketing]
                                Status: [open]

       CONFIRM: This is the Requisition you wish to match to
                available Applicants. If not, press F4-Abort NOW
                and re-enter the Requisition Number.
```

Fig. 10.5 Target Requisition Confirmation Screen

145

10 DESIGNING AND IMPLEMENTING UPDATE PROGRAMS

Two different screens are used to collect the target requisition data — the initial screen (ATREQNM1, shown in Figure 10.4) contains a paragraph of literal text and a single entry field (the Key Field, REQ-NO), while the second screen (ATREQNM2, shown in Figure 10.5) contains several fields to display requisition data elements. Once the user enters a target requisition number and presses the **F1-Get Requisition** key, the script reads the Requisition Masterfile (ATRQMSTR) for that record (again, refer to Figure 10.3).

If a record is found, the EDIT-RECORD procedure is executed. This procedure (see Figure 10.6) moves selected data fields from the link format to the screen format, and displays the second screen. The user is required to confirm that the selected Requisition is the one to use as the update target by pressing the **F1-Go** key. If any other key is pressed on the second screen, the selection is aborted and the initial screen is re-displayed[2] allowing another Requisition number to be entered. If the **F1-Go** key is pressed, the program variable MODE-FLAG is set to "SERCH" so that, upon return from the EDIT-RECORD procedure, the **DO LOOP** will be terminated and the continuation script will be executed (see the command **RUN "ATSRCH1"** in Figure 10.3). All of this is done in the post processing SET-TERM-KEY procedure (see Figure 10.6) that is executed upon leaving the REQ-NO field.

The rest of the primary script contains the various procedures to handle missing or busy records, redisplay of the screen after **HELP** is requested, etc. The screen layouts and actual message text can be found in the various appendices at the end of the book, or can be seen by executing the search application function in the demonstration software.

Searching for Matching Applicants

The first step in the continuation script (ATSRCH1) is to clear out the temporary file, ATAPTEMP (see Figure 10.7). This is accomplished by **OPEN**ing the link with the **CLEAR** option. This cleans out any existing records and sets it up for having new records **ADD**ed to it. Then a message that the update is in progress is printed on the screen (Prompting Message #20), and a record counter (NO-RECORDS) is set to zero.

The Applicant masterfile is **READ** with a **SELECT WHEN** clause that looks complicated but really is not (see Figure 10.8). In English, the script is searching for: Applicants whose Current Positions match the Requisition's Job Title, or whose Current Experience Code matches the Req's Primary Experience Code, and whose Current Salary falls within the Req's Maximum and Minimum Salary range (inclusive), and who

```
Script: AT SRCH0    Type: 1
Desc: Search for Appl By Req - Setup (Prim)                         Page: 2
Last Change Date: 04/19/88    Last Compile Date: 04/13/88
            Time: 12:41:32              Time: 18:09:03    Date: 04/19/88
================================================================================

    EDIT-RECORD
    * MOVE DATA RECORD TO SCREEN FORMAT
        LET ATREQUIS.REQ-NO = ATRQMSTR.REQ-NO,
            ATREQUIS.REQ-DATE = ATRQMSTR.REQ-DATE,
            ATREQUIS.DEPARTMENT = ATRQMSTR.DEPARTMENT,
            ATREQUIS.JOB-TITLE = ATRQMSTR.JOB-TITLE,
            ATREQUIS.REQ-STATUS = ATRQMSTR.REQ-STATUS,
            MODE-FLAG = "EDIT "
    * DISPLAY SCREEN AND MESSAGES
        PRINT 'CS'
        PRINT SCREEN ATREQNM2
        PRINT MESSAGE "P,17" USING "ATMSGS"
        PRINT MESSAGE "P,18" USING "ATMSGS"
    * DISPLAY DATA AND ALLOW INPUT OF KEY FIELD ONLY
        PRINT SCREEN ATREQNM2 DATA
        INPUT SCREEN ATREQNM2 DATA-NAME LIST REQ-NO
            POST        PROCESS REQ-NO, SET-TERM-KEY
            POST-HELP PROCESS REDO-SCREEN
        IF MODE-FLAG = "ABORT" THEN
            PRINT 'CS'
        ENDIF

    SET-TERM-KEY
    * SET APPROPRIATE MODE BASED ON OPERATOR RESPONSE
        IF TERM-KEY = 1 THEN
            LET ATREQNM2.FIELD = 99
            LET MODE-FLAG = "SERCH"
        ELSE
            IF TERM-KEY = 4 THEN
                LET ATREQNM2.FIELD = 99
                LET MODE-FLAG = "ABORT"
                LET TERM-KEY = 0
            ELSE
                LET ATREQNM2.FIELD = 0
            ENDIF
        ENDIF
```

Fig. 10.6 EDIT-RECORD and SET-TERM-KEY Procedures from ATSRCH0

have an Education Level Achievement at least as high as that specified on the Req, and who have not already been hired (DISP-CODE not equal to "HI"), or who have the target Requisition number in their Applicant record.

```
Script: AT SRCH1    Type: 2
Desc: Search for Appl By Req - Cont #1                          Page: 1
Last Change Date: 04/19/88    Last Compile Date: 04/13/88
           Time: 12:42:58                 Time: 18:09:48        Date: 04/19/88
=============================================================================
     * FIRST CONTINUATION SCRIPT FOR SEARCH FOR APPL BY REQ FUNCTION
     * THE FOLLOWING INCLUDE SCRIPT CONTAINS THE REQUIRED DATA DEFINITIONS
           INCLUDE ATSRCHDS

     MAIN-PROCEDURE
     *     SETTRACE PAUSE DIRECTIVE
     * OPEN TEMPORARY APPLICANT FILE AND CLEAR EXISTING RECORDS
           OPEN ATAPTEMP CLEAR
     * ISSUE MESSAGE THAT UPDATE IS IN PROCESS
           PRINT @(0,1), 'CL'
           PRINT MESSAGE "P,20" USING "ATMSGS"
     * SET RECORD COUNTER TO ZERO
           LET NO-RECORDS = 0
```

Fig. 10.7 Continuation Update Script — Part 1

For every record found that matches these criteria, the COPY-RECORD procedure is executed. This procedure copies the Applicant record's format into the ATAPTEMP link's format, adds one to the record counter, and **ADDs** the record to the ATAPTEMP link (file).

After all records in the file have been checked, the script prints a message (**INPUT MESSAGE**) on the screen indicating how many Applicants were found that were matches, and waits for the user to press the **ENTER** key. The script then executes a **PRINT VIEW** that displays the selected applicant records in a window on the screen. After the **PRINT VIEW**, the primary script is re-executed, taking the user back to the beginning of the function.

```
Script: AT SRCH1    Type: 2
Desc: Search for Appl By Req - Cont #1                    Page: 2
Last Change Date: 04/19/88    Last Compile Date: 04/13/88
          Time: 12:42:58              Time: 18:09:48      Date: 04/19/88
==============================================================================

    * FIND RECORDS TO COPY (ATRQMSTR CONTAINS THE TARGET REQ RECORD)
        READ ATAPMSTR USING KEY RANGE ALL
            PROCESSING IS COPY-RECORD
            BUSY       IS BUSY-RECORD
            SELECT WHEN ATRQMSTR.JOB-TITLE = ATAPMSTR.CUR-POSITION
                    OR ATRQMSTR.PRIM-EXP-CODE = ATAPMSTR.CUR-EXP-CODE
                   AND ATRQMSTR.SALARY-MIN <= ATAPMSTR.CUR-SALARY
                   AND ATRQMSTR.SALARY-MAX >= ATAPMSTR.CUR-SALARY
                   AND ATRQMSTR.EDUC-LEVEL <= ATAPMSTR.EDUC-LVL-ACH
                    OR ATRQMSTR.REQ-NO = ATAPMSTR.REQ-NO
                   AND ATAPMSTR.DISP-CODE <> "HI"
    * ISSUE A MESSAGE THAT 'n' RECORDS HAVE BEEN FOUND
        INPUT MESSAGE "N,7,,,." + STR(NO-RECORDS) INTO MSG-RESP
                USING "ATMSGS"
        PRINT VIEW ATATMPVW USING KEY RANGE FROM "" TO "zzzzzz"
            WINDOW LINE IS 14
                   COLUMN IS 3
                   CHARACTERS ARE 73
                   HEADING IS "Y"
                   BORDER TYPE IS "R"
                   NUMBER LINES ARE 7
        RUN "ATSRCH0"

COPY-RECORD
* ADD A COPY OF APPLICANT RECORD TO TEMP FILE
      LET ATAPTEMP = ATAPMSTR
      LET NO-RECORDS = NO-RECORDS + 1
      ADD ATAPTEMP USING KEY ATAPTEMP.IDENT
* NO DUPLICATE ERROR PROCEDURE IS SPECIFIED, SO SCRIPT JUST KEEPS GOING
```

Fig. 10.8 Continuation Update Script — Part 2

10 DESIGNING AND IMPLEMENTING UPDATE PROGRAMS

Once more, the rest of the script contains procedures to handle error conditions and the like. However, you will note the absence of an End-of-File procedure on the **READ**. This is because you do not need one with SCRIPT-IV, if you want the script simply to continue to the next command when the end of the file is encountered. This is a very useful default for this, as well as other, "error" conditions that can occur in file handling.

Finally, you will notice on the ATS Main Menu a "View Selected Applicants" function grouped with the "Search" function. This allows further study of the currently selected applicant records that were displayed in the **PRINT VIEW** at the end of the search.

Conclusions

The example update application described in this chapter is not a very complicated one, but is a fair representative of the type of update functions required for business systems. It is amazing that some supposedly full-function 4GLs make it so hard for the application designer to create even this simple program.

It should be obvious to you from the structure of this example that the data entry portion of the update process is not included as a result of a language requirement, but as a requirement of the program's function. The actual update portion could easily have been created to execute independently of any screens or user interaction, assuming, of course, that the parameters for finding the records to update could be "hardcoded" in the script.

The **SELECT WHEN** clause in the **READ** and **CHANGE** commands of SCRIPT-IV combined with the **PROCESSING IS** procedure make creating pure update processes, as well as update portions of more generalized processes, as easy as it can get. This type of language structure is so simple once you see it implemented, but unfortunately seems to be beyond the grasp of some Fourth Generation Language designers. Not so with the designers of SCRIPT-IV.

Notes and References

[1] A "match" is found if the attributes in the list match between the requisition record and an applicant record **OR** if the target requisition number exists in the applicant record. This allows the Human Resources Department to take applicants for a specific job opening as well as "general" applicants for consideration for any applicable job openings.

[2]Note the use of the directive **PRINT 'CS'**. The mnemonic **'CS'** clears the screen completely, and is used here as two different screens are employed to collect the required data. If the **'CS'** was not done, each portion of the screen image would have to be cleared separately.

APPENDICES

1. ATS Global Dictionary

2. ATS Format Definitions

3. ATS Message Dictionary

4. ATS Link Definitions

5. ATS Screen Definitions

6. ATS Data Entry Scripts

7. ATS Sample Code File Data

8. ATS Report Specifications

9. ATS Report Definitions and Sample Output

10. ATS Menu Definitions

Appendix 1

ATS GLOBAL DICTIONARY

```
GLOBAL DICTIONARY REPORT                                          Page:      1
                                                                  Date: 06/09/88

                                            E   N   P   D   Y      Variable
    Data Element        Length       HELP   T   T   D   T   N        Name
================================================================================
    ADDRESS..........     30         ADDRES  -   -   -   -   -
    ADVERT...........     10.2       ADVERT  -   1   -   -   -
    AGENCY-FEES......     10.2       AGENCY  -   1   -   -   -
    AVAIL-DATE.......     6          AVAIL   1   -   -   1   -
    BIRTH-DATE.......     6          BIRTH   1   -   -   1   -
    CITY.............     20         CITY    -   -   -   -   -
    COMMENTS.........     1          COMNTS  -   -   6   -   -

        Valid Value---: 3,A,60,4,3,19,R,-----APPLICANT COMMENTS-----

    COMPANY..........     30         COMPAN  -   -   -   -   -
    CUR-ADDRESS......     30         ADDRES  -   -   -   -   -
    CUR-CITY.........     20         CITY    -   -   -   -   -
    CUR-EXP-CODE.....     2          EXPCOD  1   -   -   -   -

        Valid Value---: 2,ATEXPCDE,1

    CUR-EXT..........     4          EXTENS  -   -   -   -   -
    CUR-HIRED........     6          CURHIR  1   -   -   1   -
    CUR-PHONE........     10         PHONE   1   -   4   -   -
    CUR-POSITION.....     20         CURPOS  -   -   -   -   -
    CUR-SALARY.......     9.2        SALARY  -   1   -   -   -
    CUR-STATE........     2          STATE   1   -   -   -   -
    CUR-ZIPCODE......     10         ZIPCD   -   -   -   -   -
    DATE-ENTERED.....     6          DTENTR  1   -   -   1   -
    DEPARTMENT.......     20         DEPTMT  -   -   -   -   -
    DIPLOMA..........     5          DIPLOM  -   -   -   -   -
    DISP-CODE........     2          DISPCD  1   -   -   -   -

        Valid Value---: 2,ATDISPCD,1

    DISP-DATE........     6          DISPDT  1   -   -   1   -
    DISP-DESC........     30         DESCRP  -   -   -   -   -
    DIVISION.........     15         DIVISN  -   -   -   -   -
    EDUC-LEVEL.......     1          EDUCLV  -   -   -   -   -

        Valid Value---: 0,0,1,2,3,4,5,6

    EEO-CODE.........     1          EEOCDE  3   -   -   -   -

        Valid Value---: 0,0,1,2,3,4
```

APPENDIX 1: ATS GLOBAL DICTIONARY

```
Data Element            Length        HELP      E   N   P   D   Y   Variable
                                                T   T   D   T   N   Name
==============================================================================

    EEOC-JOB-CAT........    1          EEOCJC   3   -   -   -   -

        Valid Value---: 0,A,B,C,D,E,F,G,H,J,K,M

    EMPLOYEE-REFERRAL...   10.2        EMPREF   -   1   -   -   -
    EXEMPT-CLASS........    1          EXEMPT   3   -   -   -   -

        Valid Value---: 0,E,N,H

    EXP-CODE............    2          EXPCD1   -   -   -   -   -

        Valid Value---: 2,ATEXPCDE,1

    EXP-DESC............   30          DESCRP   -   -   -   -   -
    EXPER-CODE..........    2          EXPCD1   -   -   -   -   -

        Valid Value---: 2,ATEXPCDE,1

    EXPER-DESC..........   30          DESCRP   -   -   -   -   -
    FROM-DATE...........    6          FROMDT   1   -   -   1   -
    GRAD-DATE...........    6          GRADDT   1   -   -   1   -
    GRAD-HS.............    1          GRADHS   1   -   -   -   Y
    IDENT...............    6          IDENT    3   -   -   -   -
    INTERNAL-REC........    1          INTREC   1   -   -   -   -

        Preset Values-: Y

    INTERNAL-SRCH.......    1          INTSCH   1   -   -   -   Y
    JOB-CODE............    4          JOBCDE   -   -   -   -   -

        Valid Value---: 2,ATJOBCDE,1

    JOB-STATUS..........    2          JOBSTS   3   -   -   -   -

        Preset Values-: FT
        Valid Value---: 0,FT,PT

    JOB-TITLE...........   25          POSITN   -   -   -   -   -
    LOCATION............   15          LOCATN   -   -   -   -   -
    MAJOR...............   20          MAJOR    -   -   -   -   -
    NAME................   30          NAME     -   -   -   -   -
    NEW-POSITION........    1          NEWPOS   1   -   -   -   -

        Preset Values-: N

    NO-DAYS-TO-FILL.....    4.0        NODAYS   -   1   -   -   -
    OTHER-REC-EXP.......   10.2        OTHEXP   -   1   -   -   -
    PHONE...............   10          PHONE    1   -   4   -   -
    POSITION............   25          POSITN   -   -   -   -   -
    PT-RATE.............   10.2        PTRATE   -   1   1   -   -
    RECRUITER...........    6          RECRUT   1   -   -   -   -

        Valid Value---: 2,ATRECRUT,0

    RECRUT-NAME.........   30          RECNME   -   -   -   -   -
    RECRUT-RATE.........    7.2        RECRAT   -   1   -   -   -
    RELOCATION-EXP......   10.2        RELOC    -   1   -   -   -
    REPLACEMENT-DATE....    6          RPLDAT   1   -   -   1   -
    REQ-APPROVAL-DATE...    6          REQAPD   1   -   -   1   -
```

APPENDIX 1: ATS GLOBAL DICTIONARY

```
                                            E  N  P  D  Y   Variable
Data Element         Length       HELP      T  T  D  T  N     Name
================================================================================
   REQ-APPROVER........   20       REQAPP    -  -  -  -  -
   REQ-APPROVER-TITLE..   10       REQAPT    -  -  -  -  -
   REQ-DATE............    6       REQDAT    1  -  -  1  -
   REQ-DISP-DATE.......    6       REQDDT    1  -  -  1  -
   REQ-NO..............    4       REQNO     -  -  3  -  -

      Valid Value---: 2,ATRQMSTR,1

   REQ-STATUS..........    9       REQSTS    -  -  -  -  -

      Preset Values-: open
      Valid Value---: 0,open      ,closed   ,cancelled,on hold  ,re-opened

   SALARY-DESC.........   30       DESCRP    -  -  -  -  -
   SALARY-GRADE........    2       SALGRD    -  -  -  -  -

      Valid Value---: 2,ATSALGRD,1

   SALARY-MAX..........   10.2     HISAL     -  1  -  -  -
   SALARY-MIN..........   10.2     LOWSAL    -  1  -  -  -
   SCHOOL-NAME.........   30       SCHOOL    -  -  -  -  -
   SEX.................    1       SEX       3  -  -  -  -

      Valid Value---: 0,M,F

   SHIFT...............    7       SHIFT     -  -  -  -  -

      Preset Values-: Daily
      Valid Value---: 0,Daily    ,Evening,Night

   SKILL...............   20       SKILL     -  -  -  -  -
   SOURCE..............   20       SOURCE    -  -  -  -  -
   SSN.................    9       SSN       1  -  5  -  -
   STATE...............    2       STATE     3  -  -  -  -
   TITLE...............   10       TITLE     -  -  -  -  -
   TO-DATE.............    6       TODATE    1  -  -  1  -
   TOTAL-REC-EXP.......   10.2     TOTEXP    -  1  -  -  -
   TVL-LODG-EXP........   10.2     TNLEXP    -  1  -  -  -
   VETERAN.............    1       VETERN    -  -  -  -  -
   ZIPCODE.............   10       ZIPCD     -  -  -  -  -
```

Appendix 2

ATS FORMAT DEFINITIONS

All definitions from the sample Applicant Tracking System are from the AT library.

APCOST	Applicant Recruitment Costs Screen Format
APGENL	Applicant General Information Screen Format
APMSTR	Applicant Master File Format
APTEMP	Applicant Search File Format (same as APMSTR)
DISPCD	Disposition Code File Format
EXPCDE	Experience Code File Format
EXPCDP	Experience Code File Format For Reports
JOBCDE	Job Code File Format
RECRUT	Recruiter Code File Format
REQUIS	Employment Requisitions Screen Format
RQMSTR	Employment Requisitions Masterfile Format
SALGRD	Salary Grade File Format

APPENDIX 2: ATS FORMAT DEFINITIONS

```
Name: ATAPCOST, Appl. Recruitment Costs Screen Fmt

        Record Information:                        Lst Chg Date: 06/06/88
           Key Size-0      #FldSep-0               Lst Chg Time: 08:53:09
           Rec Size-173    #KeyInd-0               Created Date: 07/10/87

                                     F     KENPDY     --- Position ----
    Data Element        Length       S  HELP YTTDTN   Record    Internal
================================================================================
 1 ADVERT..............  10.2        - ADVERT --1---    1-10      1-10
 2 AGENCY-FEES.........  10.2        - AGENCY --1---   11-10     11-10
 3 EMPLOYEE-REFERRAL...  10.2        - EMPREF --1---   21-10     21-10
 4 RELOCATION-EXP......  10.2        - RELOC  --1---   31-10     31-10
 5 TVL-LODG-EXP........  10.2        - TNLEXP --1---   41-10     41-10
 6 OTHER-REC-EXP.......  10.2        - OTHEXP -21---   51-10     51-10
 7 TOTAL-REC-EXP.......  10.2        - TOTEXP --1---   61-10     61-10
 8 NO-DAYS-TO-FILL.....   4.0        - NODAYS --1---   71-4      71-4
 9 IDENT...............   6          - IDENT  ------   75-6      75-6
10 NAME................  30          - NAME   ------   81-30     81-30
11 RECRUITER...........   6          - RECRUT -1----  111-6     111-6
12 JOB-TITLE...........  25          - JOBTIT ------  117-25    117-25
13 AVAIL-DATE..........   6          - AVAIL  -1--1-  142-6     142-6
14 SEX.................   1          - SEX    -3----  148-1     148-1

      Valid Value---: 0,M,F

15 EEO-CODE............   1          - EEOCDE -3----  149-1     149-1

      Preset Values-: 0
      Valid Value---: 0,0,1,2,3,4

16 SSN.................   9          - SSN    -1-5--  150-9     150-9
17 BIRTH-DATE..........   6          - BIRTH  -1--1-  159-6     159-6
18 VETERAN.............   1          - VETERN -----Y  165-1     165-1
19 NEXT-SCRN-NO........   2.0        - NXTSCR --1---  166-2     166-2


Name: ATAPGENL, Appl. General Infor. Screen Format

        Record Information:                        Lst Chg Date: 06/06/88
           Key Size-6      #FldSep-0               Lst Chg Time: 08:55:15
           Rec Size-365    #KeyInd-1               Created Date: 06/26/87

 1 IDENT...............   6          - IDENT  Y-----    1-6       1-6
 2 NAME................  30          - NAME   ------    7-30      7-30
 3 ADDRESS.............  30          - ADDRES ------   37-30     37-30
 4 CITY................  20          - CITY   ------   67-20     67-20
 5 STATE...............   2          - STATE  ------   87-2      87-2
 6 ZIPCODE.............  10          - ZIPCD  ------   89-10     89-10
 7 PHONE...............  10          - PHONE  -1-4--   99-10     99-10
 8 CUR-HIRED...........   6          - CURHIR -1--1-  109-6     109-6
 9 COMPANY.............  30          - COMPAN ------  115-30    115-30
10 CUR-ADDRESS.........  30          - ADDRES ------  145-30    145-30
11 CUR-CITY............  20          - CITY   ------  175-20    175-20
12 CUR-STATE...........   2          - STATE  -1----  195-2     195-2
13 CUR-ZIPCODE.........  10          - ZIPCD  ------  197-10    197-10
14 CUR-PHONE...........  10          - PHONE  -1-4--  207-10    207-10
15 CUR-EXT.............   4          - EXTENS ------  217-4     217-4
16 CUR-POSITION........  25          - CURPOS ------  221-25    221-25
17 CUR-SALARY..........   9.2        - SALARY --1---  246-9     246-9
18 CUR-EXP-CODE........   2          - EXPCOD -2----  255-2     255-2
19 RECRUITER...........   6          - RECRUT ------  257-6     257-6
20 SOURCE..............  20          - SOURCE ------  263-20    263-20
21 REQ-NO..............   4          - REQNO  ---3--  283-4     283-4
22 COMMENTS............   1          - COMNTS ---6--  287-1     287-1

      Valid Value---: 3,A,60,4,3,19,R,-----APPLICANT COMMENTS-----
```

APPENDIX 2: ATS FORMAT DEFINITIONS

```
                                     F           KENPDY     --- Position ----
   Data Element         Length       S   HELP    YTTDTN     Record    Internal
===============================================================================
23 AVAIL-DATE.........    6          -   AVAIL   -1--1-     288-6      288-6
24 DISP-CODE..........    2          -   DISPCD  ------     294-2      294-2
25 DISP-DATE..........    6          -   DISPDT  -1--1-     296-6      296-6
26 DATE-ENTERED.......    6          -   DTENTR  -1--1-     302-6      302-6
27 JOB-TITLE..........   25          -   JOBTIT  ------     308-25     308-25
28 DISP-DESC..........   30          -   DESCRP  ------     333-30     333-30
29 EDUC-LVL-ACH.......    1          -   EDUCLV  ------     363-1      363-1

      Valid Value---: 0,0,1,2,3,4,5,6

30 NEXT-SCRN-NO.......    2.0        -   NXTSCR  --1---     364-2      364-2
```

Name: ATAPMSTR, Applicant Master File Format
      ATAPTEMP, Applicant Search File Format
   Record Information: Lst Chg Date: 06/06/88
      Key Size-6   #FldSep-0   Lst Chg Time: 08:56:59
      Rec Size-394   #KeyInd-1   Created Date: 06/26/87

```
                                     F           KENPDY     --- Position ----
   Data Element         Length       S   HELP    YTTDTN     Record    Internal
===============================================================================
 1 IDENT..............    6          -   IDENT   Y2----       1-6        1-6
 2 NAME...............   30          -   NAME    ------       7-30       7-30
 3 ADDRESS............   30          -   ADDRES  ------      37-30      37-30
 4 CITY...............   20          -   CITY    ------      67-20      67-20
 5 STATE..............    2          -   STATE   ------      87-2       87-2
 6 ZIPCODE............   10          -   ZIPCD   ------      89-10      89-10
 7 PHONE..............   10          -   PHONE   -1-4--      99-10      99-10
 8 CUR-HIRED..........    6          -   CURHIR  -1--1-     109-6      109-6
 9 COMPANY............   30          -   COMPAN  ------     115-30     115-30
10 CUR-ADDRESS........   30          -   ADDRES  ------     145-30     145-30
11 CUR-CITY...........   20          -   CITY    ------     175-20     175-20
12 CUR-STATE..........    2          -   STATE   -1----     195-2      195-2
13 CUR-ZIPCODE........   10          -   ZIPCD   ------     197-10     197-10
14 CUR-PHONE..........   10          -   PHONE   -1-4--     207-10     207-10
15 CUR-EXT............    4          -   EXTENS  ------     217-4      217-4
16 CUR-POSITION.......   25          -   CURPOS  ------     221-25     221-25
17 CUR-SALARY.........    9.2        -   SALARY  --1---     246-9      246-9
18 CUR-EXP-CODE.......    2          -   EXPCOD  -2----     255-2      255-2
19 SOURCE.............   20          -   SOURCE  ------     257-20     257-20
20 REQ-NO.............    4          -   REQNO   ---3--     277-4      277-4
21 COMMENTS...........    1          -   COMNTS  ---6--     281-1      281-1

      Valid Value---: 3,A,60,4,3,19,R,-----APPLICANT COMMENTS-----

22 AVAIL-DATE.........    6          -   AVAIL   -1--1-     282-6      282-6
23 DISP-CODE..........    2          -   DISPCD  ------     288-2      288-2
24 DISP-DATE..........    6          -   DISPDT  -1--1-     290-6      290-6
25 ADVERT.............   10.2        -   ADVERT  --1---     296-10     296-10
26 AGENCY-FEES........   10.2        -   AGENCY  --1---     306-10     306-10
27 EMPLOYEE-REFERRAL..   10.2        -   EMPREF  --1---     316-10     316-10
28 RELOCATION-EXP.....   10.2        -   RELOC   --1---     326-10     326-10
29 TVL-LODG-EXP.......   10.2        -   TNLEXP  --1---     336-10     336-10
30 OTHER-REC-EXP......   10.2        -   OTHEXP  --1---     346-10     346-10
31 TOTAL-REC-EXP......   10.2        -   TOTEXP  --1---     356-10     356-10
32 NO-DAYS-TO-FILL....    4.0        -   NODAYS  --1---     366-4      366-4
33 DATE-ENTERED.......    6          -   DTENTR  -1--1-     370-6      370-6
34 EDUC-LVL-ACH.......    1          -   EDUCLV  ------     376-1      376-1

      Valid Value---: 0,0,1,2,3,4,5,6

35 SEX................    1          -   SEX     ------     377-1      377-1

      Valid Value---: 0,M,F
```

2-3

APPENDIX 2: ATS FORMAT DEFINITIONS

```
                                    F             KENPDY    --- Position ----
   Data Element         Length      S   HELP      YTTDTN    Record    Internal
  ================================================================================
  36 EEO-CODE..........    1            - EEOCDE  ------    378-1     378-1

       Valid Value---: 0,0,1,2,3,4

  37 SSN...............    9            - SSN     -1-5--    379-9     379-9
  38 BIRTH-DATE........    6            - BIRTH   -1--1-    388-6     388-6
  39 VETERAN...........    1            - VETERN  -1---Y    394-1     394-1



  Name: ATDISPCD, Disposition Code File Format

       Record Information:                        Lst Chg Date: 05/20/88
          Key Size-2        #FldSep-0             Lst Chg Time: 14:04:59
          Rec Size-32       #KeyInd-1             Created Date: 06/27/87

                                    F             KENPDY    --- Position ----
   Data Element         Length      S   HELP      YTTDTN    Record    Internal
  ================================================================================
  1 DISP-CODE..........    2            - DISPCD  Y1----    1-2       1-2
  2 DISP-DESC..........   30            - DESCRP  ------    3-30      3-30



  Name: ATEXPCDE, Experience Code File Format

       Record Information:                        Lst Chg Date: 05/20/88
          Key Size-2        #FldSep-0             Lst Chg Time: 14:05:03
          Rec Size-32       #KeyInd-1             Created Date: 06/26/87

                                    F             KENPDY    --- Position ----
   Data Element         Length      S   HELP      YTTDTN    Record    Internal
  ================================================================================
  1 EXPER-CODE.........    2            - EXPCD1  Y-----    1-2       1-2
  2 EXPER-DESC.........   30            - DESCRP  ------    3-30      3-30



  Name: ATEXPCDP, Exper Code File Fmt For Reports

       Record Information:                        Lst Chg Date: 05/20/88
          Key Size-2        #FldSep-0             Lst Chg Time: 18:46:11
          Rec Size-32       #KeyInd-1             Created Date: 06/26/87

                                    F             KENPDY    --- Position ----
   Data Element         Length      S   HELP      YTTDTN    Record    Internal
  ================================================================================
  1 PRIM-EXP-CODE......    2            - EXPCD1  Y-----    1-2       1-2
  2 EXPER-DESC.........   30            - DESCRP  ------    3-30      3-30
```

APPENDIX 2: ATS FORMAT DEFINITIONS

```
Name: ATJOBCDE, Job Code File Format

        Record Information:                           Lst Chg Date: 05/20/88
           Key Size-4       #FldSep-0                 Lst Chg Time: 14:05:27
           Rec Size-33      #KeyInd-1                 Created Date: 09/25/87

                                         F         KENPDY    --- Position ----
   Data Element          Length          S  HELP   YTTDTN    Record   Internal
   =============================================================================
   1 JOB-CODE..........    4                - JOBCDE Y--3--    1-4      1-4

      Valid Value---: 1,0001,9999

   2 JOB-TITLE.........   25                - JOBTIT ------    5-25     5-25
   3 EEOC-JOB-CAT......    1                - EEOCJC -3----   30-1     30-1

      Valid Value---: 0,A,B,C,D,E,F,G,H,J,K,M

   4 JOB-STATUS........    2                - JOBSTS -3----   31-2     31-2

      Preset Values-: FT
      Valid Value---: 0,FT,PT

   5 EXEMPT-CLASS......    1                - EXEMPT -3----   33-1     33-1

      Valid Value---: 0,E,N,H


Name: ATRECRUT, Recruiter Code File Format

        Record Information:                           Lst Chg Date: 06/06/88
           Key Size-6       #FldSep-0                 Lst Chg Time: 08:59:38
           Rec Size-55      #KeyInd-1                 Created Date: 06/26/87

                                         F         KENPDY    --- Position ----
   Data Element          Length          S  HELP   YTTDTN    Record   Internal
   =============================================================================
   1 RECRUITER.........    6                - RECRUT Y1----    1-6      1-6
   2 RECRUT-NAME.......   30                - RECNME ------    7-30     7-30
   3 RECRUT-RATE.......    8.2              - RECRAT --1---   37-8     37-8
   4 RECRUT-PHONE......   10                - PHONE  -1-4--   45-10    45-10
   5 INTERNAL-REC......    1                - INTREC -1---Y   55-1     55-1

      Preset Values-: Y

Name: ATREQUIS, Emplmt Requisitions Screen Format

        Record Information:                           Lst Chg Date: 06/06/88
           Key Size-4       #FldSep-0                 Lst Chg Time: 09:00:30
           Rec Size-333     #KeyInd-1                 Created Date: 10/15/87

                                         F         KENPDY    --- Position ----
   Data Element          Length          S  HELP   YTTDTN    Record   Internal
   =============================================================================
   1 REQ-NO............    4                - REQNUM Y--3--    1-4      1-4

      Valid Value---: 1,0001,9999

   2 REQ-DATE..........    6                - REQDAT -1--1-    5-6      5-6
   3 JOB-CODE..........    4                - JOBCDE -2-3--   11-4     11-4
   4 JOB-TITLE.........   25                - JOBTIT -2----   15-25    15-25
   5 SALARY-GRADE......    2                - SALGRD -2----   40-2     40-2
   6 PT-RATE...........   10.2              - PTRATE --11--   42-10    42-10
   7 DEPARTMENT........   20                - DEPTMT ------   52-20    52-20
   8 SHIFT.............    7                - SHIFT  ------   72-7     72-7

      Preset Values-: Daily
      Valid Value---: 0,Daily   ,Evening,Night
```

2-5

APPENDIX 2: ATS FORMAT DEFINITIONS

```
                                     F           KENPDY    --- Position ----
      Data Element        Length     S   HELP    YTTDTN    Record   Internal
===============================================================================

    9 LOCATION.........   15           - LOCATN ------      79-15    79-15
   10 EEOC-JOB-CAT.....    1           - EEOCJC ------      94-1     94-1
   11 RECRUITER........    6           - RECRUT -2----      95-6     95-6
   12 INTERNAL-SRCH....    1           - INTSCH -1---Y     101-1    101-1

       Preset Values-: Y

   13 NEW-POSITION.....    1           - NEWPOS -1---Y     102-1    102-1

       Preset Values-: N

   14 REPLACEMENT-DATE.    6           - RPLDAT -1--1-     103-6    103-6
   15 REPLACEMENT-FOR..    6           - RPLFOR ------     109-6    109-6
   16 REQ-STATUS.......    9           - REQSTS ------     115-9    115-9

       Valid Value---: 0,open      ,closed    ,cancelled,on hold  ,re-opened

   17 REQ-DISP-DATE....    6           - REQDDT -1--1-     124-6    124-6
   18 TOTAL-REC-EXP....   10.2         - TOTEXP --1---     130-10   130-10
   19 REQ-APPROVER.....   20           - REQAPP ------     140-20   140-20
   20 REQ-APPROVER-TITLE. 10           - REQAPT ------     160-10   160-10
   21 REQ-APPROVAL-DATE.   6           - REQAPD -1--1-     170-6    170-6
   22 JOB-STATUS.......    2           - JOBSTS -1----     176-2    176-2

       Preset Values-: FT
       Valid Value---: 0,FT,PT

   23 NO-DAYS-TO-FILL..    4.0         - NODAYS --1---     178-4    178-4
   24 EDUC-LEVEL.......    1           - EDUCLV ------     182-1    182-1

       Valid Value---: 0,0,1,2,3,4,5,6

   25 IDENT............    6           - FILLED ------     183-6    183-6

   26 PRIM-EXP-CODE....    2           - EXPCD1 -2----     189-2    189-2
   27 SEC-EXP-CODE.....    2           - EXPCD1 ------     191-2    191-2
   28 EXEMPT-CLASS.....    1           - EXEMPT ------     193-1    193-1
   29 SALARY-MAX.......   10.2         - HISAL  --1---     194-10   194-10
   30 SALARY-MIN.......   10.2         - LOWSAL --1---     204-10   204-10
   31 PRIM-EXP-DESC....   30           - DESCRP ------     214-30   214-30
   32 SEC-EXP-DESC.....   30           - DESCRP ------     244-30   244-30
   33 RECRUT-NAME......   30           - RECNME ------     274-30   274-30
   34 NAME.............   30           - NAME   ------     304-30   304-30
```

APPENDIX 2: ATS FORMAT DEFINITIONS

```
Name: ATRQMSTR, Emplmt Requisitions Masterfile Fmt

        Record Information:                            Lst Chg Date: 06/06/88
        Key Size-4        #FldSep-0                    Lst Chg Time: 09:00:54
        Rec Size-199      #KeyInd-1                    Created Date: 10/15/87

                                          F          KENPDY      --- Position ----
     Data Element            Length       S   HELP   YTTDTN      Record    Internal
     ================================================================================
   1 REQ-NO..........        4                - REQNO   Y--3--    1-4        1-4

       Valid Value---: 1,0001,9999

   2 REQ-DATE.........       6                - REQDAT  -1--1-    5-6        5-6
   3 JOB-CODE.........       4                - JOBCDE  ------    11-4       11-4
   4 JOB-TITLE........       25               - JOBTIT  -2----    15-25      15-25
   5 SALARY-GRADE.....       2                - SALGRD  -2----    40-2       40-2
   6 PT-RATE..........       10.2             - PTRATE  --11--    42-10      42-10
   7 DEPARTMENT.......       20               - DEPTMT  ------    52-20      52-20
   8 SHIFT............       7                - SHIFT   ------    72-7       72-7

       Preset Values-: Daily
       Valid Value---: 0,Daily   ,Evening,Night

   9 LOCATION.........       15               - LOCATN  ------    79-15      79-15
  10 EEOC-JOB-CAT.....       1                - EEOCJC  -3----    94-1       94-1

       Valid Value---: 0,A,B,C,D,E,F,G,H,J,K,M

  11 RECRUITER........       6                - RECRUT  -2----    95-6       95-6
  12 INTERNAL-SRCH....       1                - INTSCH  -1---Y    101-1      101-1
  13 NEW-POSITION.....       1                - NEWPOS  -1---Y    102-1      102-1

       Preset Values-: N

  14 REPLACEMENT-DATE.       6                - RPLDAT  -1--1-    103-6      103-6
  15 REPLACEMENT-FOR..       6                - RPLFOR  ------    109-6      109-6
  16 REQ-STATUS.......       9                - REQSTS  ------    115-9      115-9

       Preset Values-: open
       Valid Value---: 0,open      ,closed    ,cancelled,on hold   ,re-opened

  17 REQ-DISP-DATE....       6                - REQDDT  -1--1-    124-6      124-6
  18 REQ-APPROVER.....       20               - REQAPP  ------    130-20     130-20
  19 REQ-APPROVER-TITLE..    10               - REQAPT  ------    150-10     150-10
  20 REQ-APPROVAL-DATE...    6                - REQAPD  -1--1-    160-6      160-6
  21 JOB-STATUS.......       2                - JOBSTS  -3----    166-2      166-2

       Preset Values-: FT
       Valid Value---: 0,FT,PT

  22 EDUC-LEVEL.......       1                - EDUCLV  ------    168-1      168-1

       Valid Value---: 0,0,1,2,3,4,5,6

  23 IDENT............       6                - FILLED  ------    169-6      169-6

  24 PRIM-EXP-CODE....       2                - EXPCD1  -2----    175-2      175-2
  25 SEC-EXP-CODE.....       2                - EXPCD1  ------    177-2      177-2
  26 EXEMPT-CLASS.....       1                - EXEMPT  -3----    179-1      179-1

       Valid Value---: 0,E,N,H

  27 SALARY-MAX.......       10.2             - HISAL   --1---    180-10     180-10
  28 SALARY-MIN.......       10.2             - LOWSAL  --1---    190-10     190-10
```

APPENDIX 2: ATS FORMAT DEFINITIONS

```
Name: ATSALGRD, Salary Grade File Format

        Record Information:                          Lst Chg Date: 05/20/88
          Key Size-2        #FldSep-0                Lst Chg Time: 14:59:44
          Rec Size-52       #KeyInd-1                Created Date: 07/10/87

                                     F        KENPDY     --- Position ----
      Data Element         Length    S  HELP  YTTDTN    Record    Internal
    =============================================================================
    1 SALARY-GRADE........    2       - SALGRD Y-----     1-2        1-2
    2 SALARY-DESC.........   30       - DESCRP ------     3-30       3-30
    3 SALARY-MAX..........   10.2     - HISAL  --1---    33-10      33-10
    4 SALARY-MIN..........   10.2     - LOWSAL --1---    43-10      43-10
```

Appendix 3

ATS MESSAGE DICTIONARY

All definitions from the sample Appplicant Tracking System are from the AT library.

```
MESSAGE REPORT - Prompts and Constants                      Page:          1
                                                            Date:    05/31/88
NAME: ATMSGS         Desc: Sample Applicant Tracking System MsgList

                                                    Lst Chg Date:   04/18/88
                                                    Lst Chg Time:   13:55:52
                                                    Created Date:   07/10/87
===============================================================================
Msg    -Screen-                          Max  Scn  Num  Typ  Pad  Dat
Nbr    Col  Lin  Mode  Clr  HlpCde       Len  Len  Typ  Inp  Ind  Ind
===============================================================================
YN (Y/N)?
  1     0    0    R     B

, RETURN to continue.
  2     0    0    R     B

:
  3     0    0    R     B

F4-END   F6-HELP
  4     0    99   R     B

Specified Record is Missing; try again.
  5     0    0    R     B

F1-Next  F2-Prev  F4-End  F6-Help  F7-Copy  F8-Lookup  F10-GoTo
  6     0    1    R     B

Enter *1 to search (F1, 2, or 10), F8 to display list or F3 to add recd
  7     0    0    R     B

F1-Next  F2-Prev  F3-Add  F4-End  F6-Help  F8-Lookup  F10-Find Rec
  8     0    1    R     B

F1-Next  F2-Prev  F3-Delete  F4-End  F6-Help  F7-Copy  F8-Lookup  F10-GoTo
  9     0    1    R     B

F4-End   F6-Help  F8-Lookup  F10-GoTo
 10     0    1    R     B

F1-Next  F2-Prev  F4-End  F6-Help
 11     0    1    R     B

Enter data into fields for new record; press F6 for help.
 12     0    0    R     B

Enter starting *1 value; RETURN to continue, F4 to Abort Sequence.
 13     0    0    R     B
```

3-1

APPENDIX 3: ATS MESSAGE DICTIONARY

```
MESSAGE REPORT - Prompts and Constants                    Page:           2
                                                          Date:    05/31/88
NAME: ATMSGS       Desc: Sample Applicant Tracking System MsgList
                                                  Lst Chg Date:    04/18/88
                                                  Lst Chg Time:    13:55:52
                                                  Created Date:    07/10/87
===============================================================================
Msg     -Screen-                    Max   Scn   Num   Typ   Pad   Dat
Nbr    Col  Lin  Mode   Clr  HlpCde  Len   Len   Typ   Inp   Ind   Ind
===============================================================================

F4-End   F6-Help
   14     0    1    R    B

Enter new *1 value; RETURN to continue, F4 to Abort Copy.
   15     0    0    R    B

F1-Get Requisition  F4-Abort  F6-Help
   16     0    1    R    B

F1-Go  F4-Abort  F6-Help
   17     0    1    R    B

Press F1 to Start Search; F4 to Re-enter Req No.
   18     0    0    R    B

Press F1 to Get Requisition Record; F4 to Abort Search
   19     0    0    R    B

Search for matching Applicants NOW IN PROGRESS...
   20     0    0    R    B

F1-Next F2-Prev F3-Delete F4-End F6-Help F7-Copy F8-Lookup F9-Nxt Scr F10-GoTo
   21     0    1    R    B

COMPANY: *1              *2           DATE: *3
   22     0    0    R    B

Place Cursor on the *1 you wish to retrieve and press F1-Choose
   23     0    0    R    B

Use scrolling keys to view existing *1 records; press F4 to Exit
   24     0    0    R    B

This record is now reserved by you for editing
   25     0    0    R    B

F1-Next F2-Prev F3-Delete F4-End F6-Help F7-Copy F9-Nxt Scr F10-GoTo
   26     0    1    R    B

F1-Choose *1  F4-End/Close  F10-GoTo Rec  Use Scroll Keys to View Recds
   27     0    1    R    B

Press RETURN to Edit Record, or choose one of the following functions
   28     0    0    R    B

F4-End/Close  F10-GoTo Rec
   29     0    1    R    B

ATS - Salary Grade Masterfile Maintenance
   30     0    2    R    B

F3-Delete Record  F4-End  F6-Help  F10-GoTo Field
   31     0    1    R    B
```

APPENDIX 3: ATS MESSAGE DICTIONARY

```
MESSAGE REPORT - Non-Input Messages                    Page:           1
                                                       Date:    05/31/88
NAME: ATMSGS       Desc: Sample Applicant Tracking System MsgList
                                               Lst Chg Date:    04/18/88
                                               Lst Chg Time:    13:55:52
                                               Created Date:    07/10/87
=============================================================================
Msg     -Screen-                        Max  Scn  Num  Typ  Pad  Dat
Nbr     Col  Lin  Mode  Clr  HlpCde     Len  Len  Typ  Inp  Ind  Ind
=============================================================================
'RB'Specified *1 Record is Missing
   1     0    0    R     A

'RB'You have reached the End of the *1 File
   2     0    0    R     A

Press RETURN for next *1 Record
   3     0    0    R     A

'RB'CANNOT Add this *1; a duplicate key exists
   4     0    0    R     A

'RB'*1 Record is Busy; try again later
   5     0    0    R     A

'RB'Continuation Script *1 is Missing
   6     0    0    R     A

*1 matching Applicant records found
   7     0    0    R     A

'RB'Overlay Script *1 is Missing
   8     0    0    R     A

'RB'You have reached the Beginning of the *1 File
   9     0    0    R     A

'RB'CANNOT Delete this *1; in use in *2 File
  10     0    0    R     A

'RB'You MUST enter a valid *1
  11     0    0    R     A

'RB'You tried to overwrite an existing *1; this is NOT allowed
  12     0    0    R     A

'RB'An error occurred trying to update this *1; your changes may be LOST
  13     0    0    R     A

'RB'The *1 file is busy and CANNOT be accessed now
  14     0    0    R     A

'RB'An error occurred trying to open the *1 file
  15     0    0    R     A

'RB'Maximum Salary MUST BE > Minimum Salary
  16     0    0    R     A
```

APPENDIX 3: ATS MESSAGE DICTIONARY

```
MESSAGE REPORT - Yes/No Messages                         Page:           1
                                                         Date:    05/31/88
NAME: ATMSGS      Desc: Sample Applicant Tracking System MsgList

                                             Lst Chg Date:    04/18/88
                                             Lst Chg Time:    13:55:52
                                             Created Date:    07/10/87
================================================================================
Msg    -Screen-                       Max  Scn  Num  Typ  Pad  Dat
Nbr    Col  Lin  Mode  Clr  HlpCde    Len  Len  Typ  Inp  Ind  Ind
================================================================================
'RB'Save changes to this record
  1     0    0    R    A

'RB'Are you SURE you want to delete this record
  2     0    0    R    A

'RB'Add this record to the file
  3     0    0    R    A

'RB'Are you SURE you want to change the key to this record
  4     0    0    R    A

'RB'Replace *1: *2 with *3
  5     0    0    R    A

'RB'Is this a new *1 record
  6     0    0    R    A



MESSAGE REPORT - Input Messages                          Page:           1
                                                         Date:    05/31/88
NAME: ATMSGS      Desc: Sample Applicant Tracking System MsgList

                                             Lst Chg Date:    04/18/88
                                             Lst Chg Time:    13:55:52
                                             Created Date:    07/10/87
================================================================================
Msg    -Screen-                       Max  Scn  Num  Typ  Pad  Dat
Nbr    Col  Lin  Mode  Clr  HlpCde    Len  Len  Typ  Inp  Ind  Ind
================================================================================
Enter Sequence Number to use; press F6 for help
  1     0    0    R    A   TSTCUS     2    3    1    2    3
       Valid Value---: 0,0,1

Enter Sequence Number to use; press F6 for help
  2     0    0    R    A   REQSRT     2    3    1    2    3
       Valid Value---: 0,0,1,2

Enter Sequence Number to use; press F6 for help
  3     0    0    R    A   APSORT     2    3    1    2    3
       Valid Value---: 0,0,1

|General Data - Screen 1|  |Recruitment Costs - Screen 2|
  4     0    0    S    A   APSCRN     1    1
       Valid Value---: 012
```

Appendix 4

ATS LINK DEFINITIONS

All definitions from the sample Applicant Tracking System are from the AT library.

APMSTR	Applicant Master File Link
APTEMP	Applicant Search File Link
DISPCD	Disposition Code File Link
EXPCDE	Experience Code File Link
EXPCDP	Experience Code File Link for Reports
JOBCDE	Job Code File Link
RECRUT	Recruiter Code File Link
RQMSTR	Employment Requisitions File Link
SALGRD	Salary Grade File Link

```
NAME: ATAPMSTR, Applicant Master File Link

  Password:        Data File: ATAPMSTR   Scrn:        Lst Chg Date:  10/14/87
                   Format...: ATAPMSTR   View:        Lst Chg Time:  13:20:46
                   Audit....: N                       Created Date:  06/26/87
===============================================================================
Secondary Keys: SORT1 DISP-CODE; SORT2 SOURCE; SORT3 REQ-NO


NAME: ATAPTEMP, Applicant Search File Link

  Password:        Data File: ATAPTEMP   Scrn:        Lst Chg Date:  05/20/88
                   Format...: ATAPTEMP   View:        Lst Chg Time:  18:51:15
                   Audit....: N                       Created Date:  12/02/87
===============================================================================
Secondary Keys: SORT1 NAME; SORT2 SOURCE
```

APPENDIX 4: ATS LINK DEFINITIONS

```
NAME: ATDISPCD, Disposition Code File Link

    Password:        Data File: ATDISPCD  Scrn:      Lst Chg Date:  05/12/88
                     Format...: ATDISPCD  View:      Lst Chg Time:  11:58:09
                     Audit....: N                    Created Date:  06/27/87
===============================================================================


NAME: ATEXPCDE, Experience Code File Link

    Password:        Data File: ATEXPCDE  Scrn:      Lst Chg Date:  05/12/88
                     Format...: ATEXPCDE  View:      Lst Chg Time:  11:59:19
                     Audit....: N                    Created Date:  10/13/87
===============================================================================

NAME: ATEXPCDP, Exper Code File Link For Reports

    Password:        Data File: ATEXPCDE  Scrn:      Lst Chg Date:  05/20/88
                     Format...: ATEXPCDP  View:      Lst Chg Time:  18:51:30
                     Audit....: N                    Created Date:  10/13/87
===============================================================================

NAME: ATJOBCDE, Job Code File Link

    Password:        Data File: ATJOBCDE  Scrn:      Lst Chg Date:  05/12/88
                     Format...: ATJOBCDE  View:      Lst Chg Time:  12:01:05
                     Audit....: N                    Created Date:  10/04/87
===============================================================================

NAME: ATRECRUT, Recruiter Code File Link

    Password:        Data File: ATRECRUT  Scrn:      Lst Chg Date:  05/12/88
                     Format...: ATRECRUT  View:      Lst Chg Time:  12:01:40
                     Audit....: N                    Created Date:  06/26/87
===============================================================================

NAME: ATRQMSTR, Employment Requisitions File Link

    Password:        Data File: ATRQMSTR  Scrn:      Lst Chg Date:  10/15/87
                     Format...: ATRQMSTR  View:      Lst Chg Time:  20:44:00
                     Audit....: N                    Created Date:  10/15/87
===============================================================================

Secondary Keys: SORT1 DEPARTMENT; SORT2 RECRUITER; SORT3 IDENT

NAME: ATSALGRD, Salary Grade File Link

    Password:        Data File: ATSALGRD  Scrn:      Lst Chg Date:  05/12/88
                     Format...: ATSALGRD  View:      Lst Chg Time:  12:02:18
                     Audit....: N                    Created Date:  07/10/87
===============================================================================
```

Appendix 5

ATS SCREEN DEFINITIONS

All definitions from the sample Applicant Tracking System are from the AT library.

*APCOST	Applicant Recruitment Costs Screen
APCOSh	Applicant Recruitment Costs Help Refresh Screen
*APGENL	Applicant General Information Screen
APGENh	Applicant General Information Help Refresh Screen
APGEN1	Applicant General Information View Refresh Screen
DISPCD	Disposition Code Screen
EXPCDE	Experience Code Screen
JOBCDE	Job Code Screen
**MENU01	Applicant Tracking System Main Menu Screen
**MENU02	Applicant and Requisitions Report Menu Screen
RECRUT	Recruiter Code Screen
REQNM1	Requisition Number Input Screen #1
REQNM2	Requisition Number Input Screen #2
REQUIS	Employment Requisitions Screen
REQUIh	Employment Requisitions Help Refresh Screen
REQUIr	Employment Requisitions View Refresh Screen
SALGRD	Salary Grade Screen

*Refer to Chapter 6, "Database Maintenance Implementation and Use" for a representation of the screen definition.

**Refer to Appendix 10, "ATS Menu Definitions", for the screen definitions.

5-1

APPENDIX 5: ATS SCREEN DEFINITIONS

```
Name: ATAPCOST, Appl. Recruitment Costs Screen

    Link/Frmt         Screen----------  HELP-----------  Lst Chg Date:  05/20/88
    ATAPCOST    Size: chrs-80  lns-16   chrs-73  lns-4   Lst Chg Time:  18:47:11
                Home: col--0   lin-2    col--3   lin-18  Created Date:  06/27/87
=================================================================================
{ATAPCOST            APPLICANT RECRUITMENT COSTS        TODAY'S DATE: /d        ~
{
{ID:~_____(        Name:~_____(        Recruiter:~____( ~
>    L                    M                                            R
 (            Seeking Position:~_____(       Avail:~_____( ~
 >                              N                                    O
 (                                                                              ~
 {   Enter Recruitment Costs, as required    *******************************~
 {              Advertising:~ _____  ( *   Voluntary Disclosure Data    *~
 >                            A
 {              Agency Fees:~ _____  ( *             Sex:~_             (*~
 >                            B                              G
 {       Employee Referral Fee:~ _____ ( *         EEO Code:~_            (*~
 >                              C                             H
 {        Relocation Expenses:~ _____ ( *              SSN:~_____     (*~
 >                              D                              I
 { Travel & Lodging Expenses:~ _____( *       Birth Date:~_____      (*~
 >                             E                                J
 (Other Recruitment Expenses:~ _____( *         Veteran:~_             (*~
 >                             F                             K
 {                             ========    * BY FEDERAL LAW THIS DATA MAY NOT *~
 (Total Recruitment Expenses:~ _____( * BE USED IN THE HIRING DECISION!! *~
 >                             P
 (# of Days To Fill Position:~ ____     ( *******************************~
 >                             Q
 (                      Next Screen Number:~__(                           ~
 >                                            S

    Formulas:

        A - ADVERT              K - VETERAN
        B - AGENCY-FEES         L - IDENT
        C - EMPLOYEE-REFERRAL   M - NAME
        D - RELOCATION-EXP      N - JOB-TITLE
        E - TVL-LODG-EXP        O - /FIELD(8)=AVAIL-DATE
        F - OTHER-REC-EXP       P - TOTAL-REC-EXP
        G - SEX                 Q - NO-DAYS-TO-FILL
        H - EEO-CODE            R - RECRUITER
        I - /FIELD(11)=SSN      S - NEXT-SCRN-NO
        J - /FIELD(8)=BIRTH-DATE


Name: ATAPCOSh, Appl. Rec Costs Help Refresh Screen

    Link/Frmt         Screen----------  HELP-----------  Lst Chg Date:  05/20/88
    ATAPCOST    Size: chrs-80  lns-16   chrs-73  lns-4   Lst Chg Time:  18:49:21
                Home: col--0   lin-17   col--3   lin-18  Created Date:  06/27/87
=================================================================================
(                      Next Screen Number:~   (                           ~
```

SCREEN DISPLAY CODES USED:

{ - Start Reverse Video Background	/d - Terminal Date
~ - End Reverse Video Bascground	> - Identifies a Field for the Report (not in screen definition)

5-2

APPENDIX 5: ATS SCREEN DEFINITIONS

```
Name: ATAPGENL, Appl. General Information Screen

    Link/Frmt       Screen---------   HELP-----------   Lst Chg Date:  05/20/88
    ATAPGENL   Size: chrs-80  lns-15  chrs-73  lns-5    Lst Chg Time:  18:49:30
               Home: col--0   lin-2   col--3   lin-17  Created Date:  06/26/87
================================================================================
(ATAPGENL           APPLICANT GENERAL INFORMATION          TODAY'S DATE: /d    ~
(                                                                              ~
(          Name and Address Information           Current Employment           ~
(ID Code:~_____ (Date Entered:~_____ ( Hired:~_____   (Avail:~_____  ( ~
>             A                   B               J                 K
(   Name:~_____(Company:~_____     ( ~
>            C                                    L
(Address:~_____(Address:~_____     ( ~
>          D                                      M
(   City:~_____      (   City:~_____   ( ~
>          E                                      N
(  State:~__  (Zip:~_____            (  State:~__  (Zip:~_____          ( ~
>          F        G                              O        P
(  Phone:~_____                    (  Phone:~_____   (Ext:~____    ( ~
>          H                                      Q                  R
(Education Level Achieved:~ _           (Position:~_____  ( ~
>                          I                       S
(        Job Seeking Information         Salary:~_____(Exp Code:~__       ( ~
>                                                T                  U
(Source:~_____(Req'st #:~____(       Disposition of Applicant          ~
>        V                       W
(Recruiter:~_____ (Comments:~_         ( Disp Code:~__ (Disp Date:~_____  ( ~
>           b                Z                      X                Y
(Job Title:~_____( Disp Desc:~_____  ( ~
>           c                                        a
(                   Next Screen Number:~__(                                    ~
>                                        d

     Formulas:

         A - IDENT                       P - CUR-ZIPCODE
         B - /FIELD(8)=DATE-ENTERED      Q - /FIELD(12)=CUR-PHONE
         C - NAME                        R - CUR-EXT
         D - ADDRESS                     S - CUR-POSITION
         E - CITY                        T - CUR-SALARY
         F - STATE                       U - CUR-EXP-CODE
         G - ZIPCODE                     V - /FIELD(15)=SOURCE
         H - /FIELD(12)=PHONE            W - REQ-NO
         I - EDUC-LVL-ACH                X - DISP-CODE
         J - /FIELD(8)=CUR-HIRED         Y - /FIELD(8)=DISP-DATE
         K - /FIELD(8)=AVAIL-DATE        Z - COMMENTS
         L - /FIELD(27)=COMPANY          a - /FIELD(24)=DISP-DESC
         M - /FIELD(27)=CUR-ADDRESS      b - RECRUITER
         N - CUR-CITY                    c - JOB-TITLE
         O - CUR-STATE                   d - NEXT-SCRN-NO
```

SCREEN DISPLAY CODES USED:

{ - Start Reverse Video Background   /d - Terminal Date
~ - End Reverse Video Basckground   > - Identifies a Field for the Report
                                               (not in screen definition)

5-3

APPENDIX 5: ATS SCREEN DEFINITIONS

```
Name: ATAPGENh, Appl. Gen Infor Help Refresh Screen

    Link/Frmt         Screen---------    HELP----------   Lst Chg Date:  05/20/88
    ATAPGENL    Size: chrs-80  lns-1     chrs-72  lns-5   Lst Chg Time:  18:49:35
                Home: col--0   lin-16    col--3   lin-17  Created Date:  06/26/87
================================================================================
{                        Next Screen Number:~   {                              ~


Name: ATAPGENl, Appl. Gen Infor View Refresh Screen

    Link/Frmt         Screen---------    HELP----------   Lst Chg Date:  05/20/88
    ATAPGENL    Size: chrs-80  lns-4     chrs-73  lns-5   Lst Chg Time:  18:49:36
                Home: col--0   lin-13    col--3   lin-17  Created Date:  06/26/87
================================================================================
{Source:~              {Req'stn #:~    (       Disposition of Applicant      ~
{Recruiter:~       {Comments:~             ( Disp Code:~
{Job Title:~                               ( Disp Desc:~
{                        Next Screen Number:~   {                              ~

Name: ATDISPCD, Disposition Code Screen

    Link/Frmt         Screen---------    HELP----------   Lst Chg Date:  05/20/88
    ATDISPCD    Size: chrs-80  lns-24    chrs-72  lns-10  Lst Chg Time:  14:08:43
                Home: col--0   lin-0     col--3   lin-9   Created Date:  07/10/87
================================================================================




{Disposition Code:~__
>                     A
{      Description:~_____
>                     B

    Formulas:

      A - DISP-CODE
      B - DISP-DESC

Name: ATEXPCDE, Experience Code Screen

    Link/Frmt         Screen---------    HELP----------   Lst Chg Date:  05/20/88
    ATEXPCDE    Size: chrs-80  lns-24    chrs-72  lns-10  Lst Chg Time:  14:08:49
                Home: col--0   lin-0     col--3   lin-9   Created Date:  07/10/87
================================================================================




{Experience Code:~__
>                    A
{      Description:~_____
>                    B

    Formulas:

      A - EXPER-CODE
      B - EXPER-DESC
```

SCREEN DISPLAY CODES USED:

| { - Start Reverse Video Background | /d - Terminal Date |
| ~ - End Reverse Video Basckground | > - Identifies a Field for the Report (not in screen definition) |

APPENDIX 5: ATS SCREEN DEFINITIONS

```
Name: ATJOBCDE, Job Code Screen

    Link/Frmt        Screen---------  HELP-----------  Lst Chg Date:  05/20/88
    ATJOBCDE   Size: chrs-80  lns-24  chrs-72  lns-10  Lst Chg Time:  14:08:56
               Home: col--0   lin-0   col--3   lin-9   Created Date:  09/25/87
================================================================================


{       Job Code:~_____
>                    A
{Job Title/Position:~_____
>                    B
{ EEOC Job Category:~_
>                    C
{      Job Status:~_
>                  D
{    Exempt Class:~_
>                  E

   Formulas:

     A - JOB-CODE
     B - JOB-TITLE
     C - EEOC-JOB-CAT
     D - JOB-STATUS
     E - EXEMPT-CLASS

Name: ATRECRUT, Recruiter Code Screen

    Link/Frmt        Screen---------  HELP-----------  Lst Chg Date:  01/22/88
    ATRECRUT   Size: chrs-80  lns-24  chrs-72  lns-10  Lst Chg Time:  13:57:56
               Home: col--0   lin-0   col--3   lin-9   Created Date:  07/10/87
================================================================================


{   Recruiter Id:~_____
>                 A
{           Name:~_____
>                 B
{      Telephone:~_____
>                 C
{           Rate:~_____
>                 D
{  Internal (Y/N):~_
>                  E

   Formulas:

     A - RECRUITER
     B - RECRUT-NAME
     C - /FIELD(12)=RECRUT-PHONE
     D - RECRUT-RATE
     E - INTERNAL-REC
```

SCREEN DISPLAY CODES USED:

{ - Start Reverse Video Background
~ - End Reverse Video Basckground
/d - Terminal Date
> - Identifies a Field for the Report (not in screen definition)

5-5

APPENDIX 5: ATS SCREEN DEFINITIONS

```
Name: ATREQNM1, Requisition Number Input Screen #1

    Link/Frmt      Screen--------   HELP-----------   Lst Chg Date:  05/20/88
    ATREQUIS  Size: chrs-80 lns-15  chrs-72 lns-10    Lst Chg Time:  14:09:53
              Home: col--0  lin-2   col--3  lin-9     Created Date:  07/10/87
================================================================================
{ATREQNM1            APPLICANT SEARCH INPUT SCREEN        TODAY'S DATE: /d    ~
{                                                                              ~
{                 Requisition Number to Match:~____{                           ~
>                                               A
{
{         Enter the number of the Employment Requisition for which you         ~
{         you wish Applicants matched.  Any matching applicant records         ~
{         will be placed in the Temporary Applicant File for your review.      ~
{         This review may be done after this program has terminated using      ~
{         the View Matched Applicant Records function on the main ATS          ~
{         menu.  WARNING: EACH time this program is executed, the Temp-        ~
{         orary Applicant File is CLEARED; any existing records are            ~
{         REMOVED.  Press F4-Abort NOW, if records exist in the Temporary      ~
{         Applicant File that you wish to save.                                ~
{                                                                              ~

    Formulas:

       A - REQ-NO

Name: ATREQNM2, Requisition Number Input Screen #2

    Link/Frmt      Screen--------   HELP-----------   Lst Chg Date:  05/20/88
    ATREQUIS  Size: chrs-80 lns-18  chrs-72 lns-10    Lst Chg Time:  14:10:00
              Home: col--0  lin-2   col--3  lin-9     Created Date:  07/10/87
================================================================================
{ATREQNM2            APPLICANT SEARCH INPUT SCREEN        TODAY'S DATE: /d    ~
{                                                                              ~
{                 Requisition Number to Match:~____     {                      ~
>                                               A
{
{                         Job Title:~_____{                       ~
>                                    B
{
{                         Req Date:~_____           {                       ~
>                                   C
{
{                       Department:~_____{                       ~
>                                   D
{
{                           Status:~_____          {                       ~
>                                   E
{
{         CONFIRM: This is the Requisition you wish to match to                ~
{                  available Applicants.  If not, press F4-Abort NOW           ~
{                  and re-enter the Requisition Number.                        ~
{

    Formulas:

       A - REQ-NO              D - DEPARTMENT
       B - JOB-TITLE           E - REQ-STATUS
       C - /FIELD(8)=REQ-DATE
```

+---+
| **SCREEN DISPLAY CODES USED**: |
| { - Start Reverse Video Background   /d - Terminal Date |
| ~ - End Reverse Video Basckground   > - Identifies a Field for the Report |
| (not in screen definition)|
+---+

APPENDIX 5: ATS SCREEN DEFINITIONS

```
Name: ATREQUIS, Employment Requisitions Screen

    Link/Frmt     Screen---------    HELP-----------   Lst Chg Date:   02/23/88
    ATREQUIS    Size: chrs-80  lns-18  chrs-73  lns-6  Lst Chg Time:   15:51:20
                Home: col--0   lin-2   col--3   lin-16 Created Date:   07/10/87
=================================================================================
(ATREQUIS              EMPLOYMENT REQUISITIONS           TODAY'S DATE: /d      ~
{                                                                              ~
{ Requisition Number:~____(              Requisition Date:~_____(           ~
>                      A                                   B
{                                                                              ~
({|--------POSITION INFORMATION-----------|--PERSONNEL DEPARTMENT INFORMATION--|~
({| Job Code:~____    ({Job Status:~__    ({|Recruiter:~_____  _____({|~
>            C                     D                   N        b
({|Job Title:~_____  ({| Internal Search:~_ ({New Position:~_({|~
>            E                                               O                  P
({|   Exempt:~_      ({EEOC Job Cat:~_     ({| Replacement For:~_____         ({|~
>           V                      W                             Q
({|Salary Grade:~__                        ({|Replacement Date:~_____       ({|~
>              F                                               R
({|Sal - Min:~_____ ({Max:~_____     (---REQUISITION APPROVAL INFORMATION----
>           X              Y
({|Part Time Rate:~_____                ({|Approver Name:~_____     ({|~
>               G                                           S
({|Department:~_____      ({|Title:~_____ ({Date:~_____  ({|~
>            H                                      T              U
({|  Location:~_____             (----REQUISITION STATUS INFORMATION-----
>           I
({|    Shift:~_____                     ({|Status:~_____ ({Date:~_____({|~
>         J                                         c                d
({|Education Level Required For Job:~_     ({|Filled By:~_____ _____   ({|~
>                                  K                      e      f
({|Prim Exp Code:~_  _____     ({|No. of Days To Fill Job:~____   ({|~
>               L   Z                                                  g
({|Secd Exp Code:~_  _____     ({|Total Recruitment Costs:~_____ ({|~
>               M   a                                                  h
({|-------------------------------------|---------------------------------------|~
```

Formulas:

```
        A - REQ-NO                R - /FIELD(8)=REPLACEMENT-DATE
        B - /FIELD(8)=REQ-DATE    S - REQ-APPROVER
        C - JOB-CODE              T - REQ-APPROVER-TITLE
        D - JOB-STATUS            U - /FIELD(8)=REQ-APPROVAL-DATE
        E - JOB-TITLE             V - EXEMPT-CLASS
        F - SALARY-GRADE          W - EEOC-JOB-CAT
        G - PT-RATE               X - SALARY-MIN
        H - DEPARTMENT            Y - SALARY-MAX
        I - LOCATION              Z - /FIELD(20)=PRIM-EXP-DESC
        J - SHIFT                 a - /FIELD(20)=SEC-EXP-DESC
        K - EDUC-LEVEL            b - /FIELD(17)=RECRUT-NAME
        L - PRIM-EXP-CODE         c - REQ-STATUS
        M - SEC-EXP-CODE          d - /FIELD(8)=REQ-DISP-DATE
        N - RECRUITER             e - IDENT
        O - INTERNAL-SRCH         f - /FIELD(17)=NAME
        P - NEW-POSITION          g - NO-DAYS-TO-FILL
        Q - REPLACEMENT-FOR       h - TOTAL-REC-EXP
```

SCREEN DISPLAY CODES USED:

{ - Start Reverse Video Background   /d - Terminal Date

~ - End Reverse Video Basckground   > - Identifies a Field for the Report
                                               (not in screen definition)

APPENDIX 5: ATS SCREEN DEFINITIONS

```
Name: ATREQUIh, Emplmt Req'stns Help Refresh Screen

     Link/Frmt          Screen---------    HELP-----------  Lst Chg Date:  05/20/88
     ATREQUIS    Size:  chrs-80   lns-5    chrs-73  lns-6   Lst Chg Time:  18:50:21
                 Home:  col--0    lin-15   col--3   lin-16  Created Date:  07/10/87
===============================================================================
{|     Shift:~                              ({Status:~         (Date:~        {|~
{|Education Level Required For Job:~        (|Filled By:~                     {|~
{|Prim Exp Code:~                           (|No. of Days To Fill Job:~       {|~
{|Secd Exp Code:~                           (|Total Recruitment Costs:~       {|~
{|--------------------------------------|---------------------------------|~

Name: ATREQUIr, Emplmt Req'stns View Refresh Screen

     Link/Frmt          Screen---------    HELP-----------  Lst Chg Date:  05/20/88
     ATREQUIS    Size:  chrs-80   lns-8    chrs-73  lns-6   Lst Chg Time:  18:50:28
                 Home:  col--0    lin-12   col--3   lin-16  Created Date:  07/10/87
===============================================================================
                                           (|Approver Name:~                  {|~
                                           (|Title:~           (Date:~        {|~
                                           {----REQUISITION STATUS INFORMATION----~
                                           (|Status:~          (Date:~        {|~
                                           (|Filled By:~                      {|~
                                           (|No. of Days To Fill Job:~        {|~
                                           (|Total Recruitment Costs:~        {|~
{|--------------------------------------|---------------------------------|~

Name: ATSALGRD, Salary Grade Screen

     Link/Frmt          Screen---------    HELP-----------  Lst Chg Date:  03/26/88
     ATSALGRD    Size:  chrs-80   lns-24   chrs-72  lns-10  Lst Chg Time:  17:53:11
                 Home:  col--0    lin-0    col--3   lin-9   Created Date:  07/10/87
===============================================================================


{Salary Grade:~__
>                A
{ Description:~_____
>                B
{ Min. Salary:~_____
>                C
{ Max. Salary:~_____
>                D

    Formulas:

       A - SALARY-GRADE
       B - SALARY-DESC
       C - SALARY-MIN
       D - SALARY-MAX
```

SCREEN DISPLAY CODES USED:

{ - Start Reverse Video Background   /d - Terminal Date

~ - End Reverse Video Basckground   > - Identifies a Field for the Report
                                                (not in screen definition)

Appendix 6

ATS DATA ENTRY SCRIPTS

All definitions from the sample Applicant Tracking System are from the AT library.

APPLICANT MASTERFILE MAINTENANCE

APMM0	Setup	Primary
APMM1	Continuation #1	Continuation
APMM1A	Add Record	Overlay
APMM1C	Copy Record	Overlay
APMM1D	Delete Record	Overlay
APMM1E	Edit Record #1	Overlay
APMM1K	Key Change	Overlay
APMM1L	Main Lookup	Overlay
APMM1a	Requisition Number	Overlay
APMM1b	Disposition Code	Overlay
APMM1c	Experience Code	Overlay
APMM1d	Requisition Update	Overlay
APMM2E	Edit Record #2	Overlay
APMMDS	Data Section	Copy
APMMVR	View Refresh	Copy

APPENDIX 6: ATS DATA ENTRY SCRIPTS

REQUISITION MASTERFILE MAINTENANCE

RQMM0	Setup	Primary
RQMM1	Continuation #1	Continuation
RQMM1A	Add Record	Overlay
RQMM1C	Copy Record	Overlay
RQMM1D	Delete Record	Overlay
RQMM1E	Edit Record	Overlay
RQMM1K	Key Change	Overlay
RQMM1L	Main Lookup	Overlay
RQMM1a	Job Code	Overlay
RQMM1b	Salary Grade	Overlay
RQMM1c	Experience Codes	Overlay
RQMM1d	Recruiter	Overlay
RQMM1e	Applicant	Overlay
RQMMDS	Data Section	Copy
RQMMHR	Help Refresh	Copy
RQMMVR	View Refresh	Copy

APPENDIX 6: ATS DATA ENTRY SCRIPTS

APPLICANT MASTERFILE MAINTENANCE

APMM0 - Setup

```
Script: AT APMM0    Type: 1
Desc: Appl. Masterfile Mx - Setup                                  Page: 1
Last Change Date: 05/20/88    Last Compile Date: 05/26/88
              Time: 18:33:50                Time: 08:42:53    Date: 05/31/88
================================================================================
     * APPLICANT MASTERFILE MAINTENANCE PRIMARY SCRIPT
     * THE FOLLOWING INCLUDE SCRIPT CONTAINS THE REQUIRED DATA DEFINITIONS
         INCLUDE ATAPMMDS

     MAIN-PROCEDURE
     *     SETTRACE PAUSE DIRECTIVE @(0,1), "NS", NS-NO, " CS", CS-NO,
     *           " T:", TERM-KEY, " M:", MODE-FLAG
     * OPEN SCREENS, VIEWS, AND LINKS
         OPEN SCREEN ATAPGENL
         OPEN SCREEN ATAPCOST
         OPEN SCREEN ATAPGENL
         OPEN SCREEN ATAPGEN1
         OPEN SCREEN ATAPCOS1
         LET FILE-NAME = "ATAPMSTR"
         OPEN ATAPMSTR
             BUSY  IS BUSY-FILE
             ERROR IS ERROR-FILE
         LET FILE-NAME = "ATRQMSTR"
         OPEN ATRQMSTR
             BUSY  IS BUSY-FILE
             ERROR IS ERROR-FILE
         LET FILE-NAME = "ATDISPCD"
         OPEN ATDISPCD
             BUSY  IS BUSY-FILE
             ERROR IS ERROR-FILE
         LET FILE-NAME = "ATEXPCDE"
         OPEN ATEXPCDE
             BUSY  IS BUSY-FILE
             ERROR IS ERROR-FILE
     * CONTINUE WITH SCRIPT, IF FILES ARE OKAY
         IF MODE-FLAG <> "NOGO " THEN
             PRINT SCREEN ATAPGENL
             LET CS-NAME = "APGENL", SORT-NO = 0, CS-NO = 2, NS-NO = 1,
                 MODE-FLAG = "      ", D$ = DAY,
                 CURRENT-DATE = D$(1,2) + D$(4,2) + D$(7,2)
     * RUN CONTINUATION SCRIPT
             RUN "ATAPMM1"
         ENDIF
         TERMINATE

     BUSY-FILE
         INPUT MESSAGE "N,14,,,," + FILE-NAME INTO MSG-RESP USING "ATMSGS"
         LET MODE-FLAG = "NOGO "

     ERROR-FILE
         INPUT MESSAGE "N,15,,,," + FILE-NAME INTO MSG-RESP USING "ATMSGS"
         LET MODE-FLAG = "NOGO "

     END-SCRIPT
```

APPENDIX 6: ATS DATA ENTRY SCRIPTS

APMM1 - Continuation #1

```
Script: AT APMM1    Type: 2
Desc: Appl. Masterfile Mx - Cont #1                              Page: 1
Last Change Date: 05/20/88    Last Compile Date: 05/26/88
            Time: 18:30:10                Time: 08:44:04    Date: 05/31/88
================================================================================
      * APPLICANT MASTERFILE MAINTENANCE CONTINUATION SCRIPT #1
      * THE FOLLOWING INCLUDE SCRIPT CONTAINS THE REQUIRED DATA DEFINITIONS
          INCLUDE ATAPMMDS

      MAIN-PROCEDURE
      *     SETTRACE PAUSE DIRECTIVE @(0,1), "NS", NS-NO, " CS", CS-NO,
      *               " T:", TERM-KEY, " M:", MODE-FLAG
      * MAIN INPUT LOOP
          DO LOOP UNTIL MODE-FLAG = "EXIT "
              IF CS-NAME <> "APGENL" THEN
                  PRINT 'CS'
                  PRINT SCREEN ATAPGENL
              ENDIF
              LET MODE-FLAG = "INIT ", CS-NAME = "APGENL"
              PRINT MESSAGE "P,7,,,,Appl ID" USING "ATMSGS"
              PRINT MESSAGE "P,8" USING "ATMSGS"
              INPUT SCREEN ATAPGENL CLEAR KEY
                  POST-HELP PROCESS REDO-SCREEN-INIT
      * DO APPROPRIATE PROCEDURE DEPENDING ON PKKEY PRESSED
              IF TERM-KEY = 10 OR TERM-KEY = 0 THEN
                  DO FIND-EXACT-RECORD
              ELSE
                  IF TERM-KEY = 3 THEN
                      READ ATAPMSTR USING KEY ATAPGENL.IDENT
                          PROCESSING  IS EDIT-RECORD
                          MISSING KEY IS ADD-RECORD
                          BUSY        IS BUSY-RECORD
                          END         IS ADD-RECORD
                  ELSE
                      IF TERM-KEY = 8 THEN
                          DO LOOKUP-RECORDS
                          IF ATAPGENL.IDENT <> "        " THEN
                              DO FIND-EXACT-RECORD
                          ENDIF
                      ELSE
                          IF TERM-KEY = 1 OR TERM-KEY = 2 THEN
                              DO SET-RECORD
                              DO FIND-NEXT-RECORD
                          ELSE
                              IF TERM-KEY = 4 AND MODE-FLAG = "INIT " THEN
                                  LET MODE-FLAG = "EXIT "
                              ENDIF
                          ENDIF
                      ENDIF
                  ENDIF
              ENDIF
      * DO 'NEXT RECORD' EDIT UNTIL TERMINATED
              DO FIND-NEXT-RECORD WHILE
                  MODE-FLAG = "NEXT " OR MODE-FLAG = "PREV "
      * DO 'COPY RECORD' WHEN REQUESTED
              IF MODE-FLAG = "COPY " THEN
                  DO COPY-RECORD
              ENDIF
      * DO 'DELETE RECORD' WHEN REQUESTED
              IF MODE-FLAG = "DELET" THEN
                  DO DELETE-RECORD
              ENDIF
          ENDLOOP
          TERMINATE
```

APMM1 - Continuation #1 (Continued)

```
    SET-RECORD
    * SET MODE BASED ON TERM-KEY
          IF TERM-KEY = 1 THEN
              LET MODE-FLAG = "NEXT "
          ELSE
              IF TERM-KEY = 2 THEN
                  LET MODE-FLAG = "PREV "
              ENDIF
          ENDIF
    * BASED ON SORT USED, SET KEY POINTER IN LINK
    *     IF SORT-NO = 0 THEN
              READ ATAPMSTR USING KEY ATAPGENL.IDENT
    *     ELSE
    *         IF SORT-NO = 1 THEN
    *             READ ATAPMSTR USING KEY SORT SORT-NO IS SORT-NAME (NEW DN??)
    *         ENDIF
    *     ENDIF

    FIND-NEXT-RECORD
          IF MODE-FLAG = "NEXT " THEN
              READ ATAPMSTR USING KEY NEXT
                  PROCESSING  IS EDIT-RECORD
                  MISSING KEY IS MISSING-RECORD
                  BUSY        IS BUSY-RECORD
                  END         IS END-OF-MAIN-FILE
          ELSE
              IF MODE-FLAG = "PREV " THEN
                  READ ATAPMSTR USING KEY PREVIOUS
                      PROCESSING  IS EDIT-RECORD
                      MISSING KEY IS MISSING-RECORD
                      BUSY        IS BUSY-RECORD
                      END         IS BEG-OF-MAIN-FILE
              ENDIF
          ENDIF

    FIND-EXACT-RECORD
          READ ATAPMSTR USING KEY ATAPGENL.IDENT
              PROCESSING  IS EDIT-RECORD
              MISSING KEY IS MISSING-RECORD
              BUSY        IS BUSY-RECORD
              END         IS END-OF-MAIN-FILE

    ADD-RECORD
          RUN OVERLAY "ATAPMM1A"

    EDIT-RECORD

          DO LOOP UNTIL CS-NO = NS-NO OR MODE-FLAG = "END  "
              IF NS-NO = 1 THEN
                  RUN OVERLAY "ATAPMM1E"
              ELSE
                  RUN OVERLAY "ATAPMM2E"
              ENDIF
          ENDLOOP

    LOOKUP-RECORDS
          RUN OVERLAY "ATAPMM1L"

    COPY-RECORD
          RUN OVERLAY "ATAPMM1C"

    DELETE-RECORD
          RUN OVERLAY "ATAPMM1D"
```

APPENDIX 6: ATS DATA ENTRY SCRIPTS

APMM1 - Continuation #1 (Continued)

```
    BUSY-RECORD
        INPUT MESSAGE "N,5,,,,Applicant" INTO MSG-RESP USING "ATMSGS"

    MISSING-RECORD
        INPUT MESSAGE "N,1,,,,Applicant" INTO MSG-RESP USING "ATMSGS"

    END-OF-MAIN-FILE
        INPUT MESSAGE "N,2,,,,Applicant" INTO MSG-RESP USING "ATMSGS"
        LET MODE-FLAG = "EOF  "

    BEG-OF-MAIN-FILE
        INPUT MESSAGE "N,9,,,,Applicant" INTO MSG-RESP USING "ATMSGS"
        LET MODE-FLAG = "BOF  "

    REDO-SCREEN-INIT
    * REDISPLAY SCREEN AFTER HELP IS DISPLAYED FROM KEY FIELD(S)
        PRINT SCREEN ATAPGENh

    END-SCRIPT
```

APMM1A - Add Record

```
Script: AT APMM1A  Type: 3
Desc: Appl. Masterfile Mx - Add Record                           Page: 1
Last Change Date: 05/20/88    Last Compile Date: 05/26/88
            Time: 19:32:14                Time: 08:46:19    Date: 05/31/88
================================================================================
    * APPLICANT MASTERFILE MAINTENANCE OVERLAY - ADD RECORD
    * THE FOLLOWING INCLUDE SCRIPT CONTAINS THE REQUIRED DATA DEFINITIONS
        INCLUDE ATAPMMDS

    MAIN-PROCEDURE
        DO LOOP UNTIL MODE-FLAG = "END  "
            PRINT MESSAGE "P,12" USING "ATMSGS"
            PRINT MESSAGE "P,10" USING "ATMSGS"
    * CLEAR SCREEN FORMAT BEFORE ALLOWING DATA ENTRY (SAVE KEY VALUE)
            LET OLD-IDENT = ATAPGENL.IDENT
            LET ATAPGENL = ""
            LET ATAPGENL.IDENT = OLD-IDENT
    * SET FIELD DEFAULTS AND SAVE "OLD" VALUES FOR COMPARISON
            LET ATAPGENL.DATE-ENTERED = CURRENT-DATE, MODE-FLAG = "ADD  ",
                ATAPGENL.NEXT-SCRN-NO = 2
            INPUT SCREEN ATAPGENL CLEAR DATA
                PRE        PROCESS COMMENTS, SKIP-REST
                POST       PROCESS IDENT, SET-TERM-KEY,
                                   REQ-NO, GET-REQSTN-RECORD,
                                   CUR-EXP-CODE, GET-EXPCDE-RECORD,
                                   DISP-CODE, GET-DISPCD-RECORD,
                                   DISP-DATE, CK-FOR-VALID-DATE,
                                   NEXT-SCRN-NO, SKIP-BACK
                POST-HELP  PROCESS REDO-SCREEN-1
    * SET FIELD VALUES FOR SCREEN #2
            IF MODE-FLAG = "ADD  " AND TERM-KEY <> 4 THEN
                LET MODE-FLAG = "ADD2 "
                LET ATAPCOST = ""
                LET ATAPCOST.IDENT = ATAPGENL.IDENT,
                    ATAPCOST.NAME = ATAPGENL.NAME,
                    ATAPCOST.RECRUITER = ATAPGENL.RECRUITER,
                    ATAPCOST.JOB-TITLE = ATAPGENL.JOB-TITLE,
                    ATAPCOST.AVAIL-DATE = ATAPGENL.AVAIL-DATE,
                    ATAPCOST.NEXT-SCRN-NO = 2
```

APPENDIX 6: ATS DATA ENTRY SCRIPTS

APMM1A - Add Record (Continued)

```
                PRINT 'CS'
                PRINT MESSAGE "P,12" USING "ATMSGS"
                PRINT MESSAGE "P,10" USING "ATMSGS"
                PRINT SCREEN ATAPCOST
                LET CS-NAME = "APCOST"
                PRINT SCREEN ATAPCOST DATA
                INPUT SCREEN ATAPCOST DATA
                    PRE        PROCESS IDENT, SKIP-REST
                    POST       PROCESS OTHER-REC-EXP, CALC-TOTAL-EXP
                    POST-HELP PROCESS REDO-SCREEN-2
            ENDIF
    * SET MODE TO "END", IF PF4 KEY WAS PRESSED
            LET M$ = MODE-FLAG
            IF M$(1,3) = "ADD" AND TERM-KEY = 4 THEN
                LET MODE-FLAG = "END    "
            ENDIF
    * ASK TO SAVE NEW RECORD; IF "Y", MOVE SCREEN DATA TO LINK
            IF M$(1,3) = "ADD" AND TERM-KEY <> 4 THEN
                INPUT MESSAGE "Y,3" INTO MSG-RESP USING "ATMSGS"

                IF MSG-RESP = "Y" THEN
                    LET ATAPMSTR = ATAPGENL
                    LET ATAPMSTR = ATAPCOST
                    ADD ATAPMSTR USING KEY IDENT
                        DUPLICATE KEY IS DUPLICATE-RECORD
                ENDIF
            ENDIF
            IF MODE-FLAG = "ADD2 " THEN
                PRINT 'CS'
                PRINT SCREEN ATAPGENL
            ENDIF
            IF MODE-FLAG = "LKUPA" THEN DO LOOKUP-RECORDS ENDIF
        ENDLOOP

SET-TERM-KEY
    IF TERM-KEY = 8 THEN
        LET MODE-FLAG = "LKUPA", ATAPGENL.FIELD = 99
    ENDIF

LOOKUP-RECORDS
    RUN OVERLAY "ATAPMM1L"
    LET IDENT = ""

SKIP-REST
* SKIP OVER REST OF THE FIELDS ON THE SCREEN
    LET ATAPGENL.FIELD = 99, ATAPCOST.FIELD = 99

SKIP-BACK
* SKIP BACK TO LAST ENTRY FIELD, IF UP-ARROW PRESSED
    IF TERM-KEY = -4 THEN
        LET ATAPGENL.FIELD = -5
    ENDIF

GET-REQSTN-RECORD
    IF ATAPGENL.REQ-NO <> "0000" OR TERM-KEY = 8 THEN
        IF TERM-KEY = 8 THEN LET MODE-FLAG = "LKUPA" ENDIF
        RUN OVERLAY "ATAPMM1a"
        IF MODE-FLAG = "LKUPA" THEN LET MODE-FLAG = "ADD  " ENDIF
    ELSE
        IF ATAPGENL.REQ-NO = "0000" THEN
            LET ATAPGENL.RECRUITER = "", ATAPGENL.JOB-TITLE = ""
            PRINT SCREEN ATAPGENL DATA-NAME LIST RECRUITER, JOB-TITLE
        ENDIF
    ENDIF
```

APPENDIX 6: ATS DATA ENTRY SCRIPTS

APMM1A - Add Record (Continued)

```
     GET-DISPCD-RECORD
         IF ATAPGENL.DISP-CODE <> "  " OR TERM-KEY = 8 THEN
             IF TERM-KEY = 8 THEN LET MODE-FLAG = "LKUPA" ENDIF
             RUN OVERLAY "ATAPMM1b"
             IF MODE-FLAG = "LKUPA" THEN LET MODE-FLAG = "ADD  " ENDIF
         ELSE
             IF ATAPGENL.DISP-CODE = "  " THEN
                 LET ATAPGENL.DISP-DESC = ""
                 PRINT SCREEN ATAPGENL DATA-NAME LIST DISP-DESC
             ENDIF
         ENDIF

     CK-FOR-VALID-DATE
         IF ATAPGENL.DISP-CODE <> "  " AND TERM-KEY <> -4 THEN
             IF ATAPGENL.DISP-DATE = "        " THEN
                 INPUT MESSAGE "N,11,,,,Disp Date" INTO MSG-RESP USING "ATMSGS"
                 LET ATAPGENL.FIELD = 0
             ELSE
                 LET ATAPGENL.FIELD = 5
             ENDIF
         ELSE
             IF ATAPGENL.DISP-CODE = "  " AND TERM-KEY <> -4 THEN
                 LET ATAPGENL.FIELD = 5
             ENDIF
         ENDIF

     GET-EXPCDE-RECORD
         IF TERM-KEY = 8 THEN LET MODE-FLAG = "LKUPA" ENDIF
         RUN OVERLAY "ATAPMM1c"
         IF MODE-FLAG = "LKUPA" THEN LET MODE-FLAG = "ADD  " ENDIF
         IF ATAPGENL.CUR-EXP-CODE = "  " THEN LET ATAPGENL.FIELD = 0 ENDIF

     CALC-TOTAL-EXP
   * CALCULATE TOTAL REC EXPENSES AND NO DAYS TO FILL POSITION
         LET TOTAL-REC-EXP = ADVERT + AGENCY-FEES + EMPLOYEE-REFERRAL +
             RELOCATION-EXP + TVL-LODG-EXP + OTHER-REC-EXP
         PRINT SCREEN ATAPCOST DATA-NAME LIST TOTAL-REC-EXP

     DUPLICATE-RECORD
         INPUT MESSAGE "N,4,,,,Applicant" INTO MSG-RESP USING "ATMSGS"

     REDO-SCREEN-1
         PRINT SCREEN ATAPGENh
         PRINT SCREEN ATAPGENL DATA-NAME LIST NEXT-SCRN-NO

     REDO-SCREEN-2
         PRINT SCREEN ATAPCOSh
         PRINT SCREEN ATAPCOST DATA-NAME LIST NEXT-SCRN-NO

     END-SCRIPT
```

APPENDIX 6: ATS DATA ENTRY SCRIPTS

APMM1C - Copy Record

```
Script: AT APMM1C   Type: 3
Desc: Appl. Masterfile Mx - Copy Record                          Page: 1
Last Change Date: 05/20/88    Last Compile Date: 05/26/88
          Time: 19:32:27                Time: 08:47:04     Date: 05/31/88
================================================================================
    * APPLICANT MASTERFILE MAINTENANCE OVERLAY - COPY RECORD
    * THE FOLLOWING INCLUDE SCRIPT CONTAINS THE REQUIRED DATA DEFINITIONS
        INCLUDE ATAPMMDS

    MAIN-PROCEDURE
    * MAKE A COPY OF THE CURRENT RECORD
        IF CS-NAME <> "APGENL" THEN
            PRINT 'CS'
            PRINT SCREEN ATAPGENL
        ENDIF
        LET CS-NAME = "APGENL"
        PRINT MESSAGE "P,14" USING "ATMSGS"
        PRINT MESSAGE "P,15,,,,Applicant Ident" USING "ATMSGS"
        INPUT SCREEN ATAPGENL CLEAR DATA-NAME LIST IDENT
            POST-HELP PROCESS REDO-SCREEN-INIT
        IF TERM-KEY <> 4 THEN
            LET ATAPMSTR = ATAPCOST
            LET ATAPMSTR = ATAPGENL
            ADD ATAPMSTR USING KEY IDENT
            DUPLICATE KEY IS DUPLICATE-RECORD
        ENDIF

    DUPLICATE-RECORD
        INPUT MESSAGE "N,4,,,,Applicant" INTO MSG-RESP USING "ATMSGS"

    REDO-SCREEN-INIT
        PRINT SCREEN ATAPGENL

    END-SCRIPT
```

APMM1D - Delete Record

```
Script: AT APMM1D   Type: 3
Desc: Appl. Masterfile Mx - Delete Record                        Page: 1
Last Change Date: 05/20/88    Last Compile Date: 05/26/88
          Time: 18:30:49                Time: 08:47:41     Date: 05/31/88
================================================================================
    * APPLICANT MASTERFILE MAINTENANCE OVERLAY - DELETE RECORD
    * THE FOLLOWING INCLUDE SCRIPT CONTAINS THE REQUIRED DATA DEFINITIONS
        INCLUDE ATAPMMDS

    MAIN-PROCEDURE
    * DELETE THE CURRENT RECORD AFTER CONFIRM
        PRINT MESSAGE "P,14" USING "ATMSGS"
        INPUT MESSAGE "Y,2" INTO MSG-RESP USING "ATMSGS"
        IF MSG-RESP = "Y" THEN
    * CHECK REFERENTIAL INTEGRITY RULES BEFORE ALLOWING DELETE
            DO REFERENTIAL-INTEGRITY
            IF DEL-MODE = "Y" THEN
                DELETE ATAPMSTR USING KEY OLD-IDENT
                    MISSING KEY IS MISSING-RECORD
                    BUSY        IS BUSY-RECORD
            ENDIF
        ENDIF
```

APPENDIX 6: ATS DATA ENTRY SCRIPTS

APMM1D - Delete Record (Continued)

```
    REFERENTIAL-INTEGRITY
    * FIND ANY REQUISITION RECORDS THAT CONTAIN OLD-IDENT USING THE IDENT
    *   SECONDARY KEY
        LET DEL-MODE = "Y"
        READ ATRQMSTR USING KEY SORT 3 RANGE FROM OLD-IDENT TO
            OLD-IDENT + "zzzz"
            PROCESSING IS DISALLOW-DELETE
            BUSY       IS BUSY-RECORD
    * CLEAR ATRQMSTR LINK FORMAT AFTER USE
        LET ATRQMSTR = ""

    DISALLOW-DELETE
        INPUT MESSAGE "N,10,,,,Applicant,Req'stn" INTO MSG-RESP USING
            "ATMSGS"
        LET DEL-MODE = "N"
        TERMINATE

    MISSING-RECORD
        INPUT MESSAGE "N,1,,,,Applicant" INTO MSG-RESP USING "ATMSGS"

    BUSY-RECORD
        INPUT MESSAGE "N,5,,,,Applicant" INTO MSG-RESP USING "ATMSGS"

    END-SCRIPT
```

APMM1E - Edit Record #1

```
    Script: AT APMM1E   Type: 3
    Desc: Appl. Masterfile Mx - Edit Record 1                        Page: 1
    Last Change Date: 05/20/88   Last Compile Date: 05/26/88
            Time: 18:34:00                Time: 08:49:58     Date: 05/31/88
    ===============================================================================
    * APPLICANT MASTERFILE MAINTENANCE OVERLAY - EDIT RECORD #1
    * THE FOLLOWING INCLUDE SCRIPT CONTAINS THE REQUIRED DATA DEFINITIONS
        INCLUDE ATAPMMDS

    MAIN-PROCEDURE
    *    SETTRACE PAUSE DIRECTIVE @(0,1), "NS", NS-NO, " CS", CS-NO,
    *       " T:", TERM-KEY, " M:", MODE-FLAG
    * SAVE MODE FOR RETURN AFTER EDIT; SET UP SCREEN NUMBER
    * SET MODE TO DISPLAY AND SET DELETE MODE FLAG
        LET OLD-MODE-FLAG = MODE-FLAG, CS-NO = 1, MODE-FLAG = "DISPL",
            DEL-MODE = "Y"
    * CLEAR OLD SCREEN FROM TERMINAL, IF NECESSARY
        IF CS-NAME <> "APGENL" THEN
            PRINT 'CS'
        ENDIF
    * CLEAR SCREEN FORMAT BEFORE SETTING NEW RECORD INTO IT
        LET ATAPGENL = ""
    * MOVE DATA FORMAT TO BOTH SCREEN FORMATS FOR DISPLAY
        LET ATAPGENL = ATAPMSTR
        LET ATAPCOST = ATAPMSTR
    * SAVE COPY OF KEY TO DETECT KEY CHANGES; SAVE OLD FIELD VALUES
        LET OLD-IDENT = ATAPGENL.IDENT, OLD-REQ-NO = ATAPGENL.REQ-NO,
            OLD-EXP-CODE = ATAPGENL.CUR-EXP-CODE,
            OLD-DISP-CD = ATAPGENL.DISP-CODE,
            ORIG-REQ-NO = ATAPGENL.REQ-NO,
            ORIG-DISP-CD = ATAPGENL.DISP-CODE
    *GET SECONDARY RECORDS AND MOVE DATA NOT SAVED TO SCREEN FORMAT
        DO GET-REQSTN-RECORD
        DO GET-DISPCD-RECORD
    * SET SCREEN NAME AND NEXT SCREEN NUMBER
        IF CS-NAME <> "APGENL" THEN
            PRINT SCREEN ATAPGENL
        ENDIF
```

APMM1E - Edit Record #1 (Continued)

```
            LET ATAPGENL.NEXT-SCRN-NO = NS-NO, CS-NAME = "APGENL"
* PRINT APPROPRIATE PFKEY MESSAGE ('DELETE' IS ALWAYS ALLOWED)
            PRINT MESSAGE "P,28" USING "ATMSGS"
            PRINT MESSAGE "P,21" USING "ATMSGS"
* DISPLAY SCREEN DATA AND ACCEPT INPUT AT KEY FIELD ONLY
            PRINT SCREEN ATAPGENL DATA
            INPUT SCREEN ATAPGENL KEY
                POST         PROCESS IDENT, SET-TERM-KEY
                POST-HELP PROCESS REDO-SCREEN
            IF MODE-FLAG = "EDIT " THEN
                CHANGE ATAPMSTR USING KEY OLD-IDENT
                    PROCESSING   IS EDIT-RECORD
                    ERROR        IS ERROR-RECORD
                    MISSING KEY  IS MISSING-RECORD
                    BUSY         IS BUSY-RECORD
                    END          IS END-OF-MAIN-FILE
            ENDIF
* SET NEXT SCREEN FOR FURTHER DISPLAY
            IF MODE-FLAG = "NSCRN" THEN
                DO SET-NEXT-SCREEN
            ENDIF
* CHECK FOR CHANGE IN KEY VALUE & DO APPROPRIATE PROCESSING
            IF OLD-IDENT <> ATAPGENL.IDENT THEN
                DO CHANGE-KEY-VALUE
            ENDIF
* CHECK FOR DISPOSITION CODE CHANGED FROM 'HIRED' TO SOMETHING ELSE
*   OR STILL 'HIRED' BUT REQ NUMBER CHANGED
            IF (ORIG-DISP-CD = "HI" AND ATAPGENL.DISP-CODE <> "HI" AND
                ORIG-REQ-NO <> "0000") OR (ORIG-DISP-CD = "HI" AND
                ATAPGENL.DISP-CODE = "HI" AND ORIG-REQ-NO <> ATAPGENL.REQ-NO)
                THEN DO REOPEN-ORIG-REQ
            ENDIF
* CHECK FOR DISPOSITION CODE CHANGED TO 'HIRED' OR STILL 'HIRED' BUT
*   REQ NUMBER CHANGED
            IF (ORIG-DISP-CD <> "HI" AND ATAPGENL.DISP-CODE = "HI" AND
                ATAPGENL.REQ-NO <> "0000") OR (ORIG-DISP-CD = "HI" AND
                ATAPGENL.DISP-CODE = "HI" AND ORIG-REQ-NO <> ATAPGENL.REQ-NO)
                THEN DO CLOSE-CURRENT-REQ
            ENDIF
* SET MODE-FLAG BACK TO 'NEXT' OR 'PREV' AFTER EDIT
            IF (MODE-FLAG = "EDIT " OR MODE-FLAG = "NSCRN") AND
               (OLD-MODE-FLAG = "NEXT " OR OLD-MODE-FLAG = "PREV ") THEN
                LET MODE-FLAG = OLD-MODE-FLAG
            ENDIF

EDIT-RECORD
* ISSUE MESSAGE THAT RECORD IS NOW LOCKED
            PRINT MESSAGE "P,25" USING "ATMSGS"
* SAVE A COPY OF THE SCREEN FOR EDIT COMPARISONS
            LET ATAPGENL.IDENT = OLD-IDENT
            LET S$ = ATAPGENL
* COLLECT DATA FROM SCREEN AND UPDATE LINK
            PRINT SCREEN ATAPGENL DATA-NAME LIST IDENT
            INPUT SCREEN ATAPGENL DATA
                    PRE         PROCESS DATE-ENTERED, SKIP-FIELD,
                                        COMMENTS, SKIP-REST
```

APPENDIX 6: ATS DATA ENTRY SCRIPTS

APMM1E - Edit Record #1 (Continued)

```
              POST        PROCESS IDENT, SET-TERM-KEY,
                                  REQ-NO, GET-REQSTN-RECORD,
                                  CUR-EXP-CODE, GET-EXPCDE-RECORD,
                                  DISP-CODE, GET-DISPCD-RECORD,
                                  DISP-DATE, CK-FOR-VALID-DATE,
                                  NEXT-SCRN-NO, SKIP-BACK
              POST-HELP PROCESS REDO-SCREEN
* REMOVE LOCKED RECORD MESSAGE, IF STILL THERE
     PRINT @(0,0), 'CL'
* SAVE NEXT SCREEN NUMBER IN CASE USER CHANGED IT
     LET NS-NO = ATAPGENL.NEXT-SCRN-NO
     IF NS-NO > 2 THEN LET NS-NO = 2 ENDIF
     IF NS-NO < 1 THEN LET NS-NO = 1 ENDIF
* SET MODE TO "END", IF PF4 KEY WAS PRESSED
     IF MODE-FLAG = "EDIT "  AND TERM-KEY = 4 THEN
        LET MODE-FLAG = "END  "
     ENDIF
* IF KEY HAS BEEN CHANGED, CONFIRM THAT THIS IS REALLY DESIRED
     IF OLD-IDENT <> ATAPGENL.IDENT THEN
        INPUT MESSAGE "Y,4" INTO MSG-RESP USING "ATMSGS"
        IF MSG-RESP <> "Y" THEN
           LET ATAPGENL.IDENT = OLD-IDENT
           PRINT SCREEN ATAPGENL DATA-NAME LIST IDENT
        ENDIF
     ENDIF
* ASK TO SAVE CHANGES, IF NEEDED; IF "Y", MOVE SCREEN DATA TO LINK
     IF (MODE-FLAG = "EDIT " OR MODE-FLAG = "END  ") AND S$ <> ATAPGENL
        THEN
        INPUT MESSAGE "Y,1" INTO MSG-RESP USING "ATMSGS"
        IF MSG-RESP = "Y" THEN
           LET ATAPMSTR = ATAPGENL
* UPDATE NO-DAYS-TO-FILL POSITION, IF DISP CODE CHANGED
           IF ORIG-DISP-CD <> ATAPGENL.DISP-CODE THEN
              DO UPDATE-NO-DAYS
           ENDIF
        ENDIF
     ENDIF
* SET S$ TO ZERO LENGTH TO SAVE MEMORY
     LET S$ = ""

SET-TERM-KEY
* TERMINATE EDIT INPUT BASED ON PFKEY PRESSED
     IF TERM-KEY = 1 THEN
        LET ATAPGENL.FIELD = 99, MODE-FLAG = "NEXT "
     ELSE
        IF TERM-KEY = 2 THEN
           LET ATAPGENL.FIELD = 99, MODE-FLAG = "PREV "
        ELSE
           IF TERM-KEY = 3 AND DEL-MODE = "Y" THEN
              LET ATAPGENL.FIELD = 99, MODE-FLAG = "DELET"
           ELSE
              IF TERM-KEY = 7 THEN
                 LET ATAPGENL.FIELD = 99, MODE-FLAG = "COPY "
              ELSE
                 IF (TERM-KEY = 0 OR TERM-KEY = -3) AND
                    MODE-FLAG = "EDIT " THEN
                    LET ATAPGENL.FIELD = 2
                 ELSE
                    IF TERM-KEY = 9 THEN
                       LET ATAPGENL.FIELD = 99, MODE-FLAG = "NSCRN"
                    ELSE
```

APMM1E - Edit Record #1 (Continued)

```
                        IF TERM-KEY = 4 THEN
                           LET ATAPGENL.FIELD = 99, MODE-FLAG = "END  "
                        ELSE
                           IF TERM-KEY <> 6 THEN
                              LET MODE-FLAG = "EDIT "
                           ENDIF
                        ENDIF
                     ENDIF
                  ENDIF
               ENDIF
            ENDIF
         ENDIF
      ENDIF

   SET-NEXT-SCREEN
   * REQUEST WHICH 'NEXT SCREEN' THE USER WANTS TO GO TO
         LET MSG-RESP = "2"
         INPUT MESSAGE "I,4" INTO MSG-RESP USING "ATMSGS"
         IF TERM-KEY <> 4 THEN
            LET NS-NO = NUM(MSG-RESP)
         ENDIF

   CHANGE-KEY-VALUE
   * KEEP OTHER LINKS IN SYNC WITH THIS ONE AFTER CONFIRM
   * CHANGE ALL REQUISITION RECORDS CONTAINING THIS IDENT
         RUN OVERLAY "ATAPMM1E"

   SKIP-FIELD
   * SKIP OVER A 'PROTECTED' FIELD USING A PRE PROCESS
         LET ATAPGENL.FIELD = -1

   SKIP-REST
   * SKIP OVER REST OF THE FIELDS ON THE SCREEN
         LET ATAPGENL.FIELD = 99

   SKIP-BACK
   * SKIP BACK OVER SKIPPED FIELDS FROM NEXT SCREEN NO FIELD ON UP ARROW
         IF TERM-KEY = -4 THEN
            LET ATAPGENL.FIELD = -5
         ENDIF

   GET-REQSTN-RECORD
         IF TERM-KEY = 8 OR (ATAPGENL.REQ-NO <> "0000" AND OLD-REQ-NO <>
            ATAPGENL.REQ-NO) OR (ATAPGENL.REQ-NO <> "0000" AND
            MODE-FLAG = "DISPL") THEN
            IF TERM-KEY = 8 THEN LET MODE-FLAG = "LKUP " ENDIF
            RUN OVERLAY "ATAPMM1a"
            IF MODE-FLAG = "LKUP " THEN LET MODE-FLAG = "EDIT " ENDIF
         ELSE
            IF ATAPGENL.REQ-NO = "0000" AND MODE-FLAG <> "DISPL" THEN
               LET ATAPGENL.RECRUITER = "", ATAPGENL.JOB-TITLE = ""
               PRINT SCREEN ATAPGENL DATA-NAME LIST RECRUITER, JOB-TITLE
            ENDIF
         ENDIF
         LET OLD-REQ-NO = ATAPGENL.REQ-NO

   GET-DISPCD-RECORD
         IF TERM-KEY = 8 OR (ATAPGENL.DISP-CODE <> "  " AND OLD-DISP-CD <>
            ATAPGENL.DISP-CODE) OR (MODE-FLAG = "DISPL" AND
            ATAPGENL.DISP-CODE <> "  ") THEN
            IF TERM-KEY = 8 THEN LET MODE-FLAG = "LKUP " ENDIF
            RUN OVERLAY "ATAPMM1b"
```

APPENDIX 6: ATS DATA ENTRY SCRIPTS

APMM1E - Edit Record #1 (Continued)

```
                    IF MODE-FLAG = "LKUP " THEN LET MODE-FLAG = "EDIT " ENDIF
                ELSE
                    IF ATAPGENL.DISP-CODE = "  " AND MODE-FLAG <> "DISPL" THEN
                        LET ATAPGENL.DISP-DESC = "", ATAPGENL.DISP-DATE = ""
                        PRINT SCREEN ATAPGENL DATA-NAME LIST DISP-DESC,
                                                            DISP-DATE
                    ENDIF
                ENDIF
                LET OLD-DISP-CD = ATAPGENL.DISP-CODE
        CK-FOR-VALID-DATE
            IF ATAPGENL.DISP-CODE <> "  " AND TERM-KEY <> -4 THEN
                IF ATAPGENL.DISP-DATE = "        " THEN
                INPUT MESSAGE "N,11,,,,Disp Date" INTO MSG-RESP USING "ATMSGS"
                LET ATAPGENL.FIELD = 0
                ELSE
                    LET ATAPGENL.FIELD = 5
                ENDIF
            ELSE
                IF ATAPGENL.DISP-CODE = "  " AND TERM-KEY <> -4 THEN
                    LET ATAPGENL.FIELD = 5
                ENDIF
            ENDIF
        GET-EXPCDE-RECORD
            IF TERM-KEY = 8 OR OLD-EXP-CODE <> ATAPGENL.CUR-EXP-CODE THEN
                IF TERM-KEY = 8 THEN LET MODE-FLAG = "LKUP " ENDIF
                RUN OVERLAY "ATAPMM1c"
                IF MODE-FLAG = "LKUP " THEN LET MODE-FLAG = "EDIT " ENDIF
                LET OLD-EXP-CODE = ATAPGENL.CUR-EXP-CODE
            ENDIF
            IF ATAPGENL.CUR-EXP-CODE = "  " THEN LET ATAPGENL.FIELD = 0 ENDIF
    REOPEN-ORIG-REQ
        LET REQ-MODE = "REOPN"
        RUN OVERLAY "ATAPMM1d"

    CLOSE-CURRENT-REQ
        LET REQ-MODE = "CLOSE"
        RUN OVERLAY "ATAPMM1d"

    UPDATE-NO-DAYS
        IF ATAPGENL.DISP-CODE <> "HI" THEN
            LET ATAPMSTR.NO-DAYS-TO-FILL = 0
        ELSE
            LET J9$ = "AA" + ATAPGENL.DISP-DATE + "  " + CURR-REQ-DATE +
                      "  "
            CALL "IDPDT5", J9$, J9
            LET ATAPMSTR.NO-DAYS-TO-FILL = J9
        ENDIF

MISSING-RECORD
    INPUT MESSAGE "N,1,,,,Applicant" INTO MSG-RESP USING "ATMSGS"

BUSY-RECORD
    INPUT MESSAGE "N,5,,,,Applicant" INTO MSG-RESP USING "ATMSGS"

END-OF-MAIN-FILE
    INPUT MESSAGE "N,2,,,,Applicant" INTO MSG-RESP USING "ATMSGS"
```

APMM1E - Edit Record #1 (Continued)

```
    ERROR-RECORD
        IF ERR = 11 THEN
            INPUT MESSAGE "N,12,,,,Applicant" INTO MSG-RESP USING "ATMSGS"
        ELSE
            INPUT MESSAGE "N,13,,,,Applicant" INTO MSG-RESP USING "ATMSGS"
        ENDIF
        LET ATAPGENL.IDENT = OLD-IDENT, ATAPMSTR.IDENT = OLD-IDENT

    REDO-SCREEN
        PRINT SCREEN ATAPGENh
        PRINT SCREEN ATAPGENL DATA-NAME LIST NEXT-SCRN-NO

    END-SCRIPT
```

APMM1K - Key Change

```
Script: AT APMM1K   Type: 3
Desc: Appl. Masterfile Mx - Key Change                          Page: 1
Last Change Date: 05/20/88      Last Compile Date: 05/26/88
             Time: 18:31:11               Time: 08:50:31       Date: 05/31/88
================================================================================
* APPLICANT MASTERFILE MAINTENANCE OVERLAY - KEY CHANGE FROM EDIT
* THE FOLLOWING INCLUDE SCRIPT CONTAINS THE REQUIRED DATA DEFINITIONS
        INCLUDE ATAPMMDS

    MAIN-PROCEDURE
*       SETTRACE PAUSE DIRECTIVE @(0,1), "T:", TERM-KEY, " M:", MODE-FLAG
* GET ALL REQUISITION RECORDS THAT CONTAIN OLD-IDENT AND CHANGE THEM
*   USING THE IDENT SECONDARY KEY
        CHANGE ATRQMSTR USING KEY SORT 3 RANGE FROM OLD-IDENT TO OLD-IDENT
          + "zzzz"
            PROCESSING IS CHANGE-RECORD
            BUSY       IS BUSY-RECORD
* CLEAR ATRQMSTR LINK FORMAT AFTER USE
        LET ATRQMSTR = ""

    CHANGE-RECORD
        LET ATRQMSTR.IDENT = ATAPMSTR.IDENT

    BUSY-RECORD
        INPUT MESSAGE "N,5,,,,Requisition" INTO MSG-RESP USING "ATMSGS"

    END-SCRIPT
```

APPENDIX 6: ATS DATA ENTRY SCRIPTS

APMM1L - Main Lookup

```
Script: AT APMM1L  Type: 3
Desc: Appl. Masterfile Mx - Main Lookup                         Page: 1
Last Change Date: 05/20/88    Last Compile Date: 05/26/88
              Time: 18:31:34                Time: 08:51:00      Date: 05/31/88
================================================================================
     * APPLICANT MASTERFILE MAINTENANCE OVERLAY - APPLICANT LOOKUP
     * THE FOLLOWING INCLUDE SCRIPT CONTAINS THE REQUIRED DATA DEFINITIONS
          INCLUDE ATAPMMDS

     MAIN-PROCEDURE
     *    SETTRACE PAUSE DIRECTIVE @(0,1), "T:", TERM-KEY, " M:", MODE-FLAG
     * DISPLAY LIST OF RECORDS IN VIEW AS LOOKUP AID
          OPEN VIEW ATAPLKUP
          IF MODE-FLAG = "LKUPA" THEN
              PRINT MESSAGE "P,24,,,,Applicant" USING "ATMSGS"
              PRINT MESSAGE "P,29,,,,Applicant" USING "ATMSGS"
          ELSE
              PRINT MESSAGE "P,23,,,,Applicant" USING "ATMSGS"
              PRINT MESSAGE "P,27,,,,Applicant" USING "ATMSGS"
          ENDIF
          PRINT VIEW ATAPLKUP USING KEY RANGE FROM "" TO "zzzzzz"
              KEY INTO ATAPGENL.IDENT
              WINDOW LINE IS 17
                     COLUMN IS 3
                     NUMBER LINES ARE 5
                     CHARACTERS ARE 72
                     BORDER TYPE IS "R"
                     HEADING IS "Y"
          IF TERM-KEY = 4 THEN LET ATAPGENL.IDENT = "" ENDIF
     * REPRINT SCREEN AFTER VIEW
          PRINT SCREEN ATAPGENh

     END-SCRIPT
```

APMM1a - Requisition Number

```
Script: AT APMM1a  Type: 3
Desc: Appl. Masterfile Mx - Req'stn No                          Page: 1
Last Change Date: 05/20/88    Last Compile Date: 05/26/88
              Time: 18:31:42                Time: 08:51:44      Date: 05/31/88
================================================================================
     * APPLICANT MASTERFILE MAINTENANCE OVERLAY - REQ NO LOOKUP
     * THE FOLLOWING INCLUDE SCRIPT CONTAINS THE REQUIRED DATA DEFINITIONS
          INCLUDE ATAPMMDS

     MAIN-PROCEDURE
     * DISPLAY LIST OF RECORDS AS LOOKUP AID
          IF MODE-FLAG = "LKUP " OR MODE-FLAG = "LKUPA" THEN
              OPEN VIEW ATREQLVW
              LET K9$ = ATAPGENL.REQ-NO
              PRINT MESSAGE "P,23,,,,Req Num" USING "ATMSGS"
              PRINT MESSAGE "P,27,,,,Req Num" USING "ATMSGS"
              PRINT VIEW ATREQLVW USING KEY RANGE FROM "" TO "zzzz"
                  KEY INTO K9$
                  WINDOW LINE IS 17
                         COLUMN IS 3
                         NUMBER LINES ARE 5
                         CHARACTERS ARE 72
                         BORDER TYPE IS "R"
                         HEADING IS "Y"
```

APPENDIX 6: ATS DATA ENTRY SCRIPTS

APMM1a - Requisition Number (Continued)

```
    * SAVE TERM-KEY VALUE FOR USE LATER IN SCRIPT
          LET R9 = TERM-KEY
    * REPRINT PF KEY MESSAGE
          IF MODE-FLAG = "LKUP " THEN
              PRINT MESSAGE "F,21" USING "ATMSGS"
          ELSE
              PRINT MESSAGE "F,10" USING "ATMSGS"
          ENDIF
    * REPRINT SCREEN AFTER VIEW
          PRINT SCREEN ATAPGENh
          PRINT SCREEN ATAPGENL DATA-NAME LIST NEXT-SCRN-NO
          IF R9 <> 4 THEN
              IF ATAPGENL.REQ-NO <> "0000" AND ATAPGENL.REQ-NO <> K9$ THEN
                  INPUT MESSAGE "Y,5,,,,Req Num," + ATAPGENL.REQ-NO + ","
                    + K9$ INTO MSG-RESP USING "ATMSGS"
                  IF MSG-RESP = "Y" THEN
                      LET ATAPGENL.REQ-NO = K9$
                  ENDIF
              ELSE
                  LET ATAPGENL.REQ-NO = K9$
              ENDIF
          ENDIF
      ENDIF
    * LOOKUP REQ'STN RECORD & MOVE DATA INTO SCREEN & LINK FORMATS
          IF ATAPGENL.REQ-NO <> "0000" AND ATAPGENL.REQ-NO <> "    " THEN
              READ ATRQMSTR USING KEY ATAPGENL.REQ-NO
                  MISSING KEY IS MISSING-RECORD
                  BUSY        IS BUSY-RECORD
                  END         IS END-OF-FILE
              LET ATAPGENL.JOB-TITLE = ATRQMSTR.JOB-TITLE,
                  ATAPGENL.RECRUITER = ATRQMSTR.RECRUITER,
                  ATAPCOST.JOB-TITLE = ATRQMSTR.JOB-TITLE,
                  ATAPCOST.RECRUITER = ATRQMSTR.RECRUITER,
                  CURR-REQ-DATE = ATRQMSTR.REQ-DATE
              LET ATRQMSTR = ""
              IF MODE-FLAG <> "DISPL" THEN
                  PRINT SCREEN ATAPGENL DATA-NAME LIST JOB-TITLE,
                                                      RECRUITER
              ENDIF
          ENDIF

MISSING-RECORD
      INPUT MESSAGE "N,1,,,,Req'stn" INTO MSG-RESP USING "ATMSGS"

BUSY-RECORD
      INPUT MESSAGE "N,5,,,,Req'stn" INTO MSG-RESP USING "ATMSGS"

END-OF-FILE
      INPUT MESSAGE "N,2,,,,Req'stn" INTO MSG-RESP USING "ATMSGS"

END-SCRIPT
```

APPENDIX 6: ATS DATA ENTRY SCRIPTS

APMM1b - Disposition Code

```
Script: AT APMM1b  Type: 3
Desc: Appl. Masterfile Mx - Disp Code                        Page: 1
Last Change Date: 05/20/88    Last Compile Date: 05/26/88
            Time: 18:31:48                Time: 08:52:26    Date: 05/31/88
================================================================================
    * APPLICANT MASTERFILE MAINTENANCE OVERLAY - DISP CODE LOOKUP
    * THE FOLLOWING INCLUDE SCRIPT CONTAINS THE REQUIRED DATA DEFINITIONS
        INCLUDE ATAPMMDS

    MAIN-PROCEDURE
    * DISPLAY LIST OF RECORDS IN VIEW AS LOOKUP AID
        IF MODE-FLAG = "LKUP " OR MODE-FLAG = "LKUPA" THEN
            OPEN VIEW ATDISLVW
            LET K9$ = ATAPGENL.DISP-CODE
            PRINT MESSAGE "P,23,,,,Disp Code" USING "ATMSGS"
            PRINT MESSAGE "P,27,,,,Disp Code" USING "ATMSGS"
            PRINT VIEW ATDISLVW USING KEY RANGE FROM "" TO "zz"
                KEY INTO K9$
                WINDOW LINE IS 14
                       COLUMN IS 3
                       NUMBER LINES ARE 8
                       CHARACTERS ARE 35
                       BORDER TYPE IS "R"
                       HEADING IS "Y"
    * SAVE TERM-KEY VALUE FOR USE LATER IN SCRIPT
            LET R9 = TERM-KEY
    * REPRINT PF KEY MESSAGE
            IF MODE-FLAG = "LKUP " THEN
                PRINT MESSAGE "P,21" USING "ATMSGS"
            ELSE
                PRINT MESSAGE "P,10" USING "ATMSGS"
            ENDIF
    * REPRINT SCREEN AND DATA AFTER VIEW
            INCLUDE ATAPMMVR
            IF R9 <> 4 THEN
                IF ATAPGENL.DISP-CODE <> "  " AND ATAPGENL.DISP-CODE <> K9$
                THEN
                    INPUT MESSAGE "Y,5,,,,Disp Code," + ATAPGENL.DISP-CODE
                        + "," + K9$ INTO MSG-RESP USING "ATMSGS"
                    IF MSG-RESP = "Y" THEN
                        LET ATAPGENL.DISP-CODE = K9$
                    ENDIF
                ELSE
                    LET ATAPGENL.DISP-CODE = K9$
                ENDIF
            ENDIF
        ENDIF
    * LOOKUP DISP CODE RECORD & MOVE DATA INTO SCREEN FORMAT
        IF ATAPGENL.DISP-CODE <> "  " THEN
            READ ATDISPCD USING KEY ATAPGENL.DISP-CODE
                MISSING KEY IS MISSING-RECORD
                BUSY        IS BUSY-RECORD
                END         IS END-OF-FILE
            LET ATAPGENL.DISP-DESC = ATDISPCD.DISP-DESC
            LET ATDISPCD = ""
            IF MODE-FLAG <> "DISPL" THEN
                PRINT SCREEN ATAPGENL DATA-NAME LIST DISP-CODE,
                                                    DISP-DESC
```

APPENDIX 6: ATS DATA ENTRY SCRIPTS

APMM1b - Disposition Code (Continued)

```
            ENDIF
        ENDIF

    MISSING-RECORD
        INPUT MESSAGE "N,1,,,,Disp Code" INTO MSG-RESP USING "ATMSGS"

    BUSY-RECORD
        INPUT MESSAGE "N,5,,,,Disp Code" INTO MSG-RESP USING "ATMSGS"

    END-OF-FILE
        INPUT MESSAGE "N,2,,,,Disp Code" INTO MSG-RESP USING "ATMSGS"

    END-SCRIPT
```

APMM1c - Experience Code

```
Script: AT APMM1c  Type: 3
Desc: Appl. Masterfile Mx - Exper Code                      Page: 1
Last Change Date: 05/20/88     Last Compile Date: 05/26/88
                Time: 18:35:00              Time: 08:53:11    Date: 05/31/88
================================================================================
    * APPLICANT MASTERFILE MAINTENANCE OVERLAY - EXP CODE LOOKUP
    * THE FOLLOWING INCLUDE SCRIPT CONTAINS THE REQUIRED DATA DEFINITIONS
        INCLUDE ATAPMMDS

    MAIN-PROCEDURE
    *   SETTRACE PAUSE DIRECTIVE @(0,1), "T:", TERM-KEY, " M:", MODE-FLAG
    * DISPLAY LIST OF RECORDS IN VIEW AS LOOKUP AID
        IF MODE-FLAG = "LKUP " OR MODE-FLAG = "LKUPA" THEN
            OPEN VIEW ATEXPLVW
            LET K9$ = ATAPGENL.CUR-EXP-CODE
            PRINT MESSAGE "P,23,,,,Exp Code" USING "ATMSGS"
            PRINT MESSAGE "P,27,,,,Exp Code" USING "ATMSGS"
            PRINT VIEW ATEXPLVW USING KEY RANGE FROM "" TO "zz"
                KEY INTO K9$
                WINDOW LINE IS 14
                       COLUMN IS 3
                       NUMBER LINES ARE 8
                       CHARACTERS ARE 33
                       BORDER TYPE IS "R"
                       HEADING IS 'Y'
    * SAVE TERM-KEY VALUE FOR USE LATER IN SCRIPT
            LET R9 = TERM-KEY
    * REPRINT PF KEY MESSAGE
            IF MODE-FLAG = "LKUP " THEN
                PRINT MESSAGE "P,21" USING "ATMSGS"
            ELSE
                PRINT MESSAGE "P,12" USING "ATMSGS"
            ENDIF
    * REPRINT SCREEN AND DATA AFTER VIEW
            INCLUDE ATAPMMVR
            IF R9 <> 4 THEN
                IF ATAPGENL.CUR-EXP-CODE <> " " AND ATAPGENL.CUR-EXP-CODE <>
                   K9$ THEN
                    INPUT MESSAGE "Y,5,,,,Exp Code," + ATAPGENL.CUR-EXP-CODE
                        + "," + K9$ INTO MSG-RESP USING "ATMSGS"
                    IF MSG-RESP = "Y" THEN
                        LET ATAPGENL.CUR-EXP-CODE = K9$
                    ENDIF
                ELSE
                    LET ATAPGENL.CUR-EXP-CODE = K9$
                ENDIF
            ENDIF
        ENDIF
```

6-19

APPENDIX 6: ATS DATA ENTRY SCRIPTS

APMM1c - Experience Code (Continued)

```
        * LOOKUP EXP CODE RECORD & MOVE DATA INTO SCREEN FORMAT
            IF ATAPGENL.CUR-EXP-CODE <> "  " THEN
                READ ATEXPCDE USING KEY CUR-EXP-CODE
                    MISSING KEY IS MISSING-RECORD
                    BUSY        IS BUSY-RECORD
                    END         IS END-OF-FILE
                IF MODE-FLAG <> "DISPL" THEN
                    PRINT SCREEN ATAPGENL DATA-NAME LIST CUR-EXP-CODE
                ENDIF
            ENDIF

    MISSING-RECORD
            INPUT MESSAGE "N,1,,,,Exp Code" INTO MSG-RESP USING "ATMSGS"

    BUSY-RECORD
            INPUT MESSAGE "N,5,,,,Exp Code" INTO MSG-RESP USING "ATMSGS"

    END-OF-FILE
            INPUT MESSAGE "N,2,,,,Exp Code" INTO MSG-RESP USING "ATMSGS"

    END-SCRIPT
```

APMM1d - Requisition Update

```
Script: AT APMM1d  Type: 3
Desc: Appl. Masterfile Mx - Reqstn Update                       Page: 1
Last Change Date: 05/20/88    Last Compile Date: 05/26/88
            Time: 18:35:11                Time: 08:54:00        Date: 05/31/88
================================================================================
        * APPLICANT MASTERFILE MAINTENANCE OVERLAY - REQSTN UPDATE
        * THE FOLLOWING INCLUDE SCRIPT CONTAINS THE REQUIRED DATA DEFINITIONS
            INCLUDE ATAPMMDS

    MAIN-PROCEDURE
            IF REQ-MODE = "REOPN" THEN
        * CHANGE ORIGINAL REQ'STN RECORD, IF APPLICANT WAS 'HIRED' AND NOW NOT
        *   OR IF STILL 'HIRED' BUT REQ NUMBER CHANGED
                CHANGE ATRQMSTR USING KEY ORIG-REQ-NO
                    PROCESSING  IS REOPEN-ORIG-REQ
                    MISSING KEY IS MISSING-RECORD
                    BUSY        IS BUSY-RECORD
                    END         IS END-OF-FILE
            ELSE
                IF REQ-MODE = "CLOSE" THEN
        * CHANGE CURRENT REQ'STN RECORD, IF APPLICANT NOW 'HIRED' OR IF STILL
        *   'HIRED' BUT REQ NUMBER CHANGED
                    CHANGE ATRQMSTR USING KEY ATAPGENL.REQ-NO
                        PROCESSING  IS CLOSE-CURRENT-REQ
                        MISSING KEY IS MISSING-RECORD
                        BUSY        IS BUSY-RECORD
                        END         IS END-OF-FILE
                ENDIF
            ENDIF
            LET ATRQMSTR = ""

    REOPEN-ORIG-REQ
            LET ATRQMSTR.REQ-STATUS = "open        ",
                ATRQMSTR.REQ-DISP-DATE = "", ATRQMSTR.IDENT = ""
```

APPENDIX 6: ATS DATA ENTRY SCRIPTS

APMM1d - Requisition Update (Continued)

```
    CLOSE-CURRENT-REQ
        LET ATRQMSTR.REQ-STATUS = "closed    ",
            ATRQMSTR.REQ-DISP-DATE = CURRENT-DATE,
            ATRQMSTR.IDENT = ATAPMSTR.IDENT

    MISSING-RECORD
        INPUT MESSAGE "N,1,,,,Req'stn" INTO MSG-RESP USING "ATMSGS"

    BUSY-RECORD
        INPUT MESSAGE "N,5,,,,Req'stn" INTO MSG-RESP USING "ATMSGS"

    END-OF-FILE
        INPUT MESSAGE "N,2,,,,Req'stn" INTO MSG-RESP USING "ATMSGS"

    END-SCRIPT
```

APMM2E - Edit Record #2

```
Script: AT APMM2E   Type: 3
Desc: Appl. Masterfile Mx - Edit Record 2                       Page: 1
Last Change Date: 06/06/88     Last Compile Date: 05/26/88
            Time: 11:20:15                 Time: 08:55:45       Date: 06/06/88
================================================================================
    * APPLICANT MASTERFILE MAINTENANCE OVERLAY - EDIT RECORD #2
    * THE FOLLOWING INCLUDE SCRIPT CONTAINS THE REQUIRED DATA DEFINITIONS
         INCLUDE ATAPMMDS

    MAIN-PROCEDURE
    *    SETTRACE PAUSE DIRECTIVE @(0,1), "T:", TERM-KEY, " M:", MODE-FLAG
    * SAVE MODE FOR RETURN AFTER EDIT & SET SCREEN & MODE
         LET OLD-MODE-FLAG = MODE-FLAG, CS-NO = 2, MODE-FLAG = "DISPL",
             DEL-MODE = "Y"
    * CLEAR OLD SCREEN FROM TERMINAL, IF NECESSARY
         IF CS-NAME <> "APCOST" THEN
             PRINT 'CS'
         ENDIF
    * CLEAR SCREEN FORMAT BEFORE SETTING NEW RECORD INTO IT
         LET ATAPCOST = ""
    * MOVE DATA FORMAT TO BOTH SCREEN FORMATS FOR DISPLAY
         LET ATAPCOST = ATAPMSTR
         LET ATAPGENL = ATAPMSTR
    * GET SECONDARY RECORDS AND MOVE DATA NOT STORED TO SCREEN FORMAT
         DO GET-REQSTN-RECORD
    * SAVE OLD KEY VALUE TO DETECT KEY CHANGES; SET NEXT SCREEN NUMBER
         LET OLD-IDENT = ATAPCOST.IDENT, ATAPCOST.NEXT-SCRN-NO = NS-NO
    * DISPLAY SCREEN & DATA AND START INPUT AT KEY FIELD
         IF CS-NAME <> "APCOST" THEN
             PRINT SCREEN ATAPCOST
         ENDIF
         LET CS-NAME ="APCOST"
    * PRINT APPROPRIATE PFKEY MESSAGE ('DELETE' IS ALWAYS ALLOWED)
         PRINT MESSAGE "P,28" USING "ATMSGS"
         PRINT MESSAGE "P,26" USING "ATMSGS"
    * DISPLAY SCREEN DATA AND ACCEPT INPUT AT FIRST FIELD ONLY
         PRINT SCREEN ATAPCOST DATA
         INPUT SCREEN ATAPCOST DATA-NAME LIST ADVERT
             POST         PROCESS ADVERT, SET-TERM-KEY
             POST-HELP PROCESS REDO-SCREEN
         IF MODE-FLAG = "EDIT " THEN
             CHANGE ATAPMSTR USING KEY ATAPGENL.IDENT
                 PROCESSING  IS EDIT-RECORD
                 ERROR       IS ERROR-RECORD
                 MISSING KEY IS MISSING-RECORD
                 BUSY        IS BUSY-RECORD
                 END         IS END-OF-MAIN-FILE
```

APPENDIX 6: ATS DATA ENTRY SCRIPTS

APMM2E - Edit Record #2 (Continued)

```
              ENDIF
    * SET NEXT SCREEN FOR FURTHER DISPLAY
          IF MODE-FLAG = "NSCRN" THEN
              DO SET-NEXT-SCREEN
          ENDIF
    * SET MODE-FLAG BACK TO 'NEXT' OR 'PREV' AFTER EDIT
          IF (MODE-FLAG = "EDIT " OR MODE-FLAG = "NSCRN") AND
             (OLD-MODE-FLAG = "NEXT " OR OLD-MODE-FLAG = "PREV ") THEN
              LET MODE-FLAG = OLD-MODE-FLAG
          ENDIF
EDIT-RECORD
    * ISSUE MESSAGE THAT RECORD IS NOW LOCKED
          PRINT MESSAGE "P,25" USING "ATMSGS"
    * SAVE A COPY OF THE SCREEN FOR EDIT COMPARISONS
          LET S$ = ATAPCOST
    * COLLECT DATA FROM SCREEN AND UPDATE LINK
          INPUT SCREEN ATAPCOST DATA-NAME LIST ADVERT, AGENCY-FEES,
                EMPLOYEE-REFERRAL, RELOCATION-EXP, TVL-LODG-EXP,
                OTHER-REC-EXP, SEX, EEO-CODE, SSN, BIRTH-DATE, VETERAN,
                NEXT-SCRN-NO
                POST         PROCESS ADVERT, SET-TERM-KEY,
                                     OTHER-REC-EXP, CALC-TOTAL-EXP
                POST-HELP PROCESS REDO-SCREEN
    * REMOVE LOCKED RECORD MESSAGE, IF STILL THERE
          PRINT @(0,0), 'CL'
    * SAVE NEXT SCREEN NUMBER IN CASE USER OVERRODE IT
          LET NS-NO = ATAPCOST.NEXT-SCRN-NO
          IF NS-NO > 2 THEN LET NS-NO = 2 ENDIF
          IF NS-NO < 1 THEN LET NS-NO = 1 ENDIF
    * SET MODE FLAG TO "END", IF PF4 KEY WAS PRESSED
          IF MODE-FLAG = "EDIT "  AND TERM-KEY = 4 THEN
              LET MODE-FLAG = "END  "
          ENDIF
    * ASK TO SAVE CHANGES; IF "Y", MOVE SCREEN DATA TO LINK
          IF (MODE-FLAG = "EDIT " OR MODE-FLAG = "END  ") AND S$ <> ATAPCOST
          THEN
              INPUT MESSAGE "Y,1" INTO MSG-RESP USING "ATMSGS"
              IF MSG-RESP = "Y" THEN
                  LET ATAPMSTR = ATAPCOST
              ENDIF
          ENDIF
    * SET COPY OF SCREEN FORMAT TO ZERO LENGTH TO SAVE MEMORY
          LET S$ = ""

SET-TERM-KEY
    * TERMINATE EDIT INPUT BASED ON PFKEY PRESSED
          IF TERM-KEY = 1 THEN
              LET ATAPCOST.FIELD = 99, MODE-FLAG = "NEXT "
          ELSE
              IF TERM-KEY = 2 THEN
                  LET ATAPCOST.FIELD = 99, MODE-FLAG = "PREV "
              ELSE
                  IF TERM-KEY = 3 AND DEL-MODE = "Y" THEN
                      LET ATAPCOST.FIELD = 99, MODE-FLAG = "DELET"
                  ELSE
                      IF TERM-KEY = 7 THEN
                          LET ATAPCOST.FIELD = 99, MODE-FLAG = "COPY "
                      ELSE
                          IF TERM-KEY = 9 THEN
                              LET ATAPCOST.FIELD = 99, MODE-FLAG = "NSCRN"
                          ELSE
                              IF TERM-KEY = 4 THEN
                                  LET MODE-FLAG = "END  ", ATAPCOST.FIELD = 99
```

APPENDIX 6: ATS DATA ENTRY SCRIPTS

APMM2E - Edit Record #2 (Continued)

```
                        ELSE
                            IF TERM-KEY <> 6 AND MODE-FLAG <> "EDIT " THEN
                                LET MODE-FLAG = "EDIT ", ATAPCOST.FIELD = 99
                            ENDIF
                        ENDIF
                    ENDIF
                ENDIF
            ENDIF
        ENDIF
    ENDIF
SET-NEXT-SCREEN
* REQUEST WHICH 'NEXT SCREEN' THE USER WANTS TO GO TO
    LET MSG-RESP = "1"
    INPUT MESSAGE "I,4" INTO MSG-RESP USING "ATMSGS"
    IF TERM-KEY <> 4 THEN
        LET NS-NO = NUM(MSG-RESP)
    ENDIF

GET-REQSTN-RECORD
    IF ATAPGENL.REQ-NO <> "0000" THEN
        RUN OVERLAY "ATAPMM1a"
    ENDIF

CALC-TOTAL-EXP
* CALCULATE TOTAL REC EXPENSES AND NO DAYS TO FILL POSITION
    LET TOTAL-REC-EXP = ADVERT + AGENCY-FEES + EMPLOYEE-REFERRAL +
        RELOCATION-EXP + TVL-LODG-EXP + OTHER-REC-EXP
    PRINT SCREEN ATAPCOST DATA-NAME LIST TOTAL-REC-EXP

SKIP-REST
* SKIP OVER REST OF THE FIELDS ON THE SCREEN
    LET ATAPCOST.FIELD = 99

MISSING-RECORD
    INPUT MESSAGE "N,1,,,,Applicant" INTO MSG-RESP USING "ATMSGS"
BUSY-RECORD
    INPUT MESSAGE "N,5,,,,Applicant" INTO MSG-RESP USING "ATMSGS"
END-OF-MAIN-FILE
    INPUT MESSAGE "N,2,,,,Applicant" INTO MSG-RESP USING "ATMSGS"
ERROR-RECORD
    IF ERR = 11 THEN
        INPUT MESSAGE "N,12,,,,Applicant" INTO MSG-RESP USING "ATMSGS"
    ELSE
        INPUT MESSAGE "N,13,,,,Applicant" INTO MSG-RESP USING "ATMSGS"
    ENDIF
    LET ATAPGENL.IDENT = OLD-IDENT, ATAPMSTR.IDENT = OLD-IDENT
REDO-SCREEN
    PRINT SCREEN ATAPCOSh
    PRINT SCREEN ATAPCOST DATA-NAME LIST NEXT-SCRN-NO

END-SCRIPT
```

APPENDIX 6: ATS DATA ENTRY SCRIPTS

APMMDS - Data Section

```
Script: AT APMMDS  Type: 5
Desc: Appl. Masterfile Mx - Data Section                    Page: 1
Last Change Date: 05/20/88    Last Compile Date:
             Time: 18:32:12                Time:          Date: 05/31/88
================================================================================
    * INCLUDE SCRIPT FOR APPLICANT MASTERFILE MAINTENANCE FUNCTION
    * DEFINE SCREENS HERE
    SN   ATAPGENL, ATAPCOST, ATAPGENh, ATAPGEN1, ATAPCOSh
    * DEFINE LINKS HERE
    LN   ATAPMSTR, ATRQMSTR, ATDISPCD, ATEXPCDE
    * DEFINE VIEWS HERE
    VN   ATEXPLVW, ATAPLKUP, ATREQLVW, ATDISLVW
    * DEFINE DATA ELEMENTS HERE
    DN   MODE-FLAG (5), OLD-MODE-FLAG (5), FILE-NAME (8), MSG-RESP (1),
         SORT-NO (2.0), TEMP-EXPER-CODE (2)
    DN   OLD-IDENT (6), OLD-REQ-NO (4), OLD-EXP-CODE (2), OLD-DISP-CD (2),
         ORIG-REQ-NO (4), ORIG-DISP-CD (2)
    DN   CURR-REQ-DATE (6), CURRENT-DATE (6), EXP-MODE (4), DEL-MODE (1),
         REQ-MODE (5), CS-NO (2.0), NS-NO (2.0), CS-NAME (6)
```

APMMVR - View Refresh

```
Script: AT APMMVR  Type: 5
Desc: Appl. Masterfile Mx - View Refresh                    Page: 1
Last Change Date: 05/20/88    Last Compile Date:
             Time: 18:32:18                Time:          Date: 05/31/88
================================================================================
    * APPLICANT MASTERFILE MAINTENANCE - INCLUDE SCRIPT FOR VIEW REFRESH
         PRINT SCREEN ATAPGEN1
         PRINT SCREEN ATAPGENL DATA-NAME LIST SOURCE, REQ-NO, RECRUITER,
                                              JOB-TITLE, NEXT-SCRN-NO
```

APPENDIX 6: ATS DATA ENTRY SCRIPTS

REQUISITION MASTERFILE MAINTENANCE

RQMM0 - Setup

```
Script: AT RQMM0    Type: 1
Desc: Req'stn Masterfile Mx - Setup                         Page: 1
Last Change Date: 05/20/88    Last Compile Date: 05/26/88
            Time: 18:36:09                Time: 08:56:18   Date: 05/31/88
================================================================================
      * REQUISITION MASTERFILE MAINTENANCE - PRIMARY SCRIPT
      * THE FOLLOWING INCLUDE SCRIPT CONTAINS THE REQUIRED DATA DEFINITIONS
          INCLUDE ATRQMMDS

      MAIN-PROCEDURE
      *     SETTRACE PAUSE DIRECTIVE
      * OPEN SCREENS, VIEWS, AND LINKS
          OPEN SCREEN ATREQUIS
          OPEN SCREEN ATREQUIh
          OPEN SCREEN ATREQUIr
          LET FILE-NAME = "ATRQMSTR"
          OPEN ATRQMSTR
              BUSY  IS BUSY-FILE
              ERROR IS ERROR-FILE
          LET FILE-NAME = "ATJOBCDE"
          OPEN ATJOBCDE
              BUSY  IS BUSY-FILE
              ERROR IS ERROR-FILE
          LET FILE-NAME = "ATSALGRD"
          OPEN ATSALGRD
              BUSY  IS BUSY-FILE
              ERROR IS ERROR-FILE
          LET FILE-NAME = "ATEXPCDE"
          OPEN ATEXPCDE
              BUSY  IS BUSY-FILE
              ERROR IS ERROR-FILE
          LET FILE-NAME = "ATRECRUT"
          OPEN ATRECRUT
              BUSY  IS BUSY-FILE
              ERROR IS ERROR-FILE
          LET FILE-NAME = "ATAPMSTR"
          OPEN ATAPMSTR
              BUSY  IS BUSY-FILE
              ERROR IS ERROR-FILE
      * CONTINUE WITH SCRIPT, IF FILES ARE OKAY
          IF MODE-FLAG <> "NOGO " THEN
              PRINT SCREEN ATREQUIS
              LET SORT-NO = 0, MODE-FLAG = "      "
      * RUN CONTINUATION SCRIPT
              RUN "ATRQMM1"
          ENDIF
          TERMINATE

      BUSY-FILE
          INPUT MESSAGE "N,14,.,," + FILE-NAME INTO MSG-RESP USING "ATMSGS"
          LET MODE-FLAG = "NOGO "

      ERROR-FILE
          INPUT MESSAGE "N,15,.,," + FILE-NAME INTO MSG-RESP USING "ATMSGS"
          LET MODE-FLAG = "NOGO "

      END-SCRIPT
```

APPENDIX 6: ATS DATA ENTRY SCRIPTS

RQMM1 - Continuation #1

```
Script: AT RQMM1     Type: 2
Desc: Req'stn Masterfile Mx - Cont #1                              Page: 1
Last Change Date: 05/20/88     Last Compile Date: 05/26/88
            Time: 18:36:16                 Time: 08:57:19    Date: 05/31/88
================================================================================
      * REQUISITION MASTERFILE MAINTENANCE CONTINUATION SCRIPT #1
      * THE FOLLOWING INCLUDE SCRIPT CONTAINS THE REQUIRED DATA DEFINITIONS
            INCLUDE ATRQMMDS

      MAIN-PROCEDURE
      *     SETTRACE PAUSE DIRECTIVE @(0,1), "T:", TERM-KEY, " M:", MODE-FLAG
      * MAIN INPUT LOOP
            DO LOOP UNTIL MODE-FLAG = "EXIT "
                LET MODE-FLAG = "INIT "
                PRINT MESSAGE "P,7,,,,Req Num" USING "ATMSGS"
                PRINT MESSAGE "P,8" USING "ATMSGS"
                INPUT SCREEN ATREQUIS CLEAR KEY
                    POST-HELP PROCESS REDO-SCREEN-INIT
      * DO APPROPRIATE PROCEDURE DEPENDING ON PKKEY PRESSED
                IF   TERM-KEY = 10 OR TERM-KEY = 0 THEN
                    DO FIND-EXACT-RECORD
                ELSE
                    IF TERM-KEY = 3 THEN
                        READ ATRQMSTR USING KEY ATREQUIS.REQ-NO
                            PROCESSING   IS EDIT-RECORD
                            MISSING KEY  IS ADD-RECORD
                            BUSY         IS BUSY-RECORD
                            END          IS ADD-RECORD
                    ELSE
                        IF TERM-KEY = 8 THEN
                            DO LOOKUP-RECORDS
                            IF ATREQUIS.REQ-NO <> "0000" AND ATREQUIS.REQ-NO <>
                                "    " THEN
                                DO FIND-EXACT-RECORD
                            ENDIF
                        ELSE
                            IF TERM-KEY = 1 OR TERM-KEY = 2 THEN
                                DO SET-RECORD
                                DO FIND-NEXT-RECORD
                            ELSE
                                IF TERM-KEY = 4 AND MODE-FLAG = "INIT " THEN
                                    LET MODE-FLAG = "EXIT "
                                ENDIF
                            ENDIF
                        ENDIF
                    ENDIF
                ENDIF
      * DO 'NEXT RECORD' EDIT UNTIL TERMINATED
                DO FIND-NEXT-RECORD WHILE
                    MODE-FLAG = "NEXT " OR MODE-FLAG = "PREV "
      * DO 'COPY RECORD' WHEN REQUESTED
                IF MODE-FLAG = "COPY " THEN
                    DO COPY-RECORD
                ENDIF
      * DO 'DELETE RECORD' WHEN REQUESTED
                IF MODE-FLAG = "DELET" THEN
                    DO DELETE-RECORD
                ENDIF
            ENDLOOP
            TERMINATE
```

APPENDIX 6: ATS DATA ENTRY SCRIPTS

RQMM1 - Continuation #1 (Continued)

```
    SET-RECORD
    * SET MODE BASED ON TERM-KEY
        IF TERM-KEY = 1 THEN
            LET MODE-FLAG = "NEXT "
        ELSE
            IF TERM-KEY = 2 THEN
                LET MODE-FLAG = "PREV "
            ENDIF
        ENDIF
    * BASED ON SORT USED, SET KEY POINTER IN LINK
    *     IF SORT-NO = 0 THEN
              READ ATRQMSTR USING KEY ATREQUIS.REQ-NO
    *     ELSE
    *         READ ATRQMSTR USING KEY SORT SORT-NO IS SORT-NAME (NEW DN???)
    *     ENDIF

    FIND-NEXT-RECORD
        IF MODE-FLAG = "NEXT " THEN
            READ ATRQMSTR USING KEY NEXT
                PROCESSING  IS EDIT-RECORD
                MISSING KEY IS MISSING-RECORD
                BUSY        IS BUSY-RECORD
                END         IS END-OF-MAIN-FILE
        ELSE
            IF MODE-FLAG = "PREV " THEN
                READ ATRQMSTR USING KEY PREVIOUS
                    PROCESSING  IS EDIT-RECORD
                    MISSING KEY IS MISSING-RECORD
                    BUSY        IS BUSY-RECORD
                    END         IS BEG-OF-MAIN-FILE
            ENDIF
        ENDIF

    FIND-EXACT-RECORD
        READ ATRQMSTR USING KEY ATREQUIS.REQ-NO
            PROCESSING  IS EDIT-RECORD
            MISSING KEY IS MISSING-RECORD
            BUSY        IS BUSY-RECORD
            END         IS END-OF-MAIN-FILE

    ADD-RECORD
        RUN OVERLAY "ATRQMM1A"

    EDIT-RECORD
        RUN OVERLAY "ATRQMM1E"

    LOOKUP-RECORDS
        RUN OVERLAY "ATRQMM1L"

    COPY-RECORD
        RUN OVERLAY "ATRQMM1C"

    DELETE-RECORD
        RUN OVERLAY "ATRQMM1D"

    BUSY-RECORD
        INPUT MESSAGE "N,5,,,,Requisition" INTO MSG-RESP USING "ATMSGS"

    MISSING-RECORD
        INPUT MESSAGE "N,1,,,,Requisition" INTO MSG-RESP USING "ATMSGS"
```

APPENDIX 6: ATS DATA ENTRY SCRIPTS

RQMM1 - Continuation #1 (Continued)

```
    END-OF-MAIN-FILE
        INPUT MESSAGE "N,2,,,,Requisition" INTO MSG-RESP USING "ATMSGS"
        LET MODE-FLAG = "EOF  "

    BEG-OF-MAIN-FILE
        INPUT MESSAGE "N,9,,,,Requisition" INTO MSG-RESP USING "ATMSGS"
        LET MODE-FLAG = "BOF  "

    REDO-SCREEN-INIT
*   REDISPLAY SCREEN AFTER HELP IS DISPLAYED FROM KEY FIELD(S)
        PRINT SCREEN ATREQUIh

    END-SCRIPT
```

RQMM1A - Add Record

```
Script: AT RQMM1A   Type: 3
Desc: Req'stn Masterfile Mx - Add Record                         Page: 1
Last Change Date: 05/20/88    Last Compile Date: 05/26/88
           Time: 19:34:35              Time: 08:58:27       Date: 05/31/88
===============================================================================
*   REQUISITION MASTERFILE MAINTENANCE OVERLAY - ADD RECORD
*   THE FOLLOWING INCLUDE SCRIPT CONTAINS THE REQUIRED DATA DEFINITIONS
        INCLUDE ATRQMMDS

    MAIN-PROCEDURE
        DO LOOP UNTIL MODE-FLAG = "END  "
            PRINT MESSAGE "P,12" USING "ATMSGS"
            PRINT MESSAGE "P,10" USING "ATMSGS"
*   CLEAR SCREEN FORMAT BEFORE ALLOWING DATA ENTRY (SAVE KEY VALUE)
            LET OLD-REQ-NO = ATREQUIS.REQ-NO
            LET ATREQUIS = ""
            LET ATREQUIS.REQ-NO = OLD-REQ-NO
*   SET FIELD DEFAULTS AND SAVE "OLD" VALUES FOR COMPARISON
            LET ATREQUIS.REQ-STATUS = "open    ", OLD-JOB-CODE = "0000",
                MODE-FLAG = "ADD  "
            INPUT SCREEN ATREQUIS CLEAR DATA-NAME LIST REQ-NO, REQ-DATE
                  JOB-CODE, JOB-STATUS, JOB-TITLE, SALARY-GRADE, PT-RATE,
                  DEPARTMENT, LOCATION, SHIFT, EDUC-LEVEL, PRIM-EXP-CODE,
                  SEC-EXP-CODE, RECRUITER, INTERNAL-SRCH, NEW-POSITION,
                  REPLACEMENT-FOR, REPLACEMENT-DATE, REQ-APPROVER,
                  REQ-APPROVER-TITLE, REQ-APPROVAL-DATE
                  POST        PROCESS REQ-NO, SET-TERM-KEY,
                                      JOB-CODE, GET-JOBCDE-RECORD,
                                      SALARY-GRADE, GET-SALGRD-RECORD,
                                      PRIM-EXP-CODE, GET-PRIM-EXPCDE,
                                      SEC-EXP-CODE, GET-SEC-EXPCDE,
                                      RECRUITER, GET-RECRUT-RECORD
                  POST-HELP PROCESS REDO-SCREEN
*   SET MODE TO "END", IF PF4 KEY WAS PRESSED
            IF MODE-FLAG = "ADD  " AND TERM-KEY = 4 THEN
                LET MODE-FLAG = "END  "
            ENDIF
*   ASK TO SAVE NEW RECORD; IF "Y", MOVE SCREEN DATA TO LINK
            IF MODE-FLAG = "ADD  " AND TERM-KEY <> 4 THEN
                INPUT MESSAGE "Y,3" INTO MSG-RESP USING "ATMSGS"
                IF MSG-RESP = "Y" THEN
                    LET ATRQMSTR = ATREQUIS
                    ADD ATRQMSTR USING KEY REQ-NO
                        DUPLICATE KEY IS DUPLICATE-RECORD
                ENDIF
```

RQMM1A - Add Record (Continued)

```
              ENDIF
              IF MODE-FLAG = "LKUPA" THEN DO LOOKUP-RECORDS ENDIF
          ENDLOOP

     SET-TERM-KEY
          IF TERM-KEY = 8 THEN
              LET MODE-FLAG = "LKUPA", ATREQUIS.FIELD = 99
          ENDIF

     LOOKUP-RECORDS
          RUN OVERLAY "ATRQMM1L"

     * REFRESH SCREEN AFTER VIEW
          PRINT SCREEN ATREQUIh
          LET REQ-NO = ""

     GET-RECRUT-RECORD
          IF TERM-KEY = 8 THEN LET MODE-FLAG = "LKUPA" ENDIF
          RUN OVERLAY "ATRQMM1d"
          IF ATREQUIS.RECRUITER = "        " THEN LET ATREQUIS.FIELD = 0 ENDIF
          IF MODE-FLAG = "LKUPA" THEN LET MODE-FLAG = "ADD  " ENDIF

     GET-PRIM-EXPCDE
          IF TERM-KEY = 8 THEN LET MODE-FLAG = "LKUPA" ENDIF
          LET EXP-MODE = "PRIM"
          RUN OVERLAY "ATRQMM1c"
          IF ATREQUIS.PRIM-EXP-CODE = " " THEN LET ATREQUIS.FIELD = 0 ENDIF
          IF MODE-FLAG = "LKUPA" THEN LET MODE-FLAG = "ADD  " ENDIF

     GET-SEC-EXPCDE
          IF ATREQUIS.SEC-EXP-CODE <> " " OR TERM-KEY = 8 THEN
              IF TERM-KEY = 8 THEN LET MODE-FLAG = "LKUPA" ENDIF
              LET EXP-MODE = "SECD"
              RUN OVERLAY "ATRQMM1c"
              IF MODE-FLAG = "LKUPA" THEN LET MODE-FLAG = "ADD  " ENDIF
          ELSE
              IF ATREQUIS.SEC-EXP-CODE = " " THEN
                 LET SEC-EXP-DESC = ""
                 PRINT SCREEN ATREQUIS DATA-NAME LIST SEC-EXP-DESC
              ENDIF
          ENDIF

     GET-JOBCDE-RECORD
          IF TERM-KEY = 8 THEN LET MODE-FLAG = "LKUPA" ENDIF
          RUN OVERLAY "ATRQMM1a"
          IF ATREQUIS.JOB-CODE = "    " OR ATREQUIS.JOB-CODE = "0000" THEN
              LET ATREQUIS.FIELD = 0
          ENDIF
          IF MODE-FLAG = "LKUPA" THEN LET MODE-FLAG = "ADD  " ENDIF

     GET-SALGRD-RECORD
          IF TERM-KEY = 8 THEN LET MODE-FLAG = "LKUPA" ENDIF
          RUN OVERLAY "ATRQMM1b"
          IF ATREQUIS.SALARY-GRADE = " " THEN LET ATREQUIS.FIELD = 0 ENDIF
          IF MODE-FLAG = "LKUPA" THEN LET MODE-FLAG = "ADD  " ENDIF

     DUPLICATE-RECORD
          INPUT MESSAGE "N,4,,,,Requisition" INTO MSG-RESP USING "ATMSGS"

     REDO-SCREEN
          INCLUDE ATRQMMHR

     END-SCRIPT
```

APPENDIX 6: ATS DATA ENTRY SCRIPTS

RQMM1C - Copy Record

```
Script: AT RQMM1C  Type: 3
Desc: Req'stn Masterfile Mx - Copy Record                    Page: 1
Last Change Date: 05/20/88     Last Compile Date: 05/26/88
            Time: 19:34:44                 Time: 08:58:57    Date: 05/31/88
================================================================================
       * REQUISITION MASTERFILE MAINTENANCE OVERLAY - COPY RECORD
       * THE FOLLOWING INCLUDE SCRIPT CONTAINS THE REQUIRED DATA DEFINITIONS
             INCLUDE ATRQMMDS

       MAIN-PROCEDURE
       * MAKE A COPY OF THE CURRENT RECORD
             PRINT MESSAGE "P,15,,,,Requisition No." USING "ATMSGS"
             INPUT SCREEN ATREQUIS CLEAR DATA-NAME LIST REQ-NO
                 POST-HELP PROCESS REDO-SCREEN-INIT
             IF TERM-KEY <> 4 THEN
                LET ATRQMSTR = ATREQUIS
                ADD ATRQMSTR USING KEY REQ-NO
                    DUPLICATE KEY IS DUPLICATE-RECORD
             ENDIF

       DUPLICATE-RECORD
             INPUT MESSAGE "N,4,,,,Requisition" INTO MSG-RESP USING "ATMSGS"

       REDO-SCREEN-INIT
             PRINT SCREEN ATREQUIh

       END-SCRIPT
```

RQMM1D - Delete Record

```
Script: AT RQMM1D  Type: 3
Desc: Req'stn Masterfile Mx - Delete Recd                    Page: 1
Last Change Date: 05/20/88     Last Compile Date: 05/26/88
            Time: 18:36:36                 Time: 08:59:29    Date: 05/31/88
================================================================================
       * REQUISITION MASTERFILE MAINTENANCE OVERLAY - DELETE RECORD
       * THE FOLLOWING INCLUDE SCRIPT CONTAINS THE REQUIRED DATA DEFINITIONS
             INCLUDE ATRQMMDS

       MAIN-PROCEDURE
       * DELETE THE CURRENT RECORD AFTER CONFIRM
             INPUT MESSAGE "Y,2" INTO MSG-RESP USING "ATMSGS"
             IF MSG-RESP = "Y" THEN
       * CHECK REFERENTIAL INTEGRITY RULES BEFORE ALLOWING DELETE
                DO REFERENTIAL-INTEGRITY
                IF DEL-MODE = "Y" THEN
                   DELETE ATRQMSTR USING KEY OLD-REQ-NO
                       MISSING KEY IS MISSING-RECORD
                       BUSY        IS BUSY-RECORD
                ENDIF
             ENDIF

       REFERENTIAL-INTEGRITY
       * FIND ANY APPLICANT RECORDS THAT CONTAIN OLD-REQ-NO USING REQ-NO
       *    SECONDARY KEY
             LET DEL-MODE = "Y"
             READ ATAPMSTR USING KEY SORT 3 RANGE FROM OLD-REQ-NO TO OLD-REQ-NO
                + "zzzzzz"
                    PROCESSING IS DISALLOW-DELETE
                    BUSY       IS BUSY-RECORD
       * CLEAR ATAPMSTR LINK FORMAT AFTER USE
             LET ATAPMSTR = ""
```

APPENDIX 6: ATS DATA ENTRY SCRIPTS

RQMM1D - Delete Record (Continued)

```
    DISALLOW-DELETE
        INPUT MESSAGE "N,10,,,,Req'stn,Applicant" INTO MSG-RESP USING
            "ATMSGS"
        LET DEL-MODE = "N"
        TERMINATE

    MISSING-RECORD
        INPUT MESSAGE "N,1,,,,Requisition" INTO MSG-RESP USING "ATMSGS"

    BUSY-RECORD
        INPUT MESSAGE "N,5,,,,Requisition" INTO MSG-RESP USING "ATMSGS"

    END-SCRIPT
```

RQMM1E - Edit Record

```
Script: AT RQMM1E  Type: 3
Desc: Req'stn Masterfile Mx - Edit Record                           Page: 1
Last Change Date: 06/06/88     Last Compile Date: 05/26/88
                  Time: 11:25:49              Time: 09:01:18    Date: 06/06/88
================================================================================
    * REQUISITION MASTERFILE MAINTENANCE OVERLAY - EDIT RECORD
    * THE FOLLOWING INCLUDE SCRIPT CONTAINS THE REQUIRED DATA DEFINITIONS
        INCLUDE ATRQMMDS

    MAIN-PROCEDURE
    *   SETTRACE PAUSE DIRECTIVE @(0,1), "T:", TERM-KEY, " M:", MODE-FLAG
    * SAVE MODE FOR RETURN AFTER EDIT
        LET OLD-MODE-FLAG = MODE-FLAG, MODE-FLAG = "DISPL"
    * MOVE DATA RECORD TO SCREEN FORMAT & ALLOW MAINTENANCE
        LET ATREQUIS = ""
        LET ATREQUIS = ATRQMSTR
    * PRINT APPROPRIATE PFKEY MSG (WITH OR WITHOUT 'DELETE')
        PRINT MESSAGE "P,28" USING "ATMSGS"
        IF REQ-STATUS = "closed   " OR REQ-STATUS = "cancelled" THEN
            PRINT MESSAGE "P,9" USING "ATMSGS"
            LET DEL-MODE = "Y"
        ELSE
            PRINT MESSAGE "P,6" USING "ATMSGS"
            LET DEL-MODE = "N"
        ENDIF
    *GET SECONDARY RECORDS AND MOVE DATA NOT SAVED TO SCREEN FORMAT
        DO GET-RECRUT-RECORD
        DO GET-PRIM-EXPCDE
        DO GET-SEC-EXPCDE
        DO GET-APPL-RECORD
    * SAVE OLD FIELD VALUES FOR COMPARISONS
        LET OLD-JOB-CODE = ATREQUIS.JOB-CODE, OLD-REQ-NO = ATREQUIS.REQ-NO,
            OLD-RECRUT = ATREQUIS.RECRUITER,
            OLD-SALGRD = ATREQUIS.SALARY-GRADE,
            OLD-PRIM-EXP = ATREQUIS.PRIM-EXP-CODE,
            OLD-SEC-EXP = ATREQUIS.SEC-EXP-CODE
    * DISPLAY SCREEN DATA AND ACCEPT INPUT AT KEY FIELD ONLY
        PRINT SCREEN ATREQUIS DATA
        INPUT SCREEN ATREQUIS KEY
            POST          PROCESS REQ-NO, SET-TERM-KEY
            POST-HELP PROCESS REDO-SCREEN
        IF MODE-FLAG = "EDIT " THEN
            CHANGE ATRQMSTR USING KEY OLD-REQ-NO
                PROCESSING   IS EDIT-RECORD
                ERROR        IS ERROR-RECORD
                MISSING KEY  IS MISSING-RECORD
                BUSY         IS BUSY-RECORD
                END          IS END-OF-MAIN-FILE
        ENDIF
```

APPENDIX 6: ATS DATA ENTRY SCRIPTS

RQMM1E - Edit Record (Continued)

```
        * CHECK FOR CHANGE IN KEY VALUE & DO APPROPRIATE PROCESSING
             IF OLD-REQ-NO <> ATREQUIS.REQ-NO THEN
                DO CHANGE-KEY-VALUE
             ENDIF
        * SET MODE-FLAG BACK TO 'NEXT' OR 'PREV' AFTER EDIT
             IF MODE-FLAG = "EDIT " AND
                (OLD-MODE-FLAG = "NEXT " OR OLD-MODE-FLAG = "PREV ") THEN
                LET MODE-FLAG = OLD-MODE-FLAG
             ENDIF
EDIT-RECORD
        * ISSUE MESSAGE THAT RECORD IS LOCKED
             PRINT MESSAGE "P,25" USING "ATMSGS"
        * SAVE A COPY OF THE SCREEN FOR EDIT COMPARISONS
             LET ATREQUIS.REQ-NO = OLD-REQ-NO
             LET S$ = ATREQUIS
        * COLLECT DATA FROM SCREEN AND UPDATE LINK
             PRINT SCREEN ATREQUIS DATA-NAME LIST REQ-NO
             INPUT SCREEN ATREQUIS DATA-NAME LIST REQ-NO, REQ-DATE,
                   JOB-CODE, JOB-STATUS, JOB-TITLE, SALARY-GRADE, PT-RATE,
                   DEPARTMENT, LOCATION, SHIFT, EDUC-LEVEL, PRIM-EXP-CODE,
                   SEC-EXP-CODE, RECRUITER, INTERNAL-SRCH, NEW-POSITION,
                   REPLACEMENT-FOR, REPLACEMENT-DATE, REQ-APPROVER,
                   REQ-APPROVER-TITLE, REQ-APPROVAL-DATE
                   POST         PROCESS REQ-NO, SET-TERM-KEY,
                                        JOB-CODE, GET-JOBCDE-RECORD,
                                        SALARY-GRADE, GET-SALGRD-RECORD,
                                        PRIM-EXP-CODE, GET-PRIM-EXPCDE,
                                        SEC-EXP-CODE, GET-SEC-EXPCDE,
                                        RECRUITER, GET-RECRUT-RECORD
                   POST-HELP PROCESS REDO-SCREEN
        * REMOVE 'RECORD LOCKED' MESSAGE, IF STILL THERE
             PRINT @(0,0), 'CL'
        * SET MODE TO "END", IF PF4 KEY WAS PRESSED
             IF MODE-FLAG = "EDIT " AND TERM-KEY = 4 THEN
                LET MODE-FLAG = "END  "
             ENDIF
        * IF KEY HAS BEEN CHANGED, CONFIRM THAT THIS IS REALLY DESIRED
             IF OLD-REQ-NO <> ATREQUIS.REQ-NO THEN
                INPUT MESSAGE "Y,4" INTO MSG-RESP USING "ATMSGS"
                IF MSG-RESP <> "Y" THEN
                   LET ATREQUIS.REQ-NO = OLD-REQ-NO
                   PRINT SCREEN ATREQUIS DATA-NAME LIST REQ-NO
                ENDIF
             ENDIF
        * ASK TO SAVE CHANGES; IF "Y", MOVE SCREEN DATA TO LINK
             IF (MODE-FLAG = "EDIT " OR MODE-FLAG = "END  ") AND S$ <> ATREQUIS
                THEN
                INPUT MESSAGE "Y,1" INTO MSG-RESP USING "ATMSGS"
                IF MSG-RESP = "Y" THEN
                   LET ATRQMSTR = ATREQUIS
                ENDIF
             ENDIF
        * SET S$ TO ZERO LENGTH TO SAVE MEMORY
             LET S$=""

SET-TERM-KEY
        * TERMINATE EDIT INPUT BASED ON PFKEY PRESSED
             IF TERM-KEY = 1 THEN
                LET MODE-FLAG = "NEXT ", ATREQUIS.FIELD = 99
             ELSE
                IF TERM-KEY = 2 THEN
```

RQMM1E - Edit Record (Continued)

```
                    LET MODE-FLAG = "PREV ", ATREQUIS.FIELD = 99
                ELSE
                    IF TERM-KEY = 3 AND DEL-MODE = "Y" THEN
                        LET MODE-FLAG = "DELET", ATREQUIS.FIELD = 99
                    ELSE
                        IF TERM-KEY = 7 THEN
                            LET MODE-FLAG = "COPY ", ATREQUIS.FIELD = 99
                        ELSE
                            IF TERM-KEY = 4 THEN
                                LET MODE-FLAG = "END  ", ATREQUIS.FIELD = 99
                            ELSE
                                IF TERM-KEY <> 6 THEN
                                    LET MODE-FLAG = "EDIT "
                                ENDIF
                            ENDIF
                        ENDIF
                    ENDIF
                ENDIF
            ENDIF

CHANGE-KEY-VALUE
*   KEEP OTHER LINKS IN SYNC WITH THIS ONE BY CHANGING ALL APPLICANT
*   RECORDS CONTAINING OLD-REQ-NO TO THE NEW REQ-NO
        RUN OVERLAY "ATRQMM1K"

GET-RECRUT-RECORD
        IF TERM-KEY = 8 OR (MODE-FLAG = "EDIT " AND OLD-RECRUT <>
            ATREQUIS.RECRUITER) OR MODE-FLAG = "DISPL" THEN
            IF TERM-KEY = 8 THEN LET MODE-FLAG = "LKUP " ENDIF
            RUN OVERLAY "ATRQMM1d"
            IF MODE-FLAG = "LKUP " THEN LET MODE-FLAG = "EDIT " ENDIF
            LET OLD-RECRUT = ATREQUIS.RECRUITER
        ENDIF
        IF ATREQUIS.RECRUITER = "         " THEN LET ATREQUIS.FIELD = 0 ENDIF

GET-PRIM-EXPCDE
        IF TERM-KEY = 8 OR (MODE-FLAG = "EDIT " AND OLD-PRIM-EXP <>
            ATREQUIS.PRIM-EXP-CODE) OR MODE-FLAG = "DISPL" THEN
            IF TERM-KEY = 8 THEN LET MODE-FLAG = "LKUP " ENDIF
            LET EXP-MODE = "PRIM"
            RUN OVERLAY "ATRQMM1c"
            IF MODE-FLAG = "LKUP " THEN LET MODE-FLAG = "EDIT " ENDIF
            LET OLD-PRIM-EXP = ATREQUIS.PRIM-EXP-CODE
        ENDIF
        IF ATREQUIS.PRIM-EXP-CODE = "  " THEN LET ATREQUIS.FIELD = 0 ENDIF

GET-SEC-EXPCDE
        IF TERM-KEY = 8 OR (ATREQUIS.SEC-EXP-CODE <> "  " AND
            OLD-SEC-EXP <> ATREQUIS.SEC-EXP-CODE) OR (MODE-FLAG = "DISPL"
            AND ATREQUIS.SEC-EXP-CODE <> "  ") THEN
            IF TERM-KEY = 8 THEN LET MODE-FLAG = "LKUP " ENDIF
            LET EXP-MODE = "SECD"
            RUN OVERLAY "ATRQMM1c"
            IF MODE-FLAG = "LKUP " THEN LET MODE-FLAG = "EDIT " ENDIF
    ELSE
        IF ATREQUIS.SEC-EXP-CODE = "  " AND MODE-FLAG <> "DISPL" THEN
            LET SEC-EXP-DESC = ""
            PRINT SCREEN ATREQUIS DATA-NAME LIST SEC-EXP-DESC
        ENDIF
    ENDIF
    LET OLD-SEC-EXP = ATREQUIS.SEC-EXP-CODE
```

APPENDIX 6: ATS DATA ENTRY SCRIPTS

RQMM1E - Edit Record (Continued)

```
    GET-JOBCDE-RECORD
        IF TERM-KEY = 8 OR OLD-JOB-CODE <> ATREQUIS.JOB-CODE THEN
            IF TERM-KEY = 8 THEN LET MODE-FLAG = "LKUP " ENDIF
            RUN OVERLAY "ATRQMM1a"
            IF MODE-FLAG = "LKUP " THEN LET MODE-FLAG = "EDIT " ENDIF
            LET OLD-JOB-CODE = ATREQUIS.JOB-CODE
        ENDIF
        IF ATREQUIS.JOB-CODE = "    " OR ATREQUIS.JOB-CODE = "0000" THEN
            LET ATREQUIS.FIELD = 0
        ENDIF

    GET-SALGRD-RECORD
        IF TERM-KEY = 8 OR OLD-SALGRD <> ATREQUIS.SALARY-GRADE THEN
            IF TERM-KEY = 8 THEN LET MODE-FLAG = "LKUP " ENDIF
            RUN OVERLAY "ATRQMM1b"
            IF MODE-FLAG = "LKUP " THEN LET MODE-FLAG = "EDIT " ENDIF
            LET OLD-SALGRD = ATREQUIS.SALARY-GRADE
        ENDIF
        IF ATREQUIS.SALARY-GRADE = " " THEN LET ATREQUIS.FIELD = 0 ENDIF

    GET-APPL-RECORD
        IF ATREQUIS.IDENT <> "     " THEN
            RUN OVERLAY "ATRQMM1e"
        ENDIF

MISSING-RECORD
        INPUT MESSAGE "N,1,,,,Requisition" INTO MSG-RESP USING "ATMSGS"
BUSY-RECORD
        INPUT MESSAGE "N,5,,,,Requisition" INTO MSG-RESP USING "ATMSGS"
END-OF-MAIN-FILE
        INPUT MESSAGE "N,2,,,,Requisition" INTO MSG-RESP USING "ATMSGS"
ERROR-RECORD
        IF ERR = 11 THEN
            INPUT MESSAGE "N,12,,,,Requisition" INTO MSG-RESP USING "ATMSGS"
        ELSE
            INPUT MESSAGE "N,13,,,,Requisition" INTO MSG-RESP USING "ATMSGS"
        ENDIF
        LET ATREQUIS.REQ-NO = OLD-REQ-NO, ATRQMSTR.REQ-NO = OLD-REQ-NO
REDO-SCREEN
        INCLUDE ATRQMMHR

END-SCRIPT
```

APPENDIX 6: ATS DATA ENTRY SCRIPTS

RQMM1K - Key Change

```
Script: AT RQMM1K  Type: 3
Desc: Req'stn Masterfile Mx - Key Change                     Page: 1
Last Change Date: 05/20/88     Last Compile Date: 05/26/88
           Time: 18:36:56                 Time: 09:01:54     Date: 05/31/88
================================================================================
     * REQUISITION MASTERFILE MAINTENANCE OVERLAY - KEY CHANGE FROM EDIT
     * THE FOLLOWING INCLUDE SCRIPT CONTAINS THE REQUIRED DATA DEFINITIONS
         INCLUDE ATRQMMDS

     MAIN-PROCEDURE
     *   SETTRACE PAUSE DIRECTIVE @(0,1), "T:", TERM-KEY, " M:", MODE-FLAG
     * GET ALL APPLICANT RECORDS THAT CONTAIN OLD-REQ-NO AND CHANGE THEM
     *   USING THE REQ-NO SECONDARY KEY
         CHANGE ATAPMSTR USING KEY SORT 3 RANGE FROM OLD-REQ-NO TO
             OLD-REQ-NO + "zzzzzz"
             PROCESSING IS CHANGE-RECORD
             BUSY       IS BUSY-RECORD
     * CLEAR ATAPMSTR LINK FORMAT AFTER USE
         LET ATAPMSTR = ""

     CHANGE-RECORD
         LET ATAPMSTR.REQ-NO = ATRQMSTR.REQ-NO

     BUSY-RECORD
         INPUT MESSAGE "N,5,,,,Applicant" INTO MSG-RESP USING "ATMSGS"

     END-SCRIPT
```

RQMM1L - Main Lookup

```
Script: AT RQMM1L  Type: 3
Desc: Req'stn Masterfile Mx - Main Lookup                    Page: 1
Last Change Date: 05/20/88     Last Compile Date: 05/26/88
           Time: 18:37:15                 Time: 09:02:20     Date: 05/31/88
================================================================================
     * REQUISITION MASTERFILE MAINTENANCE OVERLAY - REQ'STN LOOKUP
     * THE FOLLOWING INCLUDE SCRIPT CONTAINS THE REQUIRED DATA DEFINITIONS
         INCLUDE ATRQMMDS

     MAIN-PROCEDURE
     *   SETTRACE PAUSE DIRECTIVE @(0,1), "T:", TERM-KEY, " M:", MODE-FLAG
     * DISPLAY LIST OF RECORDS IN VIEW AS LOOKUP AID
         OPEN VIEW ATREQLVW
         IF MODE-FLAG = "LKUPA" THEN
             PRINT MESSAGE "P,24,,,,Req'stn" USING "ATMSGS"
         ELSE
             PRINT MESSAGE "P,23,,,,Req'stn" USING "ATMSGS"
         ENDIF
         PRINT MESSAGE "P,27,,,,Req'stn" USING "ATMSGS"
         PRINT VIEW ATREQLVW USING KEY RANGE FROM "" TO "zzzz"
             KEY INTO ATREQUIS.REQ-NO
             WINDOW LINE IS 16
                    COLUMN IS 3
                    NUMBER LINES ARE 5
                    CHARACTERS ARE 72
                    BORDER TYPE IS "R"
                    HEADING IS "Y"
         IF TERM-KEY = 4 THEN LET ATREQUIS.REQ-NO = "" ENDIF
     * REPRINT SCREEN
         PRINT SCREEN ATREQUIh

     END-SCRIPT
```

6-35

APPENDIX 6: ATS DATA ENTRY SCRIPTS

RQMM1a - Job Code

```
Script: AT RQMM1a   Type: 3
Desc: Req'stn Masterfile Mx - Job Code                     Page: 1
Last Change Date: 05/20/88    Last Compile Date: 05/26/88
            Time: 18:37:23                  Time: 09:03:02    Date: 05/31/88
===============================================================================
     * REQUISITION MASTERFILE MAINTENANCE OVERLAY - JOB CODE LOOKUP
     * THE FOLLOWING INCLUDE SCRIPT CONTAINS THE REQUIRED DATA DEFINITIONS
         INCLUDE ATRQMMDS

         MAIN-PROCEDURE
     * DISPLAY LIST OF RECORDS IN VIEW AS LOOKUP AID
         IF MODE-FLAG = "LKUP " OR MODE-FLAG = "LKUPA" THEN
             OPEN VIEW ATJOBLVW
             LET K9$ = ATREQUIS.JOB-CODE
             PRINT MESSAGE "P,23,,,,Job Code" USING "ATMSGS"
             PRINT MESSAGE "P,27,,,,Job Code" USING "ATMSGS"
             PRINT VIEW ATJOBLVW USING KEY RANGE FROM "" TO "zzzz"
                 KEY INTO K9$
                 WINDOW LINE IS 13
                        COLUMN IS 43
                        NUMBER LINES ARE 8
                        CHARACTERS ARE 33
                        BORDER TYPE IS "R"
                        HEADING IS "Y"
     * SAVE TERM-KEY VALUE FOR USE LATER IN SCRIPT
             LET R9 = TERM-KEY
     * REPRINT CORRECT PF KEY MESSAGE BASED ON MODE-FLAG AND DEL-MODE
             IF MODE-FLAG = "LKUP " AND DEL-MODE = "Y" THEN
                 PRINT MESSAGE "P,9" USING "ATMSGS"
             ELSE
                 IF MODE-FLAG = "LKUP " AND DEL-MODE <> "Y" THEN
                     PRINT MESSAGE "P,6" USING "ATMSGS"
                 ELSE
                     IF MODE-FLAG = "LKUPA" THEN
                         PRINT MESSAGE "P,10" USING "ATMSGS"
                     ENDIF
                 ENDIF
             ENDIF
     * REPRINT SCREEN AFTER VIEW IS CLEARED
             INCLUDE ATRQMMVR
     * CHECK FOR OVERWRITE OF CODE IF WINDOW CLOSED WITHOUT PF4
             IF R9 <> 4 THEN
                 IF ATREQUIS.JOB-CODE <> "0000" AND ATREQUIS.JOB-CODE <> K9$
                 THEN
                     INPUT MESSAGE "Y,5,,,,Job Code," + ATREQUIS.JOB-CODE
                         + "," + K9$ INTO MSG-RESP USING "ATMSGS"
                     IF MSG-RESP = "Y" THEN
                         LET ATREQUIS.JOB-CODE = K9$
                     ENDIF
                 ELSE
                     LET ATREQUIS.JOB-CODE = K9$
                 ENDIF
             ENDIF
         ENDIF
     * LOOK FOR CODE RECORD & MOVE DATA INTO SCREEN FORMAT
         IF ATREQUIS.JOB-CODE <> "0000" THEN
             READ ATJOBCDE USING KEY ATREQUIS.JOB-CODE
                 MISSING KEY IS MISSING-RECORD
```

APPENDIX 6: ATS DATA ENTRY SCRIPTS

RQMM1a - Job Code (Continued)

```
Script: AT RQMM1a   Type: 3
Desc: Req'stn Masterfile Mx - Job Code                      Page: 2
Last Change Date: 05/20/88    Last Compile Date: 05/26/88
           Time: 18:37:23                Time: 09:03:02     Date: 05/31/88
================================================================================
                BUSY         IS BUSY-RECORD
                END          IS END-OF-FILE
              LET ATREQUIS = ATJOBCDE
              LET ATJOBCDE = ""
              IF MODE-FLAG <> "DISPL" THEN
                   PRINT SCREEN ATREQUIS DATA-NAME LIST JOB-CODE,
                                                       JOB-STATUS,
                                                       JOB-TITLE,
                                                       EXEMPT-CLASS,
                                                       EEOC-JOB-CAT
              ENDIF
         ENDIF

    MISSING-RECORD
         INPUT MESSAGE "N,1,,,,Job Code" INTO MSG-RESP USING "ATMSGS"

    BUSY-RECORD
         INPUT MESSAGE "N,5,,,,Job Code" INTO MSG-RESP USING "ATMSGS"

    END-OF-FILE
         INPUT MESSAGE "N,2,,,,Job Code" INTO MSG-RESP USING "ATMSGS"

    END-SCRIPT
```

RQMM1b - Salary Grade

```
Script: AT RQMM1b   Type: 3
Desc: Req'stn Masterfile Mx - Salary Grde                   Page: 1
Last Change Date: 05/20/88    Last Compile Date: 05/26/88
           Time: 18:37:47                Time: 09:03:44     Date: 05/31/88
================================================================================
     * REQUISITION MASTERFILE MAINTENANCE OVERLAY - SALARY GRADE LOOKUP
     * THE FOLLOWING INCLUDE SCRIPT CONTAINS THE REQUIRED DATA DEFINITIONS
          INCLUDE ATRQMMDS

     MAIN-PROCEDURE
     * DISPLAY LIST OF RECORDS IN VIEW AS LOOKUP AID
         IF MODE-FLAG = "LKUP " OR MODE-FLAG = "LKUPA" THEN
              OPEN VIEW ATSALLVW
              LET K9$ = ATREQUIS.SALARY-GRADE
              PRINT MESSAGE "P,23,,,,Sal Grade" USING "ATMSGS"
              PRINT MESSAGE "P,27,,,,Sal Grade" USING "ATMSGS"
              PRINT VIEW ATSALLVW USING KEY RANGE FROM "" TO "zz"
                   KEY INTO K9$
                   WINDOW LINE IS 13
                          COLUMN IS 43
                          NUMBER LINES ARE 8
                          CHARACTERS ARE 33
                          BORDER TYPE IS "R"
                          HEADING IS "Y"
     * SAVE TERM-KEY VALUE FOR USE LATER IN SCRIPT
              LET R9 = TERM-KEY
     * REPRINT CORRECT PF KEY MESSAGE BASED ON MODE-FLAG AND DEL-MODE
              IF MODE-FLAG = "LKUP " AND DEL-MODE = "Y" THEN
                   PRINT MESSAGE "P,9" USING "ATMSGS"
              ELSE
                   IF MODE-FLAG = "LKUP " AND DEL-MODE <> "Y" THEN
                        PRINT MESSAGE "P,6" USING "ATMSGS"
                   ELSE
```

6-37

APPENDIX 6: ATS DATA ENTRY SCRIPTS

RQMM1b - Salary Grade (Continued)

```
                    IF MODE-FLAG = "LKUPA" THEN
                         PRINT MESSAGE "P,10" USING "ATMSGS"
                    ENDIF
               ENDIF
          ENDIF
* REPRINT SCREEN AFTER VIEW IS CLEARED
          INCLUDE ATRQMMVR
* CHECK FOR OVERWRITE OF CODE
          IF R9 <> 4 THEN
               IF ATREQUIS.SALARY-GRADE <> "  " AND
                    ATREQUIS.SALARY-GRADE <> K9$ THEN
                    INPUT MESSAGE "Y,5,,,,Sal Grade," + ATREQUIS.SALARY-GRADE
                         + "," + K9$ INTO MSG-RESP USING "ATMSGS"
                    IF MSG-RESP = "Y" THEN
                         LET ATREQUIS.SALARY-GRADE = K9$
                    ENDIF
               ELSE
                    LET ATREQUIS.SALARY-GRADE = K9$
               ENDIF
          ENDIF
     ENDIF
* LOOK FOR CODE RECORD & MOVE DATA INTO SCREEN FORMAT
     IF ATREQUIS.SALARY-GRADE <> "  " THEN
          READ ATSALGRD USING KEY ATREQUIS.SALARY-GRADE
               MISSING KEY IS MISSING-RECORD
               BUSY        IS BUSY-RECORD
               END         IS END-OF-FILE
          LET ATREQUIS = ATSALGRD
          LET ATSALGRD = ""
          IF MODE-FLAG <> "DISPL" THEN
               PRINT SCREEN ATREQUIS DATA-NAME LIST SALARY-GRADE,
                                                   SALARY-MIN,
                                                   SALARY-MAX
          ENDIF
     ENDIF

MISSING-RECORD
     INPUT MESSAGE "N,1,,,,Salary Grade" INTO MSG-RESP USING "ATMSGS"

BUSY-RECORD
     INPUT MESSAGE "N,5,,,,Salary Grade" INTO MSG-RESP USING "ATMSGS"

END-OF-FILE
     INPUT MESSAGE "N,2,,,,Salary Grade" INTO MSG-RESP USING "ATMSGS"

END-SCRIPT
```

APPENDIX 6: ATS DATA ENTRY SCRIPTS

RQMM1c - Experience Codes

```
Script: AT RQMM1c  Type: 3
Desc: Req'stn Masterfile Mx - Exper Codes                          Page: 1
Last Change Date: 05/20/88    Last Compile Date: 05/26/88
           Time: 18:38:10                 Time: 09:04:48     Date: 05/31/88
================================================================================
      * REQUISITION MASTERFILE MAINTENANCE OVERLAY - EXP CODES LOOKUP
      * THE FOLLOWING INCLUDE SCRIPT CONTAINS THE REQUIRED DATA DEFINITIONS
            INCLUDE ATRQMMDS

        MAIN-PROCEDURE
      * ADD DISPLAY OF RECORDS IN VIEW AS LOOKUP AID
            IF MODE-FLAG = "LKUP " OR MODE-FLAG = "LKUPA" THEN
               OPEN VIEW ATEXPLVW
               LET K9$ = ATREQUIS.PRIM-EXP-CODE
               PRINT MESSAGE "P,23,,,,Exp Code" USING "ATMSGS"
               PRINT MESSAGE "P,27,,,,Exp Code" USING "ATMSGS"
               PRINT VIEW ATEXPLVW USING KEY RANGE FROM "" TO "zz"
                  KEY INTO K9$
                  WINDOW LINE IS 13
                         COLUMN IS 43
                         NUMBER LINES ARE 8
                         CHARACTERS ARE 33
                         BORDER TYPE IS "R"
                         HEADING IS "Y"
      * SAVE TERM-KEY VALUE FOR USE LATER IN SCRIPT
               LET R9 = TERM-KEY
      * REPRINT CORRECT PF KEY MESSAGE BASED ON MODE-FLAG AND DEL-MODE
               IF MODE-FLAG = "LKUP " AND DEL-MODE = "Y" THEN
                  PRINT MESSAGE "P,9" USING "ATMSGS"
               ELSE
                  IF MODE-FLAG = "LKUP " AND DEL-MODE <> "Y" THEN
                     PRINT MESSAGE "P,6" USING "ATMSGS"
                  ELSE
                     IF MODE-FLAG = "LKUPA" THEN
                        PRINT MESSAGE "P,10" USING "ATMSGS"
                     ENDIF
                  ENDIF
               ENDIF
      * REPRINT SCREEN AFTER VIEW IS CLEARED
               INCLUDE ATRQMMVR
      * CHECK FOR OVERWRITE OF CODE, IF TERM-KEY 4 NOT PRESSED
               IF R9 <> 4 THEN
                  IF EXP-MODE = "PRIM" AND ATREQUIS.PRIM-EXP-CODE <> " "
                                       AND ATREQUIS.PRIM-EXP-CODE <> K9$ THEN
                     INPUT MESSAGE "Y,5,,,,Prim Exp Code," +
                        ATREQUIS.PRIM-EXP-CODE + "," + K9$ INTO MSG-RESP
                        USING "ATMSGS"
                     IF MSG-RESP = "Y" THEN
                        LET ATREQUIS.PRIM-EXP-CODE = K9$
                     ENDIF
                  ELSE
                     IF EXP-MODE = "PRIM" THEN
                        LET ATREQUIS.PRIM-EXP-CODE = K9$
                     ENDIF
                  ENDIF
                  IF EXP-MODE = "SECD" AND ATREQUIS.SEC-EXP-CODE <> " "
                                       AND ATREQUIS.SEC-EXP-CODE <> K9$ THEN
                     INPUT MESSAGE "Y,5,,,,Secd Exp Code," +
```

APPENDIX 6: ATS DATA ENTRY SCRIPTS

RQMM1c - Experience Codes (Continued)

```
                        ATREQUIS.SEC-EXP-CODE + "," + K9$ INTO MSG-RESP
                        USING "ATMSGS"
                  IF MSG-RESP = "Y" THEN
                        LET ATREQUIS.SEC-EXP-CODE = K9$
                  ENDIF
            ELSE
                  IF EXP-MODE = "SECD" THEN
                        LET ATREQUIS.SEC-EXP-CODE = K9$
                  ENDIF
            ENDIF
         ENDIF
      ENDIF
* DO APPROPRIATE PROCEDURE DEPENDING ON MODE
      IF EXP-MODE = "PRIM" THEN
            DO GET-PRIM-EXPCDE
      ELSE
            DO GET-SEC-EXPCDE
      ENDIF

GET-PRIM-EXPCDE
      LET TEMP-EXPER-CODE = PRIM-EXP-CODE
      DO GET-EXPCDE-RECORD
      LET ATREQUIS.PRIM-EXP-DESC = ATEXPCDE.EXPER-DESC
      LET ATEXPCDE = ""
      IF MODE-FLAG <> "DISPL" THEN
            PRINT SCREEN ATREQUIS DATA-NAME LIST PRIM-EXP-CODE,
                                                PRIM-EXP-DESC
      ENDIF

GET-SEC-EXPCDE
      LET TEMP-EXPER-CODE = SEC-EXP-CODE
      IF TEMP-EXPER-CODE <> "  " THEN
            DO GET-EXPCDE-RECORD
            LET ATREQUIS.SEC-EXP-DESC = ATEXPCDE.EXPER-DESC
            IF MODE-FLAG <> "DISPL" THEN
                  PRINT SCREEN ATREQUIS DATA-NAME LIST SEC-EXP-CODE,
                                                      SEC-EXP-DESC
            ENDIF
      ENDIF
      LET ATEXPCDE = ""

GET-EXPCDE-RECORD
* LOOK FOR EXP CODE RECORD
      IF TEMP-EXPER-CODE <> "  " THEN
            READ ATEXPCDE USING KEY TEMP-EXPER-CODE
                  MISSING KEY IS MISSING-RECORD
                  BUSY        IS BUSY-RECORD
                  END         IS END-OF-FILE
      ENDIF

MISSING-RECORD
      INPUT MESSAGE "N,1,,,,Exp Code" INTO MSG-RESP USING "ATMSGS"
BUSY-RECORD
      INPUT MESSAGE "N,5,,,,Exp Code" INTO MSG-RESP USING "ATMSGS"
END-OF-FILE
      INPUT MESSAGE "N,2,,,,Exp Code" INTO MSG-RESP USING "ATMSGS"

END-SCRIPT
```

APPENDIX 6: ATS DATA ENTRY SCRIPTS

RQMM1d - Recruiter

```
Script: AT RQMM1d   Type: 3
Desc: Req'stn Masterfile Mx - Recruiter                            Page: 1
Last Change Date: 05/20/88    Last Compile Date: 05/26/88
           Time: 18:38:20                Time: 09:05:42     Date: 05/31/88
================================================================================
     * REQUISITION MASTERFILE MAINTENANCE OVERLAY - RECRUITER LOOKUP
     * THE FOLLOWING INCLUDE SCRIPT CONTAINS THE REQUIRED DATA DEFINITIONS
         INCLUDE ATRQMMDS

     MAIN-PROCEDURE
     * DISPLAY LIST OF RECORDS IN VIEW AS LOOKUP AID
         IF MODE-FLAG = "LKUP " OR MODE-FLAG = "LKUPA" THEN
             OPEN VIEW ATRECLVW
             LET K9$ = ATREQUIS.RECRUITER
             PRINT MESSAGE "P,23,,,,Recruiter" USING "ATMSGS"
             PRINT MESSAGE "P,27,,,,Recruiter" USING "ATMSGS"
             PRINT VIEW ATRECLVW USING KEY RANGE FROM "" TO "zzzzzz"
                 KEY INTO K9$
                 WINDOW LINE IS 13
                        COLUMN IS 43
                        NUMBER LINES ARE 8
                        CHARACTERS ARE 33
                        BORDER TYPE IS "R"
                        HEADING IS "Y"
     * SAVE TERM-KEY VALUE FOR USE LATER IN SCRIPT
             LET R9 = TERM-KEY
     * REPRINT CORRECT PF KEY MESSAGE BASED ON MODE-FLAG AND DEL-MODE
             IF MODE-FLAG = "LKUP " AND DEL-MODE = "Y" THEN
                 PRINT MESSAGE "P,3" USING "ATMSGS"
             ELSE
                 IF MODE-FLAG = "LKUP " AND DEL-MODE <> "Y" THEN
                     PRINT MESSAGE "P,6" USING "ATMSGS"
                 ELSE
                     IF MODE-FLAG = "LKUPA" THEN
                         PRINT MESSAGE "P,10" USING "ATMSGS"
                     ENDIF
                 ENDIF
             ENDIF
     * REPRINT SCREEN AFTER VIEW IS CLEARED
             INCLUDE ATRQMMVR
     * CHECK FOR OVERWRITE OF CODE, IF TERM-KEY <> 4
             IF R9 <> 4 THEN
                 IF ATREQUIS.RECRUITER <> "      " AND
                    ATREQUIS.RECRUITER <> K9$ THEN
                     INPUT MESSAGE "Y,5,,,,Recruiter," + ATREQUIS.RECRUITER
                         + "," + K9$ INTO MSG-RESP USING "ATMSGS"
                     IF MSG-RESP = "Y" THEN
                         LET ATREQUIS.RECRUITER = K9$
                     ENDIF
                 ELSE
                     LET ATREQUIS.RECRUITER = K9$
                 ENDIF
             ENDIF
         ENDIF
     * LOOK FOR CODE RECORD & MOVE DATA INTO SCREEN FORMAT
         IF ATREQUIS.RECRUITER <> "      " THEN
             READ ATRECRUT USING KEY ATREQUIS.RECRUITER
                 MISSING KEY IS MISSING-RECORD
                 BUSY        IS BUSY-RECORD
                 END         IS END-OF-FILE
             LET ATREQUIS.RECRUT-NAME = ATRECRUT.RECRUT-NAME
             LET ATRECRUT = ""
             IF MODE-FLAG <> "DISPL" THEN
                 PRINT SCREEN ATREQUIS DATA-NAME LIST RECRUITER,
                                                      RECRUT-NAME
             ENDIF
         ENDIF
```

6-41

APPENDIX 6: ATS DATA ENTRY SCRIPTS

RQMM1d - Recruiter (Continued)

```
    MISSING-RECORD
        INPUT MESSAGE "N,1,,,,Recruiter" INTO MSG-RESP USING "ATMSGS"

    BUSY-RECORD
        INPUT MESSAGE "N,5,,,,Recruiter" INTO MSG-RESP USING "ATMSGS"

    END-OF-FILE
        INPUT MESSAGE "N,2,,,,Recruiter" INTO MSG-RESP USING "ATMSGS"

    END-SCRIPT
```

RQMM1e - Applicant

```
Script: AT RQMM1e   Type: 3
Desc: Req'stn Masterfile Mx - Applicant                         Page: 1
Last Change Date: 05/20/88    Last Compile Date: 05/26/88
           Time: 18:38:30                Time: 09:06:20    Date: 05/31/88
===============================================================================
    * REQUISITION MASTERFILE MAINTENANCE OVERLAY - APPLICANT LOOKUP
    * THE FOLLOWING INCLUDE SCRIPT CONTAINS THE REQUIRED DATA DEFINITIONS
        INCLUDE ATRQMMDS

    MAIN-PROCEDURE
    * LOOK FOR CODE RECORD & MOVE DATA INTO SCREEN FORMAT
        READ ATAPMSTR USING KEY ATREQUIS.IDENT
            MISSING KEY IS MISSING-RECORD
            BUSY        IS BUSY-RECORD
            END         IS END-OF-FILE
        LET ATREQUIS.NAME = ATAPMSTR.NAME,
            ATREQUIS.NO-DAYS-TO-FILL = ATAPMSTR.NO-DAYS-TO-FILL,
            ATREQUIS.TOTAL-REC-EXP = ATAPMSTR.TOTAL-REC-EXP
        LET ATAPMSTR = ""
        IF MODE-FLAG <> "DISPL" THEN
            PRINT SCREEN ATREQUIS DATA-NAME LIST IDENT,
                                              NAME,
                                              NO-DAYS-TO-FILL,
                                              TOTAL-REC-EXP

        ENDIF

    MISSING-RECORD
        INPUT MESSAGE "N,1,,,,Applicant" INTO MSG-RESP USING "ATMSGS"

    BUSY-RECORD
        INPUT MESSAGE "N,5,,,,Applicant" INTO MSG-RESP USING "ATMSGS"

    END-OF-FILE
        INPUT MESSAGE "N,2,,,,Applicant" INTO MSG-RESP USING "ATMSGS"

    END-SCRIPT
```

APPENDIX 6: ATS DATA ENTRY SCRIPTS

RQMMDS - Data Section

```
Script: AT RQMMDS   Type: 5
Desc: Req'stn Masterfile Mx - Data Sectn                       Page: 1
Last Change Date: 05/20/88      Last Compile Date:
             Time: 18:38:52               Time:             Date: 05/31/88
================================================================================
      * INCLUDE SCRIPT FOR REQUISITION MASTERFILE MAINTENANCE FUNCTION
      * DEFINE SCREENS HERE
      SN   ATREQUIS, ATREQUIh, ATREQUIr
      * DEFINE LINKS HERE
      LN   ATRQMSTR, ATAPMSTR, ATJOBCDE, ATSALGRD, ATEXPCDE, ATRECRUT
      * DEFINE VIEWS HERE
      VN   ATREQLVW, ATEXPLVW, ATJOBLVW, ATSALLVW, ATRECLVW
      * DEFINE DATA ELEMENTS HERE
      DN   MODE-FLAG (5), OLD-MODE-FLAG (5), FILE-NAME (8), MSG-RESP (1),
           SORT-NO (2.0), TEMP-EXPER-CODE (2), EXP-MODE (4), DEL-MODE (1)
      DN   OLD-JOB-CODE (4), OLD-REQ-NO (4), OLD-PRIM-EXP (2), OLD-SALGRD (2),
           OLD-SEC-EXP (2), OLD-RECRUT (6)
```

RQMMHR - Help Refresh

```
Script: AT RQMMHR   Type: 5
Desc: Req'stn Masterfile Mx - Help Refrsh                      Page: 1
Last Change Date: 05/20/88      Last Compile Date:
             Time: 18:39:07               Time:             Date: 05/31/88
================================================================================
      * REQUISITION MASTERFILE MAINTENANCE - INCLUDE SCRIPT FOR HELP REFRESH
             PRINT SCREEN ATREQUIh
             PRINT SCREEN ATREQUIS DATA-NAME LIST SHIFT, EDUC-LEVEL,
                                        PRIM-EXP-CODE, PRIM-EXP-DESC,
                                        SEC-EXP-CODE, SEC-EXP-DESC,
                                        REQ-STATUS, REQ-DISP-DATE,
                                        IDENT, NAME, NO-DAYS-TO-FILL,
                                        TOTAL-REC-EXP
```

RQMMVR - View Refresh

```
Script: AT RQMMVR   Type: 5
Desc: Req'stn Masterfile Mx - View Refrsh                      Page: 1
Last Change Date: 05/20/88      Last Compile Date:
             Time: 18:39:18               Time:             Date: 05/31/88
================================================================================
      * REQUISITION MASTERFILE MAINTENANCE - INCLUDE SCRIPT FOR VIEW REFRESH
             PRINT SCREEN ATREQUIr
             PRINT SCREEN ATREQUIS DATA-NAME LIST REQ-APPROVER,
                                        REQ-APPROVER-TITLE,
                                        REQ-APPROVAL-DATE, REQ-STATUS,
                                        REQ-DISP-DATE, IDENT, NAME,
                                        NO-DAYS-TO-FILL, TOTAL-REC-EXP
```

Appendix 7

ATS SAMPLE CODE FILE DATA

All definitions from the sample Applicant Tracking System are from the AT library.

ATEXPCDE	Experience Code Listing
ATDISPCD	Disposition Code Listing
ATJOBCDE	Job Code Listing
ATRECRUT	Recruiter Code Listing
ATSALGRD	Salary Grade Listing

```
06/03/88              ATEXPCDE - Experience Code Listing              Page: 1

CD DESCRIPTION
-- -----------------------------

10 Marketing
11 V.P., Marketing
12 Dir, Marketing Support
13 Dir, Product Marketing
14 Mgr, Market Planning
15 Mgr, Marketing Support
16 Mgr, Product Marketing
17 Marketing Support Analyst
18 Marketing Systems Analyst
19 Marketing Support Technician
20 Sales
30 Finance
31 V.P., Finance
32 Controller
33 Treasurer
34 Auditor
35 Accounting/Cost Manager
36 Financial Planning
37 Credit Manager
38 CPA Firm Experience
39 Big 8 Firm Experience
40 Operations
50 Manufacturing/Production
60 Engineering
70 Data Processing
80 General Management
90 Staff
```

APPENDIX 7: ATS SAMPLE CODE FILE DATA

```
06/03/88              ATDISPCD - Disposition Code Listing              Page: 1

ID DESCRIPTION
-- ------------------------------

AJ Awaiting Job
DN Do NOT Reconsider
HI Hired
NH Not Hired
NP No Position Available
NQ Not Qualified For Job
NS Hired - No Show
OM Offer Made
OR Offer Rejected
PI Pending Interviews
PR Poor References
RC Reference Checking In Progress
WA Withdrew Application


06/03/88                ATJOBCDE - Job Code Listing                    Page: 1

JOB                              J  JB E
CODE JOB TITLE                   C  ST N
---- ------------------------    -  -- -

0101 V.P., Marketing             A  FT E
0102 V.P., Marketing Oper.       B  FT E
0110 Dir, Product Marketing      B  FT E
0111 Dir, Marketing Comm.        B  FT E
0112 Dir, Marketing Support      B  FT E
0120 Mgr, Product Marketing      B  FT E
0121 Mgr, Market Planning        B  FT E
0122 Mgr, Marketing Support      B  FT E
0123 Mgr, Marketing Docum.       B  FT E
0130 Spvr, Marketing Support     C  FT E
0131 Spvr, Product Marketing     C  FT E
0132 Prin. Mktng Systems Anlst   C  FT E
0133 Prin. Technical Writer      C  FT E
0134 Prin. Mktng Support Anlst   C  FT E
0140 Sr. Mktng Systems Analyst   D  FT E
0141 Sr. Mktng Support Analyst   D  FT E
0142 Sr. Technical Writer        D  FT E
0143 Sr. Mktng Systems Tech.     E  FT N
0150 Technical Writer            E  FT E
0151 Proofreader/Editor          E  FT E
0152 Marketing Systems Analyst   E  FT E
0153 Marketing Systems Tech.     F  FT N
0154 Marketing Support Analyst   F  FT N
0155 Marketing Support Tech.     F  FT N


06/03/88              ATRECRUT - Recruiter Code Listing                Page: 1

RECRUT                                                     I
ID     RECRUITER NAME            RATE     TELEPHONE        N
------ ------------------------- -------- ------------     -

ALLENH Henry Allen               1050.00  714 577-9922     Y
ARTHUD David Arthur              1250.00  213 987-1234     N
JOHNSL Lorraine Johnson          1200.00  714 998-7763     Y
JONESS Samantha Jones            1500.00  619 776-5433     N
SMITHK Ken Smith                 1000.00  213 123-4561     N
SULLIJ John Sullivan             1100.00  714 876-5433     Y
```

APPENDIX 7: ATS SAMPLE CODE FILE DATA

```
06/03/88              ATSALGRD - Salary Grade Listing              Page: 1

SL                                   MIN         MAX
GD   DESCRIPTION                     SALARY      SALARY
--   ------------------------------  ----------  ----------

01   Grade  1                          8425.00    13520.00
02   Grade  2                          9300.00    14875.00
03   Grade  3                         10190.00    16325.00
04   Grade  4                         11230.00    17940.00
05   Grade  5                         12425.00    19865.00
06   Grade  6                         13625.00    21790.00
07   Grade  7                         14975.00    23920.00
08   Grade  8                         16430.00    26315.00
09   Grade  9                         18150.00    29015.00
10   Grade 10                         19915.00    31875.00
11   Grade 11                         21945.00    35100.00
12   Grade 12                         24125.00    38585.00
15   Grade 15                         16950.00    27175.00
16   Grade 16                         18565.00    29650.00
17   Grade 17                         20280.00    32400.00
18   Grade 18                         22100.00    35360.00
19   Grade 19                         24125.00    38585.00
20   Grade 20                         26365.00    42120.00
21   Grade 21                         28800.00    46025.00
22   Grade 22                         32500.00    50200.00
23   Grade 23                         34275.00    54800.00
24   Grade 24                         37450.00    59850.00
25   Grade 25                         40825.00    65315.00
26   Grade 26                         44675.00    71400.00
27   Grade 27                         48775.00    77950.00
28   Grade 28                         53250.00    85125.00
29   Grade 29                         58150.00    92925.00
30   Grade 30                         60000.00   120000.00
31   Grade 31                         75000.00   150000.00
```

Appendix 8

ATS REPORT SPECIFICATIONS

Report #1 - Applicants By Disposition (ATAPDSPR)

This report prints a list of applicants grouped by disposition code. Selection is for all applicants. The report is sequenced by Applicant ID within Disposition Code. The data fields printed are:

>Disp Code and Description (once for each group)
>Disp Date
>Applicant Name
>Applicant ID
>Date Entered
>Recruiter Name (from Recruiter file)
>Source
>Position Applied For (Job Title from Req, if any)
>Total Recruiting Expenses
>No. Days To Fill

Report #2 - Source Analysis Report (ATAPSRCR)

This report prints a list of applicants grouped by source. Selection is for all applicants. The report is sequenced by Applicant ID within Source. The data fields printed are:

>Source (once for each group)
>Disp Code
>Disp Date
>Applicant ID
>Applicant Name

APPENDIX 8: ATS REPORT SPECIFICATIONS

       Date Entered
       Recruiter Name (from Recruiter file)
       Req No
       Position Applied For (Job Title from Req, if any)
       Total Recruiting Expenses
       No. Days To Fill

Subtotals By Source include:

       # applicants
       Total Recruiting Expenses
       Average No. Days To Fill

Report #3 - Open Requisitions Summary Report (ATOPNRQR)

This report prints a list of all "open" requisitions grouped by department. Selection is for all requisitions with REQ-STATUS="open". The report is sequenced by Req No. The data fields printed are:

       Req No
       Req Date
       Department
       Job Title
       Salary Grade
       Min Salary
       Max Salary
       Primary Experience Code
       Recruiter ID

Report #4 - Recruiter Analysis Report (ATRECRNR)

This report prints a list of requisitions grouped by Recruiter ID. Selection is for all closed requisitions. The report is sequenced by Applicant ID within Recruiter ID. The data fields printed are:

       Recruiter ID and Name (once for each group)
       Req No

APPENDIX 8: ATS REPORT SPECIFICATIONS

>Req Date
>Disp Date
>Applicant ID
>Applicant Name
>Source
>Position Applied For (Job Title from Req, if any)
>Total Recruiting Expenses
>No. Days To Fill

Subtotals By Recruiter include:

>\# applicants
>Total Recruiting Expenses
>Average No. Days To Fill

Report #5 - Recruiter Requisition Assignment (ATRECRQR)

This report prints a list of requisitions grouped by Recruiter ID. Selection is for all requisitions with REQ-STATUS="open". The report is sequenced by Req No within Recruiter ID. The data fields printed are:

>Recruiter ID and Name (once for each group)
>Req No
>Req Date
>Job Title
>Salary Grade
>Min Salary
>Max Salary
>Department
>Primary Experience Code and Description

Report #6 - Recruitment Costs Report (ATRECCSR)

This report prints a list of closed requisitions by Department showing recruitment costs. Selection is for all closed requisitions. The report is sequenced by Req No within Department. The data fields printed are:

APPENDIX 8: ATS REPORT SPECIFICATIONS

        Department (once for each group)
        Req No
        Req Date
        Job Title
        Salary Grade
        Min Salary
        Max Salary
        Primary Exp Code and Description
        Recruiter ID and Name

Subtotals By Department include:

        # applicants hired
        Total Recruiting Expenses
        Average No. Days To Fill

Appendix 9

ATS REPORT DEFINITIONS AND SAMPLE OUTPUT

All definitions from the sample Applicant Tracking System are from the AT library.

APDSPR	Applicants by Disposition Report and Output
APSRCR	Applicant Source Analysis Report and Output
OPNRQR	Open Requisitions Summary Report and Output
RECANR	Recruiter Analysis Report and Output
RECCSR	Recruitment Costs Report and Output
RECRQR	Recruiter Requisition Assignment Report and Output

APPENDIX 9: ATS REPORT DEFINITIONS AND SAMPLE OUTPUT

REPORT DEFINITION

```
LIB: AT         TITLE: Applicants By Disposition Rpt      CREATED: 10/10/87
DEF: APDSPR     OWNER: Jeff Zickler                  LAST CHANGED: 04/13/88

06/03/88        AT-APDSPR        Applicants By Disposition Rpt        PAGE:   1
--------------------------------------------------------------------------------
! ATAPDSPR - APPLICANTS BY DISPOSITION REPORT
!           PRINTS A LIST OF APPLICANTS GROUPED BY DISPOSITION CODE
!           SORT1 OF ATAPMSTR IS DISP-CODE + IDENT

ENTRY-SECTION

FILE-SECTION
FD    ATAPMSTR  SORT BY SORT1
FD    ATRQMSTR
FD    ATDISPCD

CONTROL-SECTION
CB1   WHEN DISP-CODE CHANGES

REPORT-SECTION
H     AT-APDSPR                         Applicants By Disposition Report                                    Page: # #
H     MM/DD/YY
>     A
H                                                        DATE     DISP            RECRUI-                       REQ
H     IDENT     APPLICANT NAME                           ENTERED  DATE            TER      SOURCE               NO      JOB TITLE
H     ---------------------------------------------------------------------------------------------------------------------------------
CB1   DISPOSITION CODE: XX  XXXXXXXXXXXXXXXXXXXXXXXXXXXX
                        B   C
>
CB1
D     XXXXXX    XXXXXXXXXXXXXXXXXXXXXXXXXXXXXX           XX/XX/XX XX/XX/XX       XXXXXX   XXXXXXXXXXXXXXXXXXXX  XXXX    XXXXXXXXXXXXXXXXXXXXXXXXX
>     D         E                                        F        G               H        I                     J       K
D           TOTAL RECRUITING EXPENSES: ######0.00  NUMBER OF DAYS TO FILL POSITION: ###0
>                                      L                                           M
D

Formulas:

A  -  /FIELD(8) = DAY                                       H - RECRUITER
B  -  DISP-CODE                                             I - SOURCE
C  -  DISP-DESC                                             J - REQ-NO
D  -  IDENT                                                 K - JOB-TITLE
E  -  NAME                                                  L - TOTAL-REC-EXP
F  -  /FIELD(8) = DATE-ENTERED(1,2) + "/" + DATE-ENTERED    M - NO-DAYS-TO-FILL
      (3,2) + "/" + DATE-ENTERED(5,2)
G  -  /FIELD(8) = DISP-DATE(1,2) +"/" + DISP-DATE(3,2) +
      "/" + DISP-DATE(5,2)
```

APPENDIX 9: ATS REPORT DEFINITIONS AND SAMPLE OUTPUT

SAMPLE OUTPUT

```
AT-APDSPR                           Applicants By Disposition Report                                    Page: 1
06/03/88

                              DATE       DISP       RECRUI-                        REQ
IDENT    APPLICANT NAME       ENTERED    DATE       TER      SOURCE                NO     JOB TITLE

DISPOSITION CODE:

COLLIR   Renee Collins        11/18/87                SMITHK   Newspaper            0100   Dir, Product Marketing
         TOTAL RECRUITING EXPENSES:   0.00   NUMBER OF DAYS TO FILL POSITION:  0

GIBSOM   Melvin Gibson        11/18/87                SMITHK   Employee Referral    0151   V.P., Marketing Oper.
         TOTAL RECRUITING EXPENSES:   0.00   NUMBER OF DAYS TO FILL POSITION:  0

JONESA   Aaron Jones          11/18/87                JONESS   Employee Referral    0110   Marketing Support Analyst
         TOTAL RECRUITING EXPENSES:  2000.00  NUMBER OF DAYS TO FILL POSITION:  0

DISPOSITION CODE: AJ

ADAM3J   Jennifer Adamson     04/21/88   04/21/88                                   0000
         TOTAL RECRUITING EXPENSES:   0.00   NUMBER OF DAYS TO FILL POSITION:  0

CAMPBJ   Janet Campbell       04/21/88   04/21/88              Newspaper            0000
         TOTAL RECRUITING EXPENSES:  231.00  NUMBER OF DAYS TO FILL POSITION:  0

DEMPSY   Yolanda Dempsey      04/21/88   04/21/88              Newspaper            0000
         TOTAL RECRUITING EXPENSES:   0.00   NUMBER OF DAYS TO FILL POSITION:  0

GILLSJ   John Gills           04/21/88   04/21/88                                   0000
         TOTAL RECRUITING EXPENSES:   0.00   NUMBER OF DAYS TO FILL POSITION:  0

KATRIL   Lonnie Katrilla      04/21/88   04/21/88                                   0000
         TOTAL RECRUITING EXPENSES:   0.00   NUMBER OF DAYS TO FILL POSITION:  0

NGUYEH   Hoang Nguyen         04/21/88   04/21/88              Newspaper            0000
         TOTAL RECRUITING EXPENSES:  50.00   NUMBER OF DAYS TO FILL POSITION:  0

NICHOW   William Nichols      04/21/88   04/21/88                                   0000
         TOTAL RECRUITING EXPENSES:   0.00   NUMBER OF DAYS TO FILL POSITION:  0

DISPOSITION CODE: HI   Hired

CAMPBB   Bruce Campbell       12/14/87   02/15/88   SMITHK    Newspaper             0103   Marketing Systems Analyst
         TOTAL RECRUITING EXPENSES:  800.00  NUMBER OF DAYS TO FILL POSITION: 63

JAMESD   Donald James         11/18/87   12/04/87   JONESS    Employee Referral     0102   Marketing Support Analyst
         TOTAL RECRUITING EXPENSES:  2000.00 NUMBER OF DAYS TO FILL POSITION: 45

LOGANL   L. M. Logan          12/15/87   03/14/88   JONESS    Newspaper             0101   Sr. Technical Writer
         TOTAL RECRUITING EXPENSES:  150.00  NUMBER OF DAYS TO FILL POSITION: 101
```

9-3

APPENDIX 9: ATS REPORT DEFINITIONS AND SAMPLE OUTPUT

AT-APDSPR
06/03/88

Applicants By Disposition Report

Page: 2

IDENT	APPLICANT NAME	DATE ENTERED	DISP DATE	RECRUI-TER	SOURCE	REQ NO	JOB TITLE

DISPOSITION CODE: NP

MCLEOD	Donald McLeod	04/21/88	04/21/88		Newspaper	0000	
	TOTAL RECRUITING EXPENSES:	0.00	NUMBER OF DAYS TO FILL POSITION:			0	
TURNES	Sam Turner	04/21/88	03/01/88		Newspaper	0000	
	TOTAL RECRUITING EXPENSES:	65.00	NUMBER OF DAYS TO FILL POSITION:			0	

DISPOSITION CODE: NQ

| THOMAR | Rodney Thomas | 02/21/88 | 04/21/88 | | | 0000 | |
| | TOTAL RECRUITING EXPENSES: | 0.00 | NUMBER OF DAYS TO FILL POSITION: | | | 0 | |

DISPOSITION CODE: OM

| MESSEN | Nancy Messenger | 12/01/87 | 04/21/88 | | | 0000 | |
| | TOTAL RECRUITING EXPENSES: | 5529.00 | NUMBER OF DAYS TO FILL POSITION: | | | 0 | |

DISPOSITION CODE: OR

| GOODMA | Allen Goodman | 04/21/88 | 04/21/88 | | | 0000 | |
| | TOTAL RECRUITING EXPENSES: | 780.75 | NUMBER OF DAYS TO FILL POSITION: | | | 0 | |

DISPOSITION CODE: PI

| LERNER | Randall S. Lerner | 11/09/87 | 03/01/88 | | | 0000 | |
| | TOTAL RECRUITING EXPENSES: | 0.00 | NUMBER OF DAYS TO FILL POSITION: | | | 0 | |

DISPOSITION CODE: PR

| HEDGES | Sandra Hedgecook | 02/01/88 | 03/01/88 | | Employee Referral | 0000 | |
| | TOTAL RECRUITING EXPENSES: | 0.00 | NUMBER OF DAYS TO FILL POSITION: | | | 0 | |

DISPOSITION CODE: RC

| COLLIJ | James Collins | 04/21/88 | 04/21/88 | | Newspaper | 0000 | |
| | TOTAL RECRUITING EXPENSES: | 250.00 | NUMBER OF DAYS TO FILL POSITION: | | | 0 | |

APPENDIX 9: ATS REPORT DEFINITIONS AND SAMPLE OUTPUT

REPORT DEFINITION

```
06/03/88      AT-APSRCR      Applicant Source Analysis Rpt      PAGE:  1
-------------------------------------------------------------------------
! ATAPSRCR - APPLICANT SOURCE ANALYSIS REPORT
!     PRINTS A LIST OF APPLICANTS GROUPED BY SOURCE
!     SORT2 OF ATAPMSTR IS SOURCE + IDENT

ENTRY-SECTION
DD       COUNT(3.0)
DD       COUNT1(3.0)
I101     COUNT = 0; COUNT1 = 0

FILE-SECTION
FD       ATAPMSTR SORT BY SORT2
FD       ATRQMSTR
FD       ATRECRUT

CONTROL-SECTION
CB1      WHEN IDENT CHANGES
CB2      WHEN SOURCE CHANGES
ST1      WHEN SOURCE CHANGES; TOTAL-REC-EXP; NO-DAYS-TO-FILL

REPORT-SECTION
H                                  Applicant Source Analysis Report                               Page: #
H    AT-APSRCR
H    MM/DD/YY
>    A
H                                                    DATE      DISP.
H    IDENT   APPLICANT NAME                          ENTERED   CD DATE    RECRUITER NAME              REQ
H                                                                                                    NO    JOB TITLE
CB1C IF DISP-CODE = "H1" THEN COUNT = COUNT + 1
CB1C COUNT1 = COUNT
CB2  **** SOURCE: XXXXXXXXXXXXXXXXXXXXXX ****
                  B
CB2
D    XXXXXX  XXXXXXXXXXXXXXXXXXXXXXXXXXXXXXX         XX/XX/XX  XX XX/XX/XX  XXXXXXXXXXXXXXXXXXXXXXXXX  XXXX  XXXXXXXXXXXXXXXXXXXXXXX
>    C       D                                       E         F  G        H                          I     J
D              TOTAL RECRUITING EXPENSES: ######0.00           NUMBER OF DAYS TO FILL POSITION: ###0
>                                         K                                                       L
D
ST1C IF COUNT = 0 THEN COUNT1 = 1
ST1            TOTAL RECRUITING EXPENSES:$######0.00  AVG. NO. OF DAYS TO FILL POSITIONS: ###0   NO. OF HIRED APPLICANTS: ##0
>                                         M                                                 N                             O
ST1
```

Formulas:

```
A - /FIELD(8) = DAY                                          G - /FIELD(8) = DISP-DATE(1,2) +"/" + DISP-DATE(3,2) +
B - SOURCE                                                       "/" + DISP-DATE(5,2)
C - IDENT                                                    H - RECRUT-NAME                        M - ST1(1):"$######0.00"
D - NAME                                                     I - REQ-NO                             N - ST1(2) / COUNT1:"####0"
E - /FIELD(8) = DATE-ENTERED(1,2) + "/" + DATE-ENTERED        J - JOB-TITLE                          O - COUNT:"##0"; COUNT = 0
    (3,2) + "/" + DATE-ENTERED(5,2)                          K - TOTAL-REC-EXP
F - DISP-CODE                                                L - NO-DAYS-TO-FILL
```

9-5

APPENDIX 9: ATS REPORT DEFINITIONS AND SAMPLE OUTPUT

SAMPLE OUTPUT

```
AT-APSRCR                                    Applicant Source Analysis Report                                        Page: 1
06/03/88

                              DATE         DISP.
IDENT   APPLICANT NAME        ENTERED      CD   DATE      RECRUITER NAME                              REQ
                                                                                                      NO    JOB TITLE
---------------------------------------------------------------------------------------------------------------------------
**** SOURCE:                  ****

ADAMSJ  Jennifer Adamson       04/21/88    AJ   04/21/88                                              0000
        TOTAL RECRUITING EXPENSES:    0.00       NUMBER OF DAYS TO FILL POSITION:    0

GILLSJ  John Gills             04/21/88    AJ   04/21/88                                              0000
        TOTAL RECRUITING EXPENSES:    0.00       NUMBER OF DAYS TO FILL POSITION:    0

GOODMA  Allen Goodman          04/21/88    OR   04/21/88                                              0000
        TOTAL RECRUITING EXPENSES:  780.75       NUMBER OF DAYS TO FILL POSITION:    0

KATRIL  Lonnie Katrilla        04/21/88    AJ   04/21/88                                              0000
        TOTAL RECRUITING EXPENSES:    0.00       NUMBER OF DAYS TO FILL POSITION:    0

LERNER  Randall S. Lerner      11/09/87    PI   03/01/88                                              0000
        TOTAL RECRUITING EXPENSES:    0.00       NUMBER OF DAYS TO FILL POSITION:    0

MESSEN  Nancy Messenger        12/01/87    OM   04/21/88                                              0000
        TOTAL RECRUITING EXPENSES: 5529.00       NUMBER OF DAYS TO FILL POSITION:    0

NICHOW  William Nichols        04/21/88    AJ   04/21/88                                              0000
        TOTAL RECRUITING EXPENSES:    0.00       NUMBER OF DAYS TO FILL POSITION:    0

THOMAR  Rodney Thomas          02/21/88    NQ   04/21/88                                              0000
        TOTAL RECRUITING EXPENSES:    0.00       NUMBER OF DAYS TO FILL POSITION:    0

        TOTAL RECRUITING EXPENSES: $6309.75      AVG. NO. OF DAYS TO FILL POSITIONS:  0      NO. OF HIRED APPLICANTS:   0

**** SOURCE: Employee Referral ****

GIBSOM  Melvin Gibson          11/18/87         Ken Smith                                             0151  V.P., Marketing Oper.
        TOTAL RECRUITING EXPENSES:    0.00       NUMBER OF DAYS TO FILL POSITION:    0

HEDGES  Sandra Hedgecook       02/01/88    PR   03/01/88                                              0000
        TOTAL RECRUITING EXPENSES:    0.00       NUMBER OF DAYS TO FILL POSITION:    0

JAMESD  Donald James           11/18/87    HI   12/04/87   Samantha Jones                             0102  Marketing Support Analyst
        TOTAL RECRUITING EXPENSES: 2000.00       NUMBER OF DAYS TO FILL POSITION:   45

JONESA  Aaron Jones            11/18/87         Samantha Jones                                        0110  Marketing Support Analyst
        TOTAL RECRUITING EXPENSES: 2000.00       NUMBER OF DAYS TO FILL POSITION:    0

        TOTAL RECRUITING EXPENSES: $4000.00      AVG. NO. OF DAYS TO FILL POSITIONS: 45      NO. OF HIRED APPLICANTS:   1

**** SOURCE: Newspaper ****

CAMPBB  Bruce Campbell         12/14/87    HI   02/15/88   Ken Smith                                  0103  Marketing Systems Analyst
        TOTAL RECRUITING EXPENSES:  800.00       NUMBER OF DAYS TO FILL POSITION:   63
```

APPENDIX 9: ATS REPORT DEFINITIONS AND SAMPLE OUTPUT

AT-APSRCR
06/03/88

Applicant Source Analysis Report

Page: 2

IDENT	APPLICANT NAME	DATE ENTERED	DISP. CD	DISP. DATE	RECRUITER NAME	REQ NO	JOB TITLE
CAMPBJ	Janet Campbell	04/21/88	AJ	04/21/88		0000	
	TOTAL RECRUITING EXPENSES:	231.00		NUMBER OF DAYS TO FILL POSITION:		0	
COLLIJ	James Collins	04/21/88	RC	04/21/88		0000	
	TOTAL RECRUITING EXPENSES:	250.00		NUMBER OF DAYS TO FILL POSITION:		0	
COLLIR	Renee Collins	11/18/87			Ken Smith	0100	Dir, Product Marketing
	TOTAL RECRUITING EXPENSES:	0.00		NUMBER OF DAYS TO FILL POSITION:		0	
DEMPSY	Yolanda Dempsey	04/21/88	AJ	04/21/88		0000	
	TOTAL RECRUITING EXPENSES:	0.00		NUMBER OF DAYS TO FILL POSITION:		0	
LOGANL	L. M. Logan	12/15/87	HI	03/14/88	Samantha Jones	0101	Sr. Technical Writer
	TOTAL RECRUITING EXPENSES:	150.00		NUMBER OF DAYS TO FILL POSITION:		101	
MCLEOD	Donald McLeod	04/21/88	NP	04/21/88		0000	
	TOTAL RECRUITING EXPENSES:	0.00		NUMBER OF DAYS TO FILL POSITION:		0	
NGUYEH	Hoang Nguyen	04/21/88	AJ	04/21/88		0000	
	TOTAL RECRUITING EXPENSES:	50.00		NUMBER OF DAYS TO FILL POSITION:		0	
TURNES	Sam Turner	04/21/88	NP	03/01/88		0000	
	TOTAL RECRUITING EXPENSES:	65.00		NUMBER OF DAYS TO FILL POSITION:		0	
	TOTAL RECRUITING EXPENSES:	$1546.00		AVG. NO. OF DAYS TO FILL POSITIONS:		82	NO. OF HIRED APPLICANTS: 2

APPENDIX 9: ATS REPORT DEFINITIONS AND SAMPLE OUTPUT

REPORT DEFINITION

```
06/03/88        AT-OPNRQR       Open Requisitions Summary Rpt         PAGE:  1
-------------------------------------------------------------------------------
! ATOPNRQR - OPEN REQUISITIONS SUMMARY REPORT
!      PRINTS A LIST OF OPEN REQUISITIONS BY REQUISITION NUMBER

ENTRY-SECTION

FILE-SECTION
FD  ATRQMSTR  SELECT WHEN REQ-STATUS = "open"
CONTROL-SECTION

REPORT-SECTION
H                                                   Open Requisitions Summary Report                             Page:  #
H    AT-OPNRQR
H    MM/DD/YY
>    A
H                                                                            SAL    MINIMUM    MAXIMUM    EXP
H    REQ   REQ DATE   DEPARTMENT            POSITION TO FILL                 GRD    SALARY     SALARY     CD   RECRUITER
H
D    XXXX  XX/XX/XX   XXXXXXXXXXXXXXXXXXXX  XXXXXXXXXXXXXXXXXXXXXXXXXXXXXX   XX    ######0.00  ######0.00  XX   XXXXXX
>    B     C          D                     E                                F     G           H           I    J

Formulas:

A - /FIELD(8) = DAY                              F  -  SALARY-GRADE
B - REQ-NO                                       G  -  SALARY-MIN
C - /FIELD(8) = REQ-DATE(1,2) + "/" + REQ-DATE(3,2) +   H  -  SALARY-MAX
    "/" + REQ-DATE(5,2)                          I  -  PRIM-EXP-CODE
D - DEPARTMENT                                   J  -  RECRUITER
E - JOB-TITLE
```

SAMPLE OUTPUT

```
AT-OPNRQR                               Open Requisitions Summary Report                                  Page: 1
06/03/88

                                                              SAL   MINIMUM     MAXIMUM    EXP
REQ    REQ DATE   DEPARTMENT    POSITION TO FILL              GRD   SALARY      SALARY     CD    RECRUITER

0100   12/03/87   Marketing     Dir, Product Marketing         24   37450.00    59850.00   13    SMITHK
0123   12/04/87   Documentation Sr. Technical Writer           16   18565.00    29650.00   19    JONESS
0151   01/15/88   Sales         V.P., Marketing Oper.          30   60000.00   120000.00   11    SMITHK
0288   02/16/88   Marketing     Dir, Product Marketing         24   37450.00    59850.00   10    JONESS
0600   04/21/88   Marketing     Mgr, Product Marketing         12   24125.00    38585.00   16    ARTHUD
0812   04/21/88   Marketing     Spvr, Marketing Support        10   19915.00    31875.00   17    JOHNSL
2010   04/20/88   Marketing     Prin. Technical Writer         09   18150.00    29015.00   10    SULLIJ
2100   04/20/88   Marketing     V.P., Marketing Oper.          25   40825.00    65315.00   11    ALLENH
3000   04/20/88   Marketing     Prin. Mktng Systems Anlst      09   18150.00    29015.00   18    JONESS
3050   04/21/88   Marketing     V.P., Marketing               25    40825.00    65315.00   11    JONESS
9013   04/21/88   Marketing     Sr. Mktng Support Analyst      15   16950.00    27175.00   17    ALLENH
```

APPENDIX 9: ATS REPORT DEFINITIONS AND SAMPLE OUTPUT

REPORT DEFINITION

```
06/03/88           AT-RECANR        Recruiter Analysis Report         PAGE:   1
--------------------------------------------------------------------------------
! ATRECANR - RECRUITER ANALYSIS REPORT
!          PRINTS A LIST OF CLOSED REQUISITIONS GROUPED BY RECRUITER ID
!          SORT2 OF ATRQMSTR IS RECRUITER + REQ-NO

ENTRY-SECTION
  DD       COUNT(3.0)
  DD       COUNT1(3.0)
  I101     COUNT = 0; COUNT1 = 0

FILE-SECTION
  FD       ATRQMSTR SORT BY SORT2
  :                 SELECT WHEN REQ-STATUS(1,6) = "closed"
  FD       ATRECRUT
  FD       ATAPMSTR

CONTROL-SECTION
  CB1      WHEN REQ-NO CHANGES
  CB2      WHEN RECRUITER CHANGES
  ST1      WHEN RECRUITER CHANGES; TOTAL-REC-EXP; NO-DAYS-TO-FILL

REPORT-SECTION
  H                                     Recruiter Analysis Report            Page: #
  H        AT-RECANR
  H        MM/DD/YY
  >                A
  H                                                      DISP                      REQ
  H        IDENT   APPLICANT NAME                        DATE   SOURCE OF APPLICANT   NO    REQ DATE   JOB TITLE
  H
  CB1C     COUNT = COUNT + 1
  CB1C     COUNT1 = COUNT
  CB2      **** RECRUITER: XXXXXX   XXXXXXXXXXXXXXXXXXXXXXXXXXXXXX ****
  >                               B                    C
  CB2
  D        XXXXXX  XXXXXXXXXXXXXXXXXXXXXXXXXXXX  XX/XX/XX  XXXXXXXXXXXXXXXXXXXX  XXXX  XX/XX/XX   XXXXXXXXXXXXXXXXXXXXXXXXXXXXXX
  >                D       E                            F              G                  H        I          J
  D                        TOTAL RECRUITING EXPENSES: ######0.00          NUMBER OF DAYS TO FILL POSITION: ###0
  >                                                       K                                                   L
  D
  ST1C     IF COUNT = 0 THEN COUNT1 = 1
  ST1                      TOTAL RECRUITING EXPENSES:$######0.00  AVG. NO. OF DAYS TO FILL POSITIONS: ###0  NO. OF HIRED APPLICANTS: ##0
  >                                                      M                                             N                              O
  ST1
```

Formulas:

```
A - /FIELD(8) = DAY                                    I - /FIELD(8) = REQ-DATE(1,2) + "/" + REQ-DATE(3,2) +
B - RECRUITER                                                          "/" + REQ-DATE(5,2)
C - RECRUIT-NAMF                                       J - JOB TITLE
D - IDENT                                              K - TOTAL-REC-EXP
E - NAME                                               L - NO-DAYS-TO-FILL
F - /FIELD(8) = DISP-DATE(1,2) +"/" + DISP-DATE(3,2) + M - ST1(1):"$######0.00"
                "/" + DISP-DATE(5,2)                   N - ST1(2) / COUNT1:"###0"
G - SOURCE                                             O - COUNT:"##0"; COUNT = 0
H - REQ-NO
```

9-9

APPENDIX 9: ATS REPORT DEFINITIONS AND SAMPLE OUTPUT

SAMPLE OUTPUT

```
AT-RECANK                                    Recruiter Analysis Report                                    Page: 1
06/03/88

                              DISP              REQ
IDENT    APPLICANT NAME       DATE    SOURCE OF APPLICANT      NO     REQ DATE    JOB TITLE
-----------------------------------------------------------------------------------------------------

**** RECRUITER: JONESS  Samantha Jones  ****

LOGANL   L. M. Logan          03/14/88  Newspaper             0101    12/04/87    Sr. Technical Writer
         TOTAL RECRUITING EXPENSES:    150.00     NUMBER OF DAYS TO FILL POSITION:    101

JAMESD   Donald James         12/04/87  Employee Referral     0102    12/03/87    Marketing Support Analyst
         TOTAL RECRUITING EXPENSES:    2000.00    NUMBER OF DAYS TO FILL POSITION:    45

         TOTAL RECRUITING EXPENSES:   $2150.00    AVG. NO. OF DAYS TO FILL POSITIONS:   73    NO. OF HIRED APPLICANTS:  2

**** RECRUITER: SMITHK  Ken Smith  ****

CAMPBB   Bruce Campbell       02/15/88  Newspaper             0103    12/14/87    Marketing Systems Analyst
         TOTAL RECRUITING EXPENSES:    800.00     NUMBER OF DAYS TO FILL POSITION:    63

         TOTAL RECRUITING EXPENSES:    $800.00    AVG. NO. OF DAYS TO FILL POSITIONS:   63    NO. OF HIRED APPLICANTS:  1
```

APPENDIX 9: ATS REPORT DEFINITIONS AND SAMPLE OUTPUT

REPORT DEFINITION

```
06/03/88      AT-RECCSR      Recruitment Costs Report                    PAGE:  1
--------------------------------------------------------------------------------
! ATRECCSR - RECRUITMENT COSTS REPORT
!   PRINTS A LIST OF CLOSED REQUISITIONS GROUPED BY DEPARTMENT
!   SORT1 OF ATRQMSTR IS DEPARTMENT + REQ-NO

ENTRY-SECTION
DD     COUNT(3.0)
DD     COUNT1(3.0)
I101   COUNT = 0;  COUNT1 = 0

FILE-SECTION
FD     ATRQMSTR SORT BY SORT1
:         SELECT WHEN REQ-STATUS(1,6) = "closed"
FD     ATRFCRUIT
FD     ATAPMSTR
FD     ATEXPCDP

CONTROL-SECTION
CB1    WHEN REQ NO CHANGES
CB2    WHEN DEPARTMENT CHANGES
ST1    WHEN DEPARTMENT CHANGES; TOTAL-REC-EXP; NO-DAYS-TO-FILL

REPORT-SECTION
H      AT-RECCSR                            Recruitment Costs Report                                    Page: #
H      MM/DD/YY
>      A
H      REQ                           SAL    MINIMUM     MAXIMUM    PRIMARY EXPERIENCE
H      NO.   REQ DATE   JOB TITLE    GRD    SALARY      SALARY     CODE AND DESCRIPTION                 RECRUITER
H
CB1C   COUNT = COUNT + 1
CB1C   COUNT1 = COUNT
CB2    **** DEPARTMENT: XXXXXXXXXXXXXXXXXXXX ****
>                       B
CB2
D      XXXX  XX/XX/XX   XXXXXXXXXXXXXXXXXXXXXXXX  XX   ######0.00  ######0.00  XX XXXXXXXXXXXXXXXXXXXXXXXXXXXXX  XXXXXX
>      C     D          E                         F    G           H           I  J                                K
D                  TOTAL RECRUITING EXPENSES: ######0.00      NUMBER OF DAYS TO FILL POSITION: ###0
>                                             L                                                M
D
ST1C   IF COUNT = 0 THEN COUNT1 = 1
ST1                TOTAL RECRUITING EXPENSES:$######0.00      AVG. NO. OF DAYS TO FILL POSITIONS: ###0   NO. OF HIRED APPLICANTS: ##0
>                                             N                                                 O                                 P
ST1

Formulas:

A - /FIELD(8) = DAY
B - DEPARTMENT
```

9-11

APPENDIX 9: ATS REPORT DEFINITIONS AND SAMPLE OUTPUT

```
C - REQ-NO                                      J - EXPER-DESC
D - /FIELD(8) = REQ-DATE(1,2) + "/" + REQ-DATE(3,2) +   K - RECRUITER
    "/" + REQ-DATE(5,2)                         L - TOTAL-REC-EXP
E - JOB-TITLE                                   M - NO-DAYS-TO-FILL
F - SALARY-GRADE                                N - ST1(1):"$######0.00"
G - SALARY-MIN                                  O - ST1(2) / COUNT1:"####0"
H - SALARY-MAX                                  P - COUNT:"##0"; COUNT = 0
I - PRIM-EXP-CODE
```

SAMPLE OUTPUT

```
AT-RECCSR                           Recruitment Costs Report                              Page: 1
06/03/88
REQ                           SAL     MINIMUM    MAXIMUM  PRIMARY EXPERIENCE
NO.   REQ DATE  JOB TITLE     GRD     SALARY     SALARY   CODE AND DESCRIPTION            RECRUITER

**** DEPARTMENT: Documentation  ****

0101  12/04/87  Sr. Technical Writer   16   18565.00   29650.00   19 Marketing Support Technician   JONESS
      TOTAL RECRUITING EXPENSES:    150.00   NUMBER OF DAYS TO FILL POSITION: 101

      TOTAL RECRUITING EXPENSES:   $150.00   AVG. NO. OF DAYS TO FILL POSITIONS: 101   NO. OF HIRED APPLICANTS: 1

**** DEPARTMENT: Marketing      ****

0102  12/03/87  Marketing Support Analyst  11   21945.00   35100.00   10 Marketing                  JONESS
      TOTAL RECRUITING EXPENSES:   2000.00   NUMBER OF DAYS TO FILL POSITION: 45

0103  12/14/87  Marketing Systems Analyst  21   28800.00   46025.00   17 Marketing Support Analyst  SMITHK
      TOTAL RECRUITING EXPENSES:    800.00   NUMBER OF DAYS TO FILL POSITION: 63

      TOTAL RECRUITING EXPENSES:  $2800.00   AVG. NO. OF DAYS TO FILL POSITIONS: 54    NO. OF HIRED APPLICANTS: 2
```

APPENDIX 9: ATS REPORT DEFINITIONS AND SAMPLE OUTPUT

REPORT DEFINITION

```
06/03/88      AT-RECRQR       Recruiter Req Assignment Rpt              PAGE:   1
----------------------------------------------------------------------------------
! ATRECRQR - RECRUITER REQUISITION ASSIGNMENT REPORT
!    PRINTS A LIST OF OPEN REQUISITIONS GROUPED BY RECRUITER ID
!    SORT2 OF ATRQMSTR IS RECRUITER + REQ-NO

ENTRY-SECTION

FILE-SECTION
FD    ATRQMSTR SORT BY SORT2
:              SELECT WHEN REQ-STATUS(1,4) = "open"
FD    ATRECRUT
FD    ATEXPCDP

CONTROL-SECTION
CB1   WHEN RECRUITER CHANGES
ST0   WHEN RECRUITER CHANGES

REPORT-SECTION
=
H     AT-RECRQR                       Recruiter Requisition Assignment Report                                    Page:  #
H     MM/DD/YY
>     A
H                                                                               SAL    MINIMUM    MAXIMUM   PRIMARY EXPERIENCE
H     REQ   REQ DATE   DEPARTMENT               POSITION TO FILL                GRD    SALARY     SALARY    CODE AND DESCRIPTION
H     --------------------------------------------------------------------------------------------------------------------------
CB1   RECRUITER: XXXXXX    XXXXXXXXXXXXXXXXXXXXXXXXXXXXXX
              B            C
>
CB1
D     XXXX  XX/XX/XX   XXXXXXXXXXXXXXXXXXXXX    XXXXXXXXXXXXXXXXXXXXXXXXXXX     XX     ######0.00  ######0.00   XX  XXXXXXXXXXXXXXXXXXXXXXXXXX
      D     E          F                        G                               H      I           J            K   L
>
ST0

Formulas:

A - /FIELD(8) = DAY                              G - JOB-TITLE
B - RECRUITER                                    H - SALARY-GRADE
C - RECRUT-NAME                                  I - SALARY-MIN
D - REQ-NO                                       J - SALARY-MAX
E - /FIELD(8) = REQ-DATE(1,2) + "/" + REQ-DATE(3,2) +     K - PRIM-EXP-CODE
    "/" + REQ-DATE(5,2)                          L - EXPER-DESC
F - DEPARTMENT
```

9-13

APPENDIX 9: ATS REPORT DEFINITIONS AND SAMPLE OUTPUT

SAMPLE OUTPUT

```
AT-RECRQR                          Recruiter Requisition Assignment Report                              Page: 1
06/03/88
                                                    SAL     MINIMUM     MAXIMUM    PRIMARY EXPERIENCE
REQ    REQ DATE   DEPARTMENT       POSITION TO FILL GRD     SALARY      SALARY     CODE AND DESCRIPTION
------------------------------------------------------------------------------------------------------------

RECRUITER: ALLENH  Henry Allen

2100   04/20/88   Marketing        V.P., Marketing Oper.      25   40825.00    65315.00    11  V.P., Marketing
9013   04/21/88   Marketing        Sr. Mktng Support Analyst  15   16950.00    27175.00    17  Marketing Support Analyst

RECRUITER: ARTHUD  David Arthur

0600   04/21/88   Marketing        Mgr, Product Marketing     12   24125.00    38585.00    16  Mgr, Product Marketing

RECRUITER: JOHNSL  Lorraine Johnson

0812   04/21/88   Marketing        Spvr, Marketing Support    10   19915.00    31875.00    17  Marketing Support Analyst

RECRUITER: JONESS  Samantha Jones

0123   12/04/87   Documentation    Sr. Technical Writer       16   18565.00    29650.00    19  Marketing Support Technician
0288   02/16/88   Marketing        Dir, Product Marketing     24   37450.00    59850.00    10  Marketing
3000   04/20/88   Marketing        Prin. Mktng Systems Anlst  09   18150.00    29015.00    18  Marketing Systems Analyst
3050   04/21/88   Marketing        V.P., Marketing            25   40825.00    65315.00    11  V.P., Marketing

RECRUITER: SMITHK  Ken Smith

0100   12/03/87   Marketing        Dir, Product Marketing     24   37450.00    59850.00    13  Dir, Product Marketing
0151   01/15/88   Sales            V.P., Marketing Oper.      30   60000.00   120000.00    11  V.P., Marketing

RECRUITER: SULLIJ  John Sullivan

2010   04/20/88   Marketing        Prin. Technical Writer     09   18150.00    29015.00    10  Marketing
```

9-14

Appendix 10

ATS MENU DEFINITIONS

All definitions from the sample Applicant Tracking System are from the AT library.

> MENU01   Applicant Tracking System Main Menu and Screen
> MENU02   Applicant and Requisition Reports Menu and Screen

Refer to Chapter 9, "Designing and Implementing Menus", for a representation of the screen definitions.

Refer to Appendix 5, "ATS Screen Definitions", for a list of screen display codes used in the definition.

APPENDIX 10: ATS MENU DEFINITIONS

```
SCREEN REPORT - Detail                                    Page:        1
                                                          Date:  05/31/88
Name: ATMENU01, Appl. Tracking Sys Main Menu Scrn

     Link/Frmt          Screen---------  HELP-----------  Lst Chg Date: 05/20/88
     IDMENUIN    Size: chrs-80  lns-24   chrs-72  lns-7   Lst Chg Time: 18:49:51
                 Home: col--0   lin-0    col--3   lin-16  Created Date: 07/31/86
=================================================================================

 /D            {                                        ~           /t
               {    Applicant Tracking System Master Menu  ~
               {                                        ~

 {       APPLICANT INFORMATION              ~  {        CODE FILES & TABLES        ~
 {   1 ~ Maintain Applicant File               {   6  ~ Disposition Codes
 {   2 ~ View Applicant Gen'l Data             {   7  ~ Experience Codes
 {   3 ~ View Applicant Cost Data              {   8  ~ Job Code Information
                                               {   9  ~ Recruiter Information
 {       REQUISITION INFORMATION           ~   {  10  ~ Salary Grade Information 1
 {   4 ~ Maintain Requisition File              {  11 ~ Salary Grade Information 2
 {   5 ~ View Requisition Records

 {       UPDATE FUNCTIONS                  ~   {        REPORTING MENU             ~
 { SAR ~ Search For Applicants by Req'stn  {   R  ~ Applicant & Requisition Rpts
 { VAR ~ View Selected Applicants



                    {        ~ Selection:  _____
 >                                    A

     Formulas:

        A - MENU-SELECTION

  MENU REPORT - Summary                                   Page:        1
                                                          Date:  06/03/88
  Name: ATMENU01, Appl. Tracking System Main Menu

     Screen Used: ATMENU01                      Lst Chg Date: 05/20/88
     Screen HELP: MENU01                        Lst Chg Time: 18:52:05
     Screen Password:                           Created Date: 06/26/87

     ------ Menu Selection ------                                Pass
     Code  Description                  Type  Action  Screen    Value   HELP  Pswd
     ==============================================================================
      1    Applicant Master File Maint...  P   ATAPMM0
      2    View Applicant Records........  F   ATAPGENL
      4    Requisition Master File Maint.  P   ATRQMM0
      5    View Requisition Records......  F   ATREQUIS
      6    Disposition Codes.............  F   ATDISPCD
      7    Experience Codes..............  F   ATEXPCDE
      8    Job Code Information..........  f   ATJOBCDE
      9    Recruiter Information.........  f   ATRECRUT
     10    Salary Grade Information 1....  f   ATSALGRD
      R    Applicant & Requisition Rpts..  M   ATMENU02
     SAR   Search For Applicants by Req..  P   ATSRCH0
      3    View Applicant Cost Data......  F   ATAPCOST
     sar   Search For Applicants By Req..  P   ATSRCH0
     VAR   View Selected Applicants......  F   ATAPTEMP
     var   View Selected Applicants......  F   ATAPTEMP
     11    Salary Grade Information 2....  P   ATSGMM0
```

APPENDIX 10: ATS MENU DEFINITIONS

```
SCREEN REPORT - Detail                                    Page:        1
                                                          Date:  05/31/88
Name: ATMENU02, Appl. & Reqstns Reports Menu Screen

    Link/Frmt          Screen---------  HELP-----------  Lst Chg Date: 05/20/83
    IDMENUIN     Size: chrs-80  lns-24  chrs-72  lns-7   Lst Chg Time:  18:50:01
                 Home: col--0   lin-0   col--3   lin-16  Created Date: 07/31/85
=================================================================================
                                                              ~         /t
    /D             {    Applicant & Requisitions Reports Menu ~
                   {                                          ~

{           APPLICANT REPORTS             ~    {       REQUISITION REPORTS           ~
{     1   ~ Applicants By Disposition          {    3  ~ Recruiter Analysis Report
{     2   ~ Source Analysis Report             {    4  ~ Open Requisitions Summary
                                                {    5  ~ Recruiter Req'stn Assignment
                                                {    6  ~ Recruitment Costs Report




                          {   ~ Selection: _____
>                                           A

    Formulas:

        A - MENU-SELECTION

    MENU REPORT - Summary                                 Page:        1
                                                          Date:  06/03/83
    Name: ATMENU02, Appl. & Requisitions Reports Menu

        Screen Used: ATMENU02                             Lst Chg Date: 05/20/83
        Screen HELP: ATMEN2                               Lst Chg Time:  18:52:15
        Screen Password:                                  Created Date: 07/03/87

    ------- Menu Selection ------------                        Pass
    Code Description                      Type  Action  Screen Value HELP  Pswd
    ============================================================================
     1    Applicants By Disposition Code    R   ATAPDSPR
     2    Source Analysis Report.......     R   ATAPSRCR
     3    Recruiter Analysis Report....     R   ATRECANR
     4    Open Requisitions Summary Rpt.    R   ATOPNRQR
     5    Recruiter Requisition Assignmt    R   ATRECRQR
     6    Recruitment Costs Report......    R   ATRECCSR
```

Index

A

Analysis, Data 16
Analyst/Designer 17, 19
Application Model 5
Application Prototype 5
Audit 63

B

Backlog, Programming 11
Batch 141
Business BASIC . . . . 1 — 3, 6, 8, 23, 35, 37, 109

C

CASE . . . . 7 - 8
CHANGE 118
COBOL . . . . 3 — 4, 8, 13
Common Functionality 51, 57
Conflict Flags 139
Conflict Processing 135, 139
Continuation Script 83
COPY 118
Copy Script 83
COUNT 117
Custom Screen . . . . 76 — 77

D

Data, Sample	6-1
Data Analysis	16, 40
Data Declaration	82
Data Dictionary	6
Data Encyclopedia	6
Data Entry Script	84 — 85, 6-1
Data Modeling, Relational	106
Data Normalization	40, 50
Data Normalization Rules	43, 45, 47, 49
Data Redundancy	48
Database Maintenance, IDOL-IV	79, 81
Database Management System	2
Date	61
DBMS	2, 8, 20
Default Screen	75
Default Values	62
DELETE	118
Dependence, Transitive	48, 50
Design, Structured	51
Development Environment, Software	25 — 26, 37
Dictionary, Data	6
Dictionary, Global	59, 61, 63, 1-1
Dictionary, Message	3-1

E

Encyclopedia, Data	6
Engineering, Information	8
Engineering, Software	7 — 8
Engines, Inference	7
Environment, Software Development	25 — 26, 37
Error Conditions	92
Expert System	7

F

Factoring, Human	6
Field	26
Field Length	60
Field Separator	65
File	26
Flags, Conflict	139
Foreign Key	41, 106
Format	26, 64 — 65, 2-1
Functional Dependence	45, 47 — 48
Functionality, Common	51, 57

G

Global Dictionary	26, 59, 61, 63

H

Help	27, 61
Housekeeping, Programmer	5
Human Factoring	6

I

IDOL-IV Database Maintenance	79, 81
Inference Engines	7
Information Engineering	8
Integrity, Referential	106, 110

K

Key 65
Key, Foreign 41, 106
Key, Primary 41
Knowledge-based System 7

L

Library 28, 64, 70
Life Cycle, Software Project . . . . . . 14 — 15, 19, 23
Link 27, 68, 4-1
LIST 117, 121
Lookup Window 101

M

Machine Independence 3
Menu . . . . 27, 135 — 136, 138, 140, 10-1
Menu Screen . . . . 136 - 137
Message List 67
Messages 27
Model, Application 5
MOVE 118

N

Non-procedural . . . . 5 - 6
Normal Form, Second 45
Normal Form, Third 48
Normalization Rules 43, 45, 47, 49
Normalization, Data 50
Numeric Field 61

O

Orthogonality 6
Overlay Script 83

P

Packaged Software 12
Padding 61
Performance Penalities 13
Portability 12
Primary Key 41
Primary Script 82
Processing, Conflict 135, 139
Processing, Transaction 13
Productivity Tradeoff 6
Productivity, Programmer 3
Profitability . . . . 21 - 22
Program, Update . . . . . 141 — 142, 144, 146, 148, 150
Programmer Housekeeping 5
Programmer Productivity 3
Programming Backlog 11
Prototype 17
Prototype, Application 5
Prototyping . . . . 17, 19 — 20, 23

R

Readability 3
Referential Integrity 106, 110
Relational Data Modeling . . . . 40 — 41, 106
Relational DBMS 57
Report . . . . . 121 — 122, 124, 126, 128, 130, 132, 9-1
Report Specifications 8-1

Requirements, User 5
Response Time . . . . 13 — 14, 23

S

Sample Data 7-1
Sample Report Output 9-1
Screen 26, 5-1
Screen Formula 78
Screen, Custom . . . . 76 — 77
Screen, Default 75
Screen, Formula 78
Screen, Menu . . . . 136 — 137
Script, Continuation 83
Script, Copy 83
Script, Data Entry . . . . 84 — 85, 6-1
Script, Overlay 83
Script, Primary 82
SCRIPT-IV Scripts . . . . 82 — 83
Second Normal Form 45
Secondary Key 69
Security 62
Software Development Environment . . . . 25 — 26, 37
Software Engineering . . . . .7 — 8
Software Project Life Cycle . . . . 14 — 15, 19, 23
Software, Packaged 12
SORT 117
Spreadsheet Metaphor 113
Structured Design .51
System, Expert 7
System, Knowledge-based 7

T

Text Field 66
Third Normal Form 48

Throughput . . . . 13 — 14
Time, Response . . . . 13 — 14, 23
Transaction Processing 13
Transitive Dependence 48, 50

U

Update Program . . . . . 141 — 142, 144, 146, 148, 150
User Requirements 5

V

Valid Entries 62
View 26, 113, 115

W

Window, Lookup .101